SIX VICTORIAN THINKERS

MALCOLM HARDMAN

Six Victorian thinkers

Manchester University Press
Manchester and New York

distributed exclusively in the USA and Canada
by St. Martin's Press

Copyright © Malcolm Hardman 1991

Published by Manchester University Press
Oxford Road, Manchester M13 9PL, UK
and Room 400, 175 Fifth Avenue, New York, NY 10010, USA

*Distributed exclusively in the USA and Canada
by* St. Martin's Press, Inc.,
175 Fifth Avenue, New York, NY 10010, USA

British Library cataloguing in publication data
Hardman, Malcolm, *1943*–
    Six Victorian thinkers
    1. Great Britain. Intellectual life, 1837–1901
    I. Title
    941.081

Library of Congress cataloging in publication data
Hardman Malcolm
    Six Victorian thinkers/Malcolm Hardman.
        p.cm.
    Includes index.
    ISBN 0–7190–2976–7
    1. English literature—19th century—History and criticism.
    2. Great Britain—Intellectual life—19th century. I. Title.
    PR461.H28 1990
    820.9'008—dc20   90–6262

ISBN 0–7190–2976–7 *hardback*

Phototypeset by Input Typesetting Ltd, London

Printed by Great Britain
by Hartnolls Limited, Bodmin, Cornwall

CONTENTS

PREFACE AND ACKNOWLEDGEMENTS

The fascination with the Victorian era continues unabated. In Britain, the failings, triumphs and 'values' of the high period of British influence are being debated anew. This is felt to be a necessary part of the sometimes unflattering process of readjustment to Britain's diminishing role, and increasingly problematic relationship with the outside world. So many of the legacies of this period – for better and worse – are still with us. The same is true of the whole world. The 'spheres of influence' established after the Second World War become daily more problematic. If we step back in imagination from the Second World War period, it is hardly possible to begin making any account of that period without going back again to the developments of the late 1860s: the reunification of Germany, the liberation of serfs in Russia, the beginnings of working-class democracy in England, the emancipation of black slaves in America. All these things remind us of the need to consider the American and French Revolutions of the eighteenth century, and the English Revolution of a century before that. Stunned with the effort of backward recall, we vaguely remember a medieval period that culminated in something called the 'Renaissance' and something called the 'Reformation'; and before that something called the 'Classical' world that culminated in the 'Fall of the Roman Empire' and the 'Dark Ages'. We have still hardly given a thought to the Oriental world.

It is just at this point, however, that we can recover some feeling of equilibrium by remembering the usefulness of Victorian literature. This was produced at a time when it first became possible really to consider, if only by an effort of imagination, the whole of the geographic globe and the vast spectrum of 'world history'. If we narrow our sights still further, we shall be able to identify a period of relative stability and reassessment for England, from about 1830 to about 1870. It was during that period that Britain's prestige and responsibilities were at their height. It was a period when England had made some reforms, in response to the developments that culminated in the French Revolution, and was biding her time before another round of reforms, made partly in response to the world developments of the 1860s. Most of the English writers of this period had the French Revolution at the back of their minds. Most of them were also middle class: they were conscious that theirs was to be a century of transition: from an old world dominated by the aristocracy and the remnants of the Church, to some new world that would probably be more democratic, perhaps more frightening, perhaps more truly enlightened than ever before. A common pattern of thinking was to have in mind the idea of developing a synthesis, for their own times and for the future, drawn from two major legacies of the past: on the one hand, the classical pre-Christian world, whose finest legacy was a literature of reason and humane discrimination; on the other hand, the spiritual legacy of Christianity, partly rooted in Judaism, with its insistence on the value and responsibility of all human souls, not merely the intelligent or the cultivated. These Victorian writers were thus preparing, for our benefit, ways of trying to reconcile, renew, and grow beyond two of the major influences on our own lives and theirs. In addition, their status as representatives of the articulate classes of a world-wide commercial empire makes them valuable focuses for us to begin to try to grasp the major problem of our day and theirs; which is how to find methods of fairness and efficiency which will maintain and replenish the organic economy of the world: however narrow the range or setting of a Victorian piece of literature, its implied subject-matter is rarely less inclusive than that. English has become more and more widely used as a language of ideas since Victorian times: and especially has contributed to that species of thinking and reaction in which political and general cultural questions come together: the area of 'liberal' ideas, in the widest sense, rather than of academic or political theory, taken in isolation.

If Victorian literature is valuable, however, and a useful source for exploring the origins of our modern ways of trying to see, and function in the world, how much of it do we need? How much of it can we begin to take on board at once? The choice is vast: many, many writers with phenomenal levels of output from the popular horrors of the *Police News* to the bulky novels of Thackeray and Trollope; from *The Origin of Species* to *Mrs. Haliburton's Troubles* or *The Ring and the Book*. Must we decide in advance that there is a shortlist of 'great works', and try to make some headway with them? What are they; and how can we read them? Even our childhood favourites like *Jane Eyre* or *Oliver Twist* turn out to be full of 'history', 'politics' and 'moral ideas' when we read them in later life.

There is a better alternative to launching unprepared into the ocean of Victorianism. Among the vast array of Victorian literary output there is a group of articulate thinkers – neither strict theorists, nor mere pragmatists – who can still be drawn upon to provide us with a map of Victorian cultural problems and concerns: questions of morality and politics, and considerations about taste and value, freedom and social coherence, and the relations between these things: questions which are still very much with us, and indeed have become particularly urgent, as might be expected at a time like ours, which is becoming a time of transition as momentous as the Victorian age itself.

I have taken the best known of these writers: commencing with Carlyle and ending, in a new generation, with Arnold. As far as I know, there has been no recent attempt to set this group of six thinkers in the context which they had in common. They are still very valuable and interesting, and becoming daily more so as so many of the things they wrote and thought about again claim to be reconsidered.

Why six? Why not more? Why so many? This group of six seems to me to be the *smallest* group of Victorian 'thinkers' of the kind I have defined which can be considered – not indeed in isolation – but as a kind of sufficient entity. What each said and thought is so helpful to understanding and sympathising with what the others said and thought.

Ever since Lytton Strachey published *Eminent Victorians* in 1918, there has been a tendency either to debunk Victorian ways of thinking altogether, or to venerate exclusive aspects or examples of Victorian thought. Claims have been made about the supposed centrality or supremacy of one or another writer, and theories have been elaborated to match the claims. Some of these views will be mentioned in my concluding chapter. Meanwhile, I have attempted, in introducing the six writers to new readers, to follow the ideal of a more measured voice from Bloomsbury. 'All this pitting of sex against sex,' wrote Virginia Woolf in *A Room of One's Own*, 'of quality against quality; all this claiming of superiority and imputing of inferiority, belong to the private-school stage of human

existence where there are "sides".' Some readers may find that I
have taken the six writers too much at their own valuation; or –
on the contrary – that my own prejudices get in the way. What I
have tried to keep in mind, however, is the quite obvious fact that
the texts of the writers themselves are the best introduction to their
significance; and that new readers (unless we despair of democracy
altogether) have the privilege and obligation of getting access to
them for themselves. Ruskin and Taylor, particularly, will convince
far more through their personal style than through any précis I
could attempt. As Mrs Woolf puts it: 'Literature is open to every-
body. I refuse to allow you, Beadle though you are, to turn me off
the grass.' The role of Beadle requires me at the least to keep my
voice down and to make an effort not to take sides.

Ruskin, Taylor, Mill and Newman benefit considerably from
being read together: Arnold and Carlyle illuminate all of them, and
are useful complements of each other.

Carlyle was the founding father of a new kind of literature
of thought, rooted in personal conviction and exploration, but
extending outwards with a fine attention to both literary and social
responsibility. He wrote well, and he said something. His principal
concern is for the renewal of individual spiritual awareness. He
challenged his successors to evolve some way of writing that would
get people's brains and hearts working towards the discovery of
some system that would combine fairness with efficiency. If democracy could not achieve that, he thought, it would not survive. He
was not sentimental about democracy.

Because I want to introduce the idea of how these six writers
round out and correct each other, I have not attempted to introduce
all their work, the whole of their lives, or the vast range of their
literary and cultural influence. The book list at the end of each
chapter introduces ways in which these things can be explored
further. What I have sought to do is to highlight, in each case,
what I consider to be the point of their greatest accessibility; by
which I mean two things in one (because, in writing an introduc-
tory book these two things come to the same thing): first: that
part of their contribution which is most immediately likely to be
important for someone approaching them for the first time; and
also, that part of their contribution which is most helpful to know
about in order to appreciate how they relate to each other.

In the case of Carlyle, it seems to be his literary career, as I have already indicated, and his challenge to his successors, which are the most useful things to consider in this respect. The literary career and challenge of all the others are important, too: but not, in considering them as a group, *the* important things.

Arnold, the last writer to be considered, may be said to stand a little beyond the high-Victorian period, as Carlyle provides the best introduction to it. Arnold makes a new beginning by opening up again, in subtler and more democratic ways, Carlyle's criterion of the reformation of the individual. Arnold's own 'point of access' – his greatest and most immediately accessible contribution – is in his poetry; so I have concentrated on the strategy of his poetry for making this appeal to the individual mind. The deepest requirements both for democracy and for literary value are realised in it. To discover this involves some close reading. Again, all the other writers benefit from such close reading. But Arnold's poetry (though not, I think, his prose) benefits most of all.

Looking at the four mid-Victorians proper, we find them engaged in a task that complements the work of Carlyle and Arnold. They all wanted to transform institutions, in order to accommodate as many kinds of individual as possible. Mill, much influenced by Carlyle to begin with, was engaged partly in theory and partly in practice. There is a sometimes ironic counterpoint between these two things in him. It is possible to outline some of his main ideas on Parliament and on women's right to enfranchisement – the latter idea very much wanting in our other male thinkers – and to contrast them with the extent to which he was able to initiate practice, as an MP. This commitment to action is a quality shared by all our thinkers: but Mill offers the most useful example of the interplay between theory and practice.

Mill's ideas on human liberation cannot really be approached without careful consideration of the character of Harriet Taylor, who was to some extent an editor, or critical reader and collaborator in his work. The 'point of access' here seems to be her character itself, her refusal to think or feel as convention demanded. This is an aspect of all our thinkers: but in the case of a woman, such persistency, in the Victorian context, was something truly heroic, and a source for the revaluation of all the male thinkers, Mill included. In considering Mill and Taylor together, it seems important to stress the value of their intellectual relationship and the fact of their collaboration. No mind works alone, and Taylor's combination of integrity and capacity for collaboration has implications beyond the question of 'feminism' in any narrow sense.

As Ruskin moved further into social questions, he became not only a close friend, but in a sense a collaborator of Carlyle. He was a transformative one, however: adapting Carlyle's authoritarian ideas into patterns that anticipate socialist forms of democracy. His 'access point' seems to me to be his *presence*, as a well-heeled maverick in the world of Victorian fine art. This is especially brought out in his performances as a lecturer: a task all our male thinkers undertook, but none with Ruskin's dedication or success.

Ruskin looked to the trade union movement as an institution that might make practical progress in the task promoted by all our thinkers: peaceful change towards fairness and efficiency. He never joined a trade union. Newman's great interest lies in the fact of his actually *joining* the world's largest institution: the Catholic Church: and in attempting to infiltrate what has often been a reactionary body with his truly liberal principle of the freedom of the individual moral conscience. His 'idea of a University' has been influential well beyond its practical context: the very partially successful attempt to found a Catholic University in Ireland.

I should like to thank the English Department, and the Departments of Fine Art and Social History at Warwick, for encouraging me to deliver papers in which some of the ideas of this book were tested. I am grateful to Manchester University Press for their forbearance and support, and to the University of Warwick for granting me study leave, part of which has been used to redraft the concluding chapter in light of the developments of 1989.

CHRONOLOGY

Note: To avoid multiplying headings, information for each year is not listed separately in strict chronological order, but grouped under each writer's name, always in order of birth-date.

1795 Thomas **Carlyle** born, Ecclefechan, Dumfriesshire.
1801 John Henry **Newman** born, London.
1806 John Stuart **Mill** born, London.
1807 Harriet **Taylor** (née Hardy) born, London.
1819 John **Ruskin** born, London.
1822 **Carlyle**'s first article on German literature published. His conversion experience on Leith Walk.
Newman elected fellow of Oriel.
Mill forms Utilitarian Society.
Matthew **Arnold** born, Laleham, Middlesex.
1823 **Mill** spends one night in prison for distributing pamphlets on birth control. Appointed junior clerk to East India Company.
1825 **Carlyle**, *Life of Schiller* appears in book form.
1826 **Carlyle** and Jane Welsh marry.
Newman appointed tutor of Oriel.
Mill's emotional crisis.
1828 **Newman** appointed Vicar of St Mary's, Oxford.
Thomas Arnold appointed Headmaster of Rugby.
1829 **Carlyle**, 'Signs of the Times'.
Catholic Relief Bill. Riots in London.
1830 **Mill** meets **Taylor**.
1831 **Carlyle**, 'Characteristics'.
1832 **Carlyle**, 'Biography' article.
Mills and **Taylor** write (unpublished) essays on marriage and divorce.
(First) Reform Act.
Tennyson's *Poems*.
1833 **Carlyle**, *Sartor Resartus* begins in *Fraser's*.
Newman's first *Tract for the Times*.
Ruskin's first continental journey.
1834 **Carlyle** moves to London.
Taylor moves to Bromley, apart from John Taylor.
Arnold's father acquires Fox How, Ambleside.
Samuel Taylor Coleridge dies.

1835 **Carlyle**'s MS of *French Revolution*, vol. 1, inadvertently destroyed in **Mill**'s father's house, probably a victim of the division of labour and absence of communication between the son and father Mill and their resentful drudges, Mill's mother and sister.

1836 **Mill** becomes editor of *London and Westminster Review*.
Ruskin admitted as gentleman commoner, Christ Church, Oxford.
Arnold at Winchester College.

1837 **Carlyle**, *French Revolution*.
Ruskin, 'The Poetry of Architecture' begins in *Architectural Magazine*.
Arnold leaves Winchester for Rugby.
Accession of Queen Victoria.

1838 **Mill**'s 'Bentham' article.

1839 **Carlyle**, 'Chartism'.
Ruskin wins Newdigate Prize for Poetry.

1840 **Mill**'s 'Coleridge' article.
Arnold's 'Alaric at Rome', Rugby prize poem.

1841 **Carlyle**, *Heroes and Hero Worship*.
Newman, 'Tract 90'.
Ruskin, 'The King of the Golden River' written.
Hong Kong is leased to Great Britain.

1843 **Carlyle**, *Past and Present*.
Newman resigns from St Mary's.
Mill, *System of Logic*.
Ruskin, *Modern Painters*, vol. 1.
Arnold wins Newdigate Prize for Poetry.
Wordsworth made Poet Laureate.

1845 **Carlyle**, *Cromwell*.
Newman received into Roman Catholic Church.
Benjamin Disraeli, *Sybil*.

1846 **Taylor**'s (anonymous) articles on male violence begin to appear.
Ruskin, *Modern Painters*, vol. 2.
Repeal of the Corn-Laws. Potato Famine in Ireland. Election of Pope Pius IX.

1847 **Newman** ordained priest at Rome.
Arnold becomes second secretary to Lord Lansdowne.
Charlotte Brontë, *Jane Eyre*. Emily Brontë, *Wuthering Heights*.
Newman establishes Oratory of St Philip Neri.

1848 **Mill**, *The Principles of Political Economy*, gift copies of which carry dedication to **Taylor**.
Ruskin and Euphemia Chalmers Gray marry.
Revolutions throughout Europe. Chartist demonstrations in London. Habeas Corpus Act suspended in Ireland.

A. H. Clough, *The Bothie*. W. M. Thackeray, *Vanity Fair*. E. C. Gaskell, *Mary Barton*.

1849 **Taylor** begins (anonymously) a second group of articles on violence. **Ruskin**, *Seven Lamps of Architecture*. **Arnold**, *The Strayed Reveller and other Poems*. Death of John Taylor. Charlotte Brontë, *Shirley*. Charles Kingsley, *Alton Locke*.

1850 **Carlyle**, *Latter-Day Pamphlets*. Queen's University in Ireland established, condemned by Catholic Synod of Thurles. Catholic hierarchy re-established in England. Royal Commission on Oxford University. Death of Sir Robert Peel. Death of Wordsworth. *The Prelude* published. Tennyson, *In Memoriam*; made Poet Laureate. First English translation, by Helen MacFarlane, of *The Communist Manifesto* (1848) appears in *Red Republican*.

1851 **Carlyle**, *Life of John Sterling*. **Mill** and **Taylor** marry. **Taylor** publishes (anonymously) *The Enfranchisement of Women*. **Ruskin**, *The Stones of Venice*, vol. 1; *Pre-Raphaelitism*. **Arnold**, now Inspector of Schools, and Frances Lucy Wightman marry. Great Exhibition. George Eliot appointed to the *Westminster Review*. Herbert Spencer, *Social Statics*.

1852 **Newman** delivers discourses as Rector-elect, Catholic University, Dublin. **Arnold**, *Empedocles on Etna and other Poems*.

1853 **Newman**, *Discourses on the Scope and Nature of University Education*. **Ruskin**, *Stones of Venice*, vols. 2 and 3. **Arnold**, *Poems, a New Edition*, with Preface explaining omission of *Empedocles*. Charlotte Brontë, *Villette*. **Newman** purchases Medical School for Catholic University.

1854 **Ruskin** and his wife collude to have their marriage annulled (divorce being impossible) by the legal fiction of his incapacity, leaving Euphemia Chalmers Gray free to marry John Everett Millais. **Arnold**, *Poems*: second series, including *Balder Dead*. Crimean War (until 1856). Religious tests for degrees abolished at Oxford. Charles Dickens, *Hard Times*. E. C. Gaskell, *North and South* (serial).

1855 **Newman** builds University Church, Dublin.
Ruskin, *Modern Painters*, vols. 3 and 4; *Academy Notes* (continued
till 1859). Landscape classes at Working Men's College, London.
Assists in organising the decoration of the Oxford Museum.
Arnold publishes *Grande Chartreuse* and *Haworth Churchyard*
in *Fraser's*.

1856 **Carlyle** begins to issue his *Collected Works*.
E. B. Browning, *Aurora Leigh*.

1857 **Newman** founds *The Atlantis* to support liberal education among
Catholics.
Ruskin, *Political Economy of Art*.
Arnold elected Oxford Professor of Poetry.
Indian Mutiny. Commercial panic. Suspension of Bank Charter
Act of 1844. First Divorce and Matrimonial Causes court
established.

1858 **Carlyle** begins to issue *Frederick the Great* (until 1865).
Newman resigns from the Catholic University.
Mill resigns as head of foreign correspondence, India House.
Taylor dies, Avignon.
Ruskin abandons his conventional Evangelical beliefs.
Jewish Disabilities Act. India Act abolishes East India Company.
A. H. Clough, *Amours de Voyage* appears serially in *Atlantic
Monthly*.

1859 **Newman**, *The Scope and Nature of University Education*, 2nd ed.
His involvement with the liberal-Catholic *Rambler* begins.
Ruskin, *The Two Paths: Lectures on Art and its Application*.
Arnold visits France, Holland and Switzerland as Foreign Assistant
Commissioner for Elementary Education.
Charles Darwin, *The Origin of Species*. George Eliot, *Adam Bede*.

1860 **Ruskin**, *Modern Painters*, vol. 5. 'Unto This Last' series on political
economy appears in *Cornhill*.
Anglo-French Commercial Treaty.
Wilkie Collins, *The Woman in White*.

1861 **Mill**, 'Utilitarianism' articles in *Fraser's* and *Considerations on
Representative Government*.
Arnold, *On Translating Homer* and *The Popular Education of
France*.
American Civil War 1861–66.
D. G. Rossetti, *The Early Italian Poets* (translations mainly from
Dante). A. H. Clough dies, Florence.

1862 **Ruskin**, 'Munera Pulveris' articles on political economy, *Fraser's*.
Arnold, 'The Twice-Revised Code' in *Fraser's*.
Cotton Famine distress in Lancashire.

William Morris founds the decorative 'firm' of Morris, Marshall, Faulkner & Co. Christina Rossetti, *Goblin Market*.

1864 **Newman**, *Apologia pro Vita Sua*.
Ruskin, *Sesame and Lilies*. Begins housing experiment with Octavia Hill.
Arnold, *A French Eton*.
Charles Dickens begins serial publication of *Our Mutual Friend*.

1865 **Mill**, *Auguste Comte and Positivism*. Elected MP for Westminster and Lord Rector of St Andrews University.
Arnold, *Essays in Criticism*, first series. Visits France, Italy, Germany and Switzerland as Foreign Assistant Commissioner on Schools.
Lewis Carroll, *Alice's Adventures in Wonderland*.

1866 **Carlyle** elected Lord Rector of Edinburgh University. Heads Eyre Defence Committee.
Newman, *The Dream of Gerontius*.
Mill forms Jamaica Committee, pledged to impeach Eyre.
Ruskin, *The Crown of Wild Olive*. **Carlyle** claims his presence on Eyre Defence Committee.
Arnold, *Thyrsis*, in *Macmillan's*.
Death of Jane Welsh Carlyle.

1867 **Carlyle**, 'Shooting Niagara: and After?', in *Macmillan's*.
Mill moves in Commons that franchise be extended to women in certain cases.
Ruskin, 'Time and Tide' newspaper articles.
Arnold, *Celtic Literature* and *New Poems*, including *Dover Beach*; retires as Professor of Poetry.
(Second) Reform Act, properly speaking, Representation of the People Act, enfranchises a million new voters (male).

1868 **Mill** loses his seat in Parliament.
Ruskin supports Trade Unions at London Social Science meeting.
Arnold, *Schools and Universities on the Continent*.
First Trade Union Congress, Manchester.
R. Browning, *The Ring and the Book*.

1869 **Mill**, *The Subjection of Women*.
Ruskin appointed Slade Professor of Art at Oxford; publishes *The Queen of the Air* on myths of Athene.
Arnold, *Culture and Anarchy*.
Disestablishment of the Church of Ireland.

1870 **Newman**, *A Grammar of Assent*.
Ruskin, *Lectures on Art*. Works on Mansion House Committee for Relief of Paris.
Arnold, *St. Paul and Prostestantism*.

Education Act. (First) Married Women's Property Act. Franco-Prussian War. Siege of Paris. End of Papal government at Rome.

1871 **Ruskin** elected Lord Rector of St Andrews – disallowed because of statute excluding English professors. Founds drawing school at Oxford; publishes *Aratra Pentelici*; commences *Fors Clavigera: Letters to the Workmen and Labourers of Great Britain* (continued at intervals till 1884).
Arnold, *Friendship's Garland*.
Trade Union Act. Commune of Paris.
George Eliot begins publication of *Middlemarch*.

1873 **Mill** dies, Avignon.
Arnold, *Literature and Dogma*.

1874 **Ruskin** lectures on 'The Schools of Florence'.
Thomas Hardy, *Far from the Madding Crowd* serialised in *Cornhill*.

1875 **Carlyle**, *Early Kings of Norway* and *Essay on the Portraits of John Knox*.
Ruskin begins publication of *Proserpina; Deucalion; Mornings in Florence*. Announces intention, achieved over subsequent years, of founding museum at Sheffield. Deeds Ruskin art collections to Oxford.
Arnold, *God and the Bible*.

1877 **Arnold** declines renomination as Oxford Professor of Poetry and nomination as Lord Rector of St Andrews.
W. H. Mallock, *The New Republic*, with satires on Carlyle, Ruskin, Arnold, etc.

1878 **Newman** made Honorary Fellow of Trinity College, Oxford.
Ruskin resigns Oxford Professorship.
Arnold, *Selected Poems*.
Election of Pope Leo XIII.

1879 **Newman** made Cardinal.

1880 **Ruskin** begins serialisation of *The Bible of Amiens* (completed 1885).

1881 **Carlyle** dies, Chelsea; burial at Ecclefechan.
W. E. Forster introduces Irish Protection Bill allowing detention without trial.
Oscar Wilde, *Poems*.

1883 **Ruskin** re-elected Professor of Art at Oxford. Lectures on 'The Art of England'.
Arnold accepts Civil List pension of £250 p.a. Begins tour of North America (October-March 1884).

1884 **Ruskin** lectures on 'The Storm-Cloud of the Nineteenth Century' at the London Institution; 'The Pleasures of England' at Oxford.

Arnold becomes Chief Inspector for Schools.
1885 Ruskin resigns his Oxford Professorship.
Arnold, *Discourses in America*.
1886 Arnold retires from Inspectorship of Schools. Second visit to North America, summer.
1887 Carlyle's *Early Letters* and *Correspondence with Goethe*, published posthumously.
1888 Arnold dies, Liverpool. *Essays in Criticism*, second series, published posthumously.
1889 Ruskin completes his autobiography, *Praeterita*.
G. R. Gissing, *The Nether World*.
1890 Newman dies, Birmingham.
William Morris, 'News from Nowhere' in *Commonweal*.
1899 Ruskin College, at Oxford, for working men, founded by Americans Walter Vrooman and C. A. Beard.
Boer War begins.
1900 Ruskin dies, Coniston.
Labour Representation Committee founded.
Elgar's *Dream of Gerontius* performed, Birmingham.

CHAPTER ONE

Introduction

Around the middle of the nineteenth century, the word 'transitional' was much in vogue. Looking back to that time, when all of our six writers were in their heyday, it is convenient to locate their work between the first Parliamentary Reform Act of 1832 which extended the vote to middle-class men in the industrial towns, and the second Reform Act of 1867 which first gave votes to working-class men in any substantial numbers. Between these punctuation marks there are two significant dates which suggest themselves.

The first date is 1846. This year saw the repeal of the Corn Laws which had protected landowners against imported grain. Though not in itself so glorious or catastrophic as contemporaries thought, this middle-class victory, won partly by motivating working-class opinion, represented a new balance of power and signalled the terms on which our writers might operate. As middle-class writers they were all conscious of the double need to advance, or ameliorate, the condition of the working classes, while coaxing the still aristocratic establishment to take the initiative. They were also conscious of their role as catalysts whose job it was to precipitate a general shift of interest from minority to majority concerns within the stable framework of some sort of equilibrium.

The second date is 1851: the Great Exhibition, and the celebration of the equilibrium. The world was held in check by the British navy; advanced to Britain's profit by British manufactures; secured by the Bank of England. But our writers did not rejoice in the Exhibition with the same aplomb as Queen Victoria or the day-trippers from the industrial towns. More than most Victorians, they had been troubled and excited by what they had seen for themselves in Europe.

1

Arnold was in France in 1846–47, where he met George Sand and other luminaries and began to read French texts seriously. He also learned to appreciate the freedom and self-respect of the average French man and woman, so different from the deferential English 'lower' class. All this had something to do with the popular institutions of Napoleonic and Republican France: a lesson Arnold would build on for the rest of his life.

Mill was conversing with French economists as a precocious teenager. After the first Reform Act of 1832, he ceased for a while to write about English politics, and made a speciality of French affairs. Later, he and Harriet Taylor, whom he eventually married, would make a home at Avignon.

Ruskin, too, was a lifelong admirer of the 'frankness' of the French; and, like Arnold, a reader of George Sand. But his main work was in Italy, which he visited regularly for long periods from 1845. Rediscovering the architectural history of Venice in crevices ignored by fashionable tourists, he encountered the poverty and resentment that festered below the veneer of the Austrian imperialists who governed it. A wealthy Englishman, he was also able to encounter at close quarters this Austrian governing class and its cosmopolitan hangers-on and form disturbing ideas about European 'culture'.

Newman was training for the priesthood at Rome in 1846–47. There was a new Pope – Pius IX – engaged in constitutional reform, which did not last. Always convinced of the need to separate secular and spiritual power – a view shared by Dante as well as by nineteenth-century Italian Nationalists – Newman regarded the temporal régime of the Pope as a mere expedient, doomed to fall.

Behind all these reflections lay the great fact of the French Revolution, and the question as to what, ultimately, would be the outcome of its demands for liberty, equality and fraternity. It was Carlyle, in his prose epic *The French Revolution* (1837), who imposed on his fellow countrymen the responsibility of thinking about this. For him, the French monarchy and most other European monarchies and aristocracies were so much 'sham', no longer functioning. They would have to go. Uniquely among the six writers, Carlyle looked with some enthusiasm to the rising power of Prussia, under which Germany was gradually united, and which, in January 1871, proclaimed its king Emperor of Germany in the Hall of Mirrors at Versailles. Perhaps because of his first-hand acquaintance with Austrian power in its elegance and rottenness, Ruskin found a phrase that went deeper than Carlyle. 'The European death of the Nineteenth Century', he concluded in *Modern Painters*, vol. 5, was the subject Turner had painted and of which his canvases still spoke. Looking back, we can see that Ruskin's phrase describes the gradual destabilisation of that reactionary European arrangement which wobbled into balance with the defeat of Napoleon and would finally smash itself, and all its emperors, in the First World War.

Their perspective on Europe helped to alienate our six writers from the blinkered view of irreversible progress dear to some Victorian politicians and journalists.

And then there was Ireland. Ireland was crippled by absentee landlordism and famine, by the destruction of its manufactures, by the alienation and exclusion from higher education of its Catholic majority, by the abolition of its parliament. As Marx did, Carlyle, Ruskin, Mill, all saw the Irish labourer as a root problem of English political economy. Newman would try to revive an educated political class in Ireland, against all odds; and rescued some of its Celtic literature from oblivion. Arnold would give the Celtic tradition its first airing in England.

The first of our two significant dates, 1846, signalled the new status of the middle classes. The second, 1851, was a time to celebrate British prosperity and peace at home and abroad. But between them, we need a third: 1848, which saw revolution in Paris, Rome, Vienna, Budapest, and State trials for 'treason' in Ireland. This 'year of revolutions' was a sharp reminder to our middle-class thinkers of the temporary nature of their special position as advocates of peaceful change. The average English gentleman read his newspaper, grateful that continental pothers could not touch him, relieved to imagine that 'Young Ireland' had been dealt with. But our six writers never forgot Ireland existed and that Britain had a European destiny.

Inevitably, their ideas were also influenced by the world beyond Europe.

Beyond Europe lay the British Empire, which was envisaged by a broad range of British opinion as a force for conservative, non-disruptive human progress. Mutiny in India, and insurrection in Jamaica, among other events, somewhat disturbed this view of Britain's destiny. More obviously challenging were the survival of more reactionary empires; and the emergence of the dynamic new capitalist democracy of the United States.

For Taylor and Mill, America offered new ideas in democracy and women's liberation. Reading de Tocqueville, they were also anxious, while there was still time, to see safeguards against the mere rule of money which might obliterate English values once nominal democracy had replaced aristocracy. Arnold shared this latter view. Carlyle and Ruskin were more widely read in America than in England: in pirated editions, for America cared nothing for British copyright. British ideas might fare better: Ruskin had at least two pioneering settlements named after him. Like Arnold, Ruskin saw the classical and European and British legacy as something to be passed on to America. Yet Arnold was happy to see civilised democratic life actually working in parts of America; and towards the end of his writing career Ruskin's American women friends the Alexanders helped him to shake off the last vestiges of Carlyle's paternalism. For Newman, America was a melting-pot where the Catholic conservatism of European and Irish immigrants might be liberalised by the traditions of English thought and language; and those traditions in turn might be enriched and spiritualised by the necessity of responding to a more modern, more prosperous Catholicism.

By and large, our middle-class writers saw North America as hopeful ground for the propagation of their ideas of peaceful change. At the same time, they realised that British imperial prestige – and with it, their own capacity to influence America – would be short-lived. The Civil War between Northern and Southern states (1861–65) kept Americans too busy at home to pursue commercial and imperial expansion abroad. But the potential of America's huge natural resources was clear: and once the North won the Civil War, the kind of capitalist democracy represented by the North was bound to exert its influence on the world.

The reactionary Empires of China, Russia and Turkey were a more ambiguous proposition. Complacent Englishmen saw China as stagnant: a vast hinterland to the British Colony of Hong Kong, and a market for opium from British India. Our writers were more alert and humane than the average: but on the whole they shared the general Western view that China was bound to become more civilised and efficient as a result of contact with the technically more 'advanced' civilisations of Europe and America. Chinese culture was little understood or appreciated, even by Ruskin or Arnold. The Western incursions which led (by 1875–76) to concessions for foreign trade and the first Chinese railway were protested against in detail by some of our six thinkers; but the overall inevitability of Western hegemony was taken for granted.

From 1854–56, England and France were involved in an ambiguous war in the Crimea, nominally in defence of Turkey against Russian aggression. British journalists managed to persuade themselves that the Orthodox Christian tyranny of the Tsars was a greater evil than the Islamic tyranny of the Sultan. Bad management of supplies by the British government led to great suffering at Sebastopol for British troops in 1855. There was a change of government; and a new impetus was given to the question of how far, and in what ways, government should interfere to ensure the welfare of troops, and of the general population from which those troops were drawn. Florence Nightingale began her campaign for medical reforms in the British Army. More general questions of morale, health, education and effective preparedness for conflict began to be raised; and were not forgotten by our writers once the Crimean War was over. Neither the Russian nor the Turkish empire seemed likely to last indefinitely. British money and diplomacy and the British Navy were able to contribute to a temporary peace in the lands of the Turkish Empire; and Tsarist reaction and inefficiency postponed the threat to British commercial hegemony posed by the underemployed natural resources of the Russian Empire. But the sense that none of these arrangements could last lent urgency to our thinkers.

Their own prestige and influence were, at the national level, the result of the intermediate nature of the British middle class. Rightly or wrongly they saw themselves as bound to articulate the needs of the hard-worked and unenfranchised majority. They tended to address those needs, however, to those above themselves in the social order: the great capitalists and landowners. They were all very aware of the ironies of this position, and there was more to their function than is implied by this pattern, baldly stated. Nevertheless, the pattern and its ambiguities were always there.

When we consider Britain's international position, it becomes clear that our writers had a special motive for supporting the continuance of the British Empire for as long as may be. Their own prestige and influence depended on it. Reading at this distance, it is easy to dismiss them as 'imperialists'. But what is remarkable about them is the degree to which they were out of step with their contemporaries in advocating change. Taylor and Carlyle were polar opposites in the kind of change they wanted. Carlyle wanted an efficient empire, and no nonsense about the rights of subject races. Taylor seems to have wanted the Empire abolished. Mill steadily pressed for liberalisation and reform, short of abolition. Arnold, Newman and Ruskin were more conscious of the inevitability of the demise of empire and more complicated in their outlook. A pattern emerges in all three of them which anticipates the views of later generations. They became less and less sure of British superiority, more and more certain that radical change would have to come.

Speculations about Europe, empire and the wider world were, in the case of each writer, connected with attitudes to the social and political realities they observed at home. Carlyle had an obsession with the natural dominance of the Saxon race, vaguely defined. He compelled Ruskin to join him in defending Governor Eyre for his suppression of Jamaica in 1865. Foolishly, Ruskin thought he could convert the issue into an attack on the capitalist world-economy – an important idea that misfired. Mill led the attack on Eyre. All of them were a sideshow to the Parliamentary routine of murmuring regret while keeping all options open.

Many male writers went into a flurry of tactical patriotism over the Indian Mutiny of 1857. They had careers to protect. Taylor, who could have no career, never let Mill (a civil servant in India House) forget the brutality at the heart of empire. Ruskin could deploy scathing denunciation and gilded encomium in adjacent sentences on the imperial issue. But his views on white domination in Africa crystallised into the negative after listening to the young daughter of Bishop Colenso, who had lived there. This response to the unregarded view was typical of him. He climaxed *Unto This Last* with a working girl's insight into what Marx would call 'surplus value' (the difference between what a worker is worth to the capitalist and what he is paid). What really is the 'natural rate of wages'? It may be that Mill and Taylor sensed this brave suggestibility in him. By 1854, they regarded him as the only real creative thinker in England apart from themselves, Carlyle, as they thought, having written himself out.

'The year of revolutions' in Europe, 1848, saw the defeat of

Chartism in England. Chartist demands, such as manhood suffrage, remained unrealised. Nevertheless democracy was coming, and Carlyle was clearer than most about that. But he saw it reductively: a levelling process from which real government by the truly strong would emerge. Ruskin never lost Carlyle's Torified enthusiasm for leaders: but was eventually to add two kinds of considerable modification: leaders should be elected, and their accounting open to public scrutiny (a liberal measure as yet unachieved); also, he envisaged them as men and women, and saw their role as the organisation of the welfare of the entire community without exception, right down, in the phrase of the parable, 'unto this last' man, woman and child: a shockingly socialist, even communist, vision to many Englishmen then and since. It was the trade unions, he thought, which would take a lead in this. Taylor and Mill wished to prepare checks and balances against the time when the masses got the vote. Proportional representation was essential to prevent a legalised *coup d'état*. Without proportional representation, it was possible for a single party to achieve a reliable majority in Parliament from a minority of the electorate. Taylor kept alive and enriched Mill's merely theoretical notion that democracy could never work on the same basis as oligarchy: it must divorce itself utterly from male hierarchy, and all the murderous advantages and disadvantages of 'family'. But Mill's proportional representation, though eventually adopted in the new Irish Republic, got nowhere in England. Votes for women came: and Britain's first woman prime minister pulled off the reactionary *coup* Mill had dreaded.

Arnold, a civil servant by profession, wished to see a core of legislation defining the functions of the State, a democracy based on right reason and the nurture of human potential. Newman, in most of his public functions, followed the usual Catholic alliance with aristocracy. But some of his thinking had a strongly democratic tendency. He revived the question of the right of the laity to be consulted on church doctrine. This 'antiquarian' plea for a return to the older and more liberal discipline of the Church remains politically relevant, if one considers (for instance) the current teaching of the Catholic hierarchy on birth control, and its political implications. As Rector of the Catholic University of Ireland, and in articles in liberal Catholic magazines, Newman essayed a model for the raising in intelligence and vitality of the whole Church. Down-to-earth initiatives included night-classes in Dublin, and the writing of statutes so that 'persons' (i.e., including women) could at least attend university lectures.

All these activities of a self-consciously 'transitional' age were set, for our writers, within a broader view of history which may be loosely described as 'Hegelian': though a similar pattern of thought seems to have been endemic with many Victorians who had never heard of G. W. F. Hegel (1770–1831). This historical pattern – famously redeployed by Marx – involved the idea of historical progression by contraries. A first condition – hypothesis – begets its opposite, or antithesis: a reaction against the first condition. From these emerges a third: a synthesis of the first two. As this synthesis fulfils itself it begins to show the germ of its *own* opposite, and the pattern is repeated, slightly differently. Hegel himself envisaged this chain-sequence as being ultimately circular. So did some Victorians, but during the mid-century it was more usual to think in terms of a 'progressive' development: 'progress' often being used in an affirmative sense. Taylor and Mill were wedded to this idea, though highly intelligent about the difficulties of progress.

At a slightly deeper, or less coherent level, writers of all kinds in England, but especially novelists, made this idea of synthesis an important and positive one, sharing Hegel's notion that this third term, because it was the *relation* between the polarities of the first and second term, was alone positive and real, and to be cultivated. Gladstone's *The State in its Relation to the Church* of 1838 is an example of this use of 'relation' in the world of political writing. Ruskin's writings are a one-man campaign to enforce awareness of relations on the British public; and Arnold's postulate of a 'best self' from which each may contribute to the progress of the community is in the same vein.

This pattern of hypothesis, antithesis, synthesis (and relation) is useful to have in mind when reading a number of Victorian works. For example, in novels which offer rich exploration of social and personal relationships such as *Our Mutual Friend* or *Middlemarch*, it is the *idea* of synthesis that matters. Dickens and Eliot show us current social relations in disarray and force us to think about some true revival of relationships that must come about *outside* the book. Mere plot solution is something they are careful to avoid. In Charlotte Brontë's *Shirley*, we are given the hypothesis of an Anglican agricultural community, governed by the Rector; and the antithesis of a new nonconformist world of industry dominated, by the end of the novel, by a 'foreign' master manufacturer, who builds his own 'alternative' village. The novel was published in 1849, but set a generation earlier, leaving the reader to ask whether synthesis had yet arrived. A clue as to a possible synthesis – one day – is the eighteenth chapter, slyly titled 'Which the genteel reader is recommended to skip, low persons being here introduced'. Outside the church, within which a visiting Anglican parson is preaching against nonconformism, the squire's heiress Shirley and the Rector's niece Caroline envision a new – or ancient – female-based myth of Nature that reconciles pagan and biblical ideas. There follows a personal dialogue between them and two working-class men, one respectable, the other not. Each person speaks from, but not merely within, gender and class roles. The chapter is full of further clues.

When reviewers described a new work, they might employ this same 'Hegelian' triad of hypothesis, antithesis and synthesis. The first complimentary review Ruskin's *Unto This Last* ever received was in *The Bradford Observer*. The reviewer seizes on Ruskin to complete a pattern. There was the violent political revolution of the seventeenth century (hypothesis); the cerebral political economy of the eighteenth century (antithesis): there is and shall be the synthesis of Ruskin's 'Christianised humanity' emerging from the nineteenth century: a reasonable revolution in which compassion and efficiency are one.

The most frequently recurring form in which this Hegelian historical pattern is used in Victorian literature is to take the pagan classical world as hypothesis; the Christian Middle Ages as antithesis; and then to offer or demand some synthesis drawn from the modern world. A most moving example of a poem whose structure owes something to this pattern is Arnold's *Dover Beach:* though as with all great poetry, no formula can account for its catalytic effect on the minds of individual readers.

The ancient classics were reaching a wider audience through translations in this period; and Bible-reading was still a regular habit. Not surprisingly, then, the 'pagan-Christian-modern' pattern of historical development was a widely familiar one. All our six thinkers studied Greek literature. Mill and Taylor fell in love with Plato and each other simultaneously. Arnold and Ruskin sometimes even write English in a way hard to fathom without familiarity with the Greek language. All of our writers were brought up learning the Bible: Mill included, who in his early days enthusiastically declared that 'the two greatest books' were Homer and the Bible: a typical Victorian choice, and an enthusiasm Mill would never show again, once his father had ripped him from his mother's faith.

The two most important figures for all of them were Socrates and Jesus: each came at the end of his civilisation, typified it at its best and was destroyed by it, preferring truth even to life. Like Socrates, our writers saw themselves as 'gadflies', goading the state into useful action. Like Christ – for the *Imitation of Christ* was a favourite book – they were determined to read for their contemporaries the 'Signs of the Times'. Indeed these words of Christ formed the title of Carlyle's article of 1829, which is the fountainhead of this kind of writing. Mill, Arnold and Ruskin, particularly, constantly think in Platonic terms in two important ways. First, open dialogue is the means towards truth. Second, ideals are important, not because they are realisable – which is a childish misapprehension – but because they are needed to inform practice. There must be this constant interplay between what we are able to conceive and what we can achieve.

Moving forward into the Christian era, the Church could be seen as an institution separate from, but informing the State: the view of Dante, another Victorian favourite. The separation of the two, and their interplay, are the creative requirements. A number of Victorian thinkers speculated about the need for a voluntary institution having a spiritual or moral role within the State. For Carlyle, an elite band of writers might form such a substitute 'Church'. Ruskin, in his later years, hoped to see trade unions fill a similar role. These two writers, particularly, but others also to a considerable degree, constantly allude to related groups of biblical texts to convey their meaning. The final paragraph of *The French Revolution* for instance, demands that we recall a whole range of biblical allusions.

Newman sought no substitute 'Church'; but found the world-wide Catholic Church. Loathing any form of persecution, and disliking political interference in religion, Newman hoped the Catholic University of Ireland would produce an educated laity capable of holding their own in State and Church, to the furtherance of international understanding and religious reconciliation. Arnold, in a cut-and-dried but handy way, used the terms 'Hellenism' and 'Hebraism' to characterise people's desires for a rational State on the one hand and for a moral consensus that would help to form a sense of duty, on the other. He thought both were vital; but felt that his contemporaries were in special need of 'Hellenism'. *Culture and Anarchy* desires to see a truly national church, rich enough to fund universities and schools; but reformed on democratic lines to allow congregations to choose their own pastors and to manage their own affairs.

Difficulties occur when these various ideas of interplay between voluntary and state institutions are placed in the historical context of Victorian England. The English Reformation had produced a State Church, subservient to the monarchy. Its clergy were educated at the ancient endowed schools, and the Universities of Oxford and Cambridge. Their task was to educate the people under the Headship of the crown. The Church of England began to fragment as soon as it was founded; but in Victorian times it remained (as it still remains) subject to Parliament and political patronage; and the endowed schools (till 1869) and the ancient universities (till 1854–56) remained exclusively Anglican preserves. Attempts by the Anglican clergy to found schools for the poor, however, were made difficult by Protestant dissenters, who opposed state funding as a matter of principle, while also making unsectarian education impossible. Obstructionistic 'liberalism' of this kind was a proper butt for Arnold.

The (Anglican) Church of Ireland remained the established church there till 1869; though it had never commanded the loyalty of more than a minority. Church of Ireland families fed their talent into the Church of England. The Brontës' father was Irish, Arnold's father partly Irish. As for Wales, an educational priority of Henry VIII's bishops had been the extirpation of the language. Its untidy survival was a theme for the contempt of *The Times* well into the 1860s.

Things were different in Scotland. Three of our writers may be said to owe their educational background to this fortunate fact. The established Church of Scotland was Presbyterian, a workable compromise wrung from its absentee Stuart monarchs by violence. Its privileges and educational dispositions were more intact than those of the English church. It had no well-connected hierarchy to milk its funds. Its universities were in populous cities. Poverty and learning might coexist in Scotland, as in medieval times. Neither Carlyle, nor Mill's father, could have bought in England the education they received at Edinburgh University; nor could Ruskin's father – the son of a Scottish minister's daughter and her English grocer husband – have afforded in England the schooling he had at Edinburgh High School.

In describing these Victorian writers of discursive prose, terms like 'sage' have been used, then and since. Attempts have been made to see them as fulfilling in part Coleridge's idea of a 'clerisy': a quasi-priestly elite acting as leaders of thought. It may, however, be more useful to see them simply as the waning, or evolving, of the clergy. An ecclesiastical connection is never far away. Carlyle, their founding father, was trained for the Presbyterian ministry and preached as a trainee. Mill's father was still expecting to be ordained, and to find a congregation, when Mill was a child. Arnold's father was an Anglican clergyman and a fellow of Oriel: Newman was both those things, too. Ruskin was intended for the church, and only after what would now be called a 'nervous breakdown' at Oxford did he – or his mother – give up the idea. Harriet Taylor was one of a band of Unitarian women, like Harriet Martineau and Mrs Gaskell, who combined religious and literary thought and practice.

What these six writers were attempting as they commenced their careers was to provide some way forward beyond the ruins of the world for which they had been exhaustively trained. Parents often took the major role in this training. Mill and Arnold were both raised by their formidable fathers on Greek literature, including the gospels. Ruskin never forgot that his father had moulded his duty, his mother his will. Taylor's father gave her a 'masculine education'. The only two to be away from home for the bulk of their schooling were Carlyle, who grimly set his formidable parents' fierce piety against the rough-and-tumble of Annan Academy; and Newman, who embraced at his little school in Ealing an Evangelical piety more tangible than his parents' casual conformity. As university students, none of them shone by any official light. Mill never did, Taylor never could, attend one. Carlyle never graduated; Newman overworked and got a Third; Arnold swotted at the last minute for a Second: a disgrace for a Balliol scholar. Ruskin promised so badly that he was only allowed to sit for a pass degree: and then did so brilliantly in both mathematics and classics that the rules were bent to give him a complimentary double Fourth.

Carlyle chose not to become the intellectual Presbyterian

preacher his parents wanted him to be. Arnold might easily have become an Anglican rector with a hobby for poetry. Ruskin would have been less disturbing as an antiquarian dean. Such were the expectations of their families. Mill and Taylor chose to subvert the Utilitarian patriarchy, the governessy Unitarian intellectuality, they were trained to promote. Newman, moving from Oxford to Rome, chose to move from the State Church of a provincial empire to the security of a world faith and the challenge of a European tradition.

Carlyle, the eldest, had to earn his living by writing. He regarded the spiritual and moral reformation of individuals as the key to all social reform. His didactic prose made a direct personal challenge to his more fortunate successors. Three of these – Ruskin, Mill and Newman – became involved in arguments about improving institutions. Practical experience was inseparable from their theory, and holding a typically mid-Victorian view of the inviolable nature of human personality and conscience, they rejected Carlyle's doctrine of obedience so far as to make creative nuisances of themselves in the areas of fine art, Parliament and the university.

Harriet Taylor – later Mrs Mill – saw institutional reform and the renewal of individual awareness as coefficients in the great task of human liberation. More radical than Mill, she was compelled, as a Victorian woman, to live within, while subverting, the institution of gender. She persistently refused to take directives from any man – even Mill – as to how she, as a woman, should think and feel. This heroic character is the key to her importance. She still provides perspectives for the reappraisal of all the male Victorian thinkers.

Finally, with Matthew Arnold, the youngest of the group, the wheel comes full circle. The liberal atmosphere of the mid-Victorian period is receding before bleaker political and theoretic confrontations. Once again, as with Carlyle, the focus is on reforming the moral and spiritual condition of the individual, rather than changing institutions. But the work of his mid-Victorian predecessors is one reason why Arnold's strategy for such individual reform is more radically humane and democratic than Carlyle's. The absolute quality of this strategy – which still speaks more searchingly to individuals than does the work of any other Victorian intellectual – is due to the fact that Arnold's true creative medium was poetry, a medium more suited to the task than Carlyle's concussive prose, and that in that medium Arnold achieved masterpieces that are still influential.

CHAPTER TWO

Thomas Carlyle: founding a new literature of thought

Introduction

Born in the eighteenth century (he was only five weeks younger than Keats), Carlyle became one of the major literary influences of the nineteenth century. At the same time he remained dominated, in important areas of his thought, by the religious politics of the seventeenth century. He was raised as a strict Presbyterian within the Burgher sect. The Burghers attempted to retain their allegiance to the Covenant as ratified by the Scottish Parliament in 1644, at the time of Cromwell's victories over the monarchy. This Covenant imposed an extreme Protestant theocracy in which state and church were indivisible. Carlyle's parents, poor but respectable farming people of the Scottish Borders, made sacrifices to send him to school and Edinburgh University, fervently hoping that he would become a Burgher minister. The peculiar political and religious outlook of the sect became untenable, however, by 1820, when Carlyle was twenty-five, and it ceased to exist as an independent body.

Only in 1822 did Carlyle begin to recover from a long spiritual crisis, renouncing formal Christianity in favour of his 'new Mythus' of Natural Supernaturalism. In a world apparently dominated by negation, 'void of Life, of Purpose, of Volition', he claimed the individual's right to affirm an 'Everlasting Yea'.[1] Henceforth, meaning and purpose must be created by an effort of human will, seeking to articulate spiritual truth in new forms beyond the collapse of old religious and political orders. Carlyle's efforts in this direction would generate a whole sequence of influential works. He would have unparalleled success in stimulating the thinking of his countless readers. Carlyle himself, however, proved incapable of breaking the grip of his early background. A critical turning-point in his career is marked by his book *On Heroes* of 1841. This was a volume of lectures: the last Victorian genre Carlyle would pioneer. The work ends with a plea for democracy to generate its own authority, and looks to the 'men of letters' to articulate the fairer and more efficient society Carlyle saw as the real demand of the French Revolution. Carlyle's own course, however, would henceforth take him more and more in an opposite direction.

While it pleads for others to generate a workable democracy – if they can – *On Heroes* was also intended to prepare the public for what was to have been Carlyle's own *magnum opus*: a biography of his greatest authoritarian hero, Oliver Cromwell. In the event, he found this impossible to write, though he produced an edition of Cromwell's letters in 1845. The year 1843 saw Carlyle's last pervasively influential work, *Past and Present*. In this, Carlyle begged his readers to generate for the future some true renewal of important principles from the Middle Ages. Spiritual meaning must be renewed, personal responsibility and an organic view of society must be reclaimed. This is the high point of Carlyle' social thinking. From that point on, he would consolidate his old ideas rather than make new explorations. Effectively isolated by his eminence as the last surviving Romantic, Carlyle lacked the humility which allowed Mill to learn from Taylor, Newman to seek precedents for his thinking, or Ruskin to give serious attention to the thoughts and feelings of his wide and varied aquaintance. Carlyle retreated into his parents' authoritarian views and his father's habit of pungent exaggeration. Indeed, as he came to seem more and more reactionary, the Liberal press made a point of linking his name almost exclusively with 'Hero-Worship', an unfair association which still continues to distort the image of Carlyle.

It is more useful to see Carlyle as the founder of a new kind of literature of thought. He profoundly influenced a whole generation of younger writers, forcing them to look at principles rather than appearances, almost challenging them to evolve some form of democracy that would satisfy the savage scepticism of a mind like his. Breaking free from conventional Christianity, while continuing to search for spiritual meaning; insisting on the performance of personal duty, while also demanding a new social order; making high claims for the men of letters while stressing the importance of practical achievements: all these living contradictions in Carlyle's work would foster a lively dialectic among his successors.

Two of these were his personal friends: Mill and Ruskin. Mill came under Carlyle's direct influence for some years after the older man's move to London in 1834. Ruskin entered Carlyle's personal circle after the publication of *The Stones of Venice*, in 1851. Partisans of Mill or Ruskin have generally praised them for the ways in which they differed from Carlyle. Some have echoed Arnold's description of Carlyle as a 'moral desperado'.[2] Yet all three, each in his different way, typified the response of Victorian thinkers to their founding father. They would develop along the lines suggested for 'men of letters' in *On Heroes*, striving to articulate some fairer and more efficient criteria for society. All three retained reservations about democracy, while moving in directions that were more liberal, and to an extent, more socialist in implication than anything Carlyle would have supported. As they did so, they inevitably came to feel less and less sympathy with what Mill called Carlyle's 'transcendentalisms' and what Ruskin regretted as Carlyle's 'howlings about Cromwell'.[3]

Sectarian background

Carlyle's parents were devout and thrifty farming people of the Scottish Borders. His father had in youth become a member of the Burgher sect, the peculiar nature of whose beliefs is significant for understanding the son.

The Burghers regarded the old Presbyterian Covenant as such a sacred thing that they were convinced allegiance was owed to it by all the descendants of all those who had ever affirmed it, even when such affirmation had been secured by force.

Their strict religious creed, combined with an equally strict regard for secular authority, placed them in a contradictory position – or, as they saw it, placed the rest of Scotland in a contradictory position. According to their reading of history, the established Presbyterian Church of Scotland had become insufficiently strict in religion by 1733, provoking the secession of a body calling themselves 'Associate' Presbyters. Then, in 1747, demands made by Parliament for oaths of religious loyalty provoked a division among these 'Associates' themselves. A loyalist group, calling themselves 'Burghers', supported the right of Parliament to demand the new oaths. But the majority, or Anti-Burghers, were averse to any use of compulsion in matters of conscience. They expanded rapidly in Scotland, Ireland and North America as an enlightened, humanitarian and (in Burgher eyes) hopelessly lax religious body.[4]

Carlyle was born in December 1795. It was the motive of his parents' existence that he should become a Burgher minister. They were members of the congregation of John Johnston, who became Carlyle's Latin tutor. This man and his memory would always be revered by Carlyle, but he could not follow in his footsteps. Loyal to his father's narrowness, Carlyle equated the 'Church' with his father's sect and retained its pattern of populism, spiritual pride and reverence for force. But the Burgher sect was doomed. The contradiction between its spiritual strictness and its respect for power was made more and more untenable by the march of events. The Burghers were in no position to reimpose the seventeenth-century Covenant on Scotland. They must either deny their religious conscience, and join the Establishment; or abandon their conviction that secular power had the right to dictate to that conscience, and join the Anti-Burghers.

Such was the background to Carlyle's decision of 1817 to renounce his intention of entering the ministry. In 1820, Burghers and Anti-Burghers were reunited in a new United Secession Church, and the Burgher sect ceased to exist as an independent body. This United Secession Church was outside the Establishment, but enjoyed access to the ancient Scottish universities: a happy compromise, it might seem, between religious conscience and participation in the state.

Such compromises did not impress Carlyle. In a sense, he never left the church of his early upbringing; never revoked his nation's pledge to the Covenant. It must rather have seemed that the march of history had compelled his church to abandon him and his nation to betray him. He would never be able to migrate from his early convictions into any laxer form of creed or any less rigorous notion of the state.

Letter writer

Carlyle learned to write, cogently, compactly, at speed, and with much of the flavour of his Lowland Scots speaking voice, by writing hundreds of letters. The fact that postage was expensive helped to give Carlyle a flair for brevity and point, which would enhance the quality of his earlier journalistic work, where space was also limited. The removal of this restriction, in some of his later books, did not improve his style. Letters, he felt, should be intimate and self-revealing; and in reading especially his controversial pamphlets it is important to remember that similar criteria obtain. In these, Carlyle honours the reader with an uncompromising, though calculated, presentation of his most characteristic thoughts, not necessarily meant to be pleasing; not veiled in shades of irony: an unembarrassed, complex bluntness, meant to provoke a response.

Finding a vocation

After four years at university it was for Carlyle as a poor Scotsman conventional to accept a post as tutor – at £70 a year – at his old school while studying externally for ordination. He began teaching at Annan in 1814; preached his first sermon that year and entered print with a letter on mathematics to a local newspaper. But his real ambitions were confided to the inside of a Greek textbook: 'Oh Fortune! . . . Grant me that with a heart of independence, unseduced by the world's smiles, and unbending to its frowns, I may attain to literary fame.'[5] The style of this inscription is deliberately burlesque yet the intention is patently sincere. It was not unusual for poor but ambitious Scots intellectuals, compelled to sell great talents cheap, to indulge in self-parody of this kind, as a form of defence against the possibility of failure.

Whatever route to fame was chosen, it was necessary to find a patron.

He removed to a better teaching post at Kirkcaldy in 1816. It was there that he met Edward Irving, who would become a friend, and in some ways a patron, too. In 1817 Carlyle renounced the ministry. By 1818 he could not face teaching either and resigned from Kirkcaldy to live on savings and short-term tutoring while pursuing his own studies and offering reviews to the press. The prospect of real recognition did not begin to open up till 1827 when he met his most significant patron, Francis Jeffrey, editor of the *Edinburgh Review*. His sectarian upbringing gave Carlyle a peculiar slant on history; but he would no longer merely teach or preach what had been said or believed in the past. His vocation would be to urge his contemporaries to renew the values he had inherited in a form viable for the future.

Translator and reviewer

During the decade 1818–28, Carlyle was based in Edinburgh. His main work was translating, reviewing, and various forms of literary hack work. Not till 1828 could he hope to 'cease *reviewing* a little, and try to give Work for reviewing'.[6] To become the known master of a subject was essential for success for a discursive writer. Mathematics was Carlyle's outstanding subject as student and tutor. But he was also interested in geology: the characteristic nineteenth-century science, with its implications for the origins and destiny of the earth: and to pursue geological theory German was necessary. Carlyle taught himself German. Before long, German language and literature became Carlyle's chief interest and a passport to success. He graduated from translating scientific papers to writing outlines and articles on the recent philosophy and literature of Germany, which was far more agreeable to the Scots mind than the alien effusions of English romantics. Carlyle became known as an expert in this field. The *Edinburgh Review* was the leading intellectual magazine of the day; and his reputation grew steadily from his first appearance in its pages in 1827.

Another Scotsman, James Fraser, gave him work for the London-based *Fraser's* which, in contrast to the serious Whig *Edinburgh Review*, was an irreverent Tory magazine. Carlyle's apprenticeship as a hack writer had made him a master of parody and pastiche; and these burlesque qualities were welcome in *Fraser's*. The *Foreign Quarterly Review* and the *London and Westminster Review* also gave him work. As was common, the books Carlyle reviewed became pegs for virtually independent articles. Less common was Carlyle's reviewing tone: always shrewd and sometimes deadly, but never trivial or cruel.

Some grandiose ideas were fostered in Carlyle by his work on German texts. The world needed strength; but it must be a pure strength. Strength would surely come to the world from a cultural alliance of the Saxon peoples in Britain, Germany and America. But Schiller taught Carlyle that strength must be purified by new ideas from outside. Very well, then, Carlyle would purify British 'Materialism' with the spirit of what he called German

'Reason', with its 'Primitive Truth', sought 'not historically and by experiment . . . but by intuition in the deepest and purest nature of Man'.[7]

Biography

Carlyle's biographies demonstrate what he thought human life really was. His contempt for 'Materialism', and his obsession with the transcendental, provide clues to his aims in writing. These aims were religious, but not Christian. Some Victorians found them shockingly anti-Christian and amoral.

For Carlyle, a man is interesting if he demonstrates the spirit of an age, good or bad. A man is great if he makes some sort of order out of chaos, by whatever means. Success of any kind in the material world is merely a reflex of some transcendental truth.

His first major piece of biography was a 'Life of Schiller', in 1824. In his closing words he begs that his hero 'be transfigured in our thoughts, and shine there without the little blemishes that clung to him in life'. It is not really Schiller the man, or even Schiller the artist, that Carlyle is interested in, but Schiller as a concept 'transfigured in our thoughts' into an emblem of transcendent truth.[8]

Carlyle's essay on 'Biography' of 1832 explains this idea further. He uses Raphael's picture of Christ's Transfiguration on the mountain top as an analogy for the biographer's 'Invention of Reality'. Raphael's painting is less important than what it depicts, Carlyle argues. But the transcendental importance of what is depicted can only be known because it is worthily depicted. Thus we have three levels of importance. First, the Divine Power of God; next, Christ, important only because transfigured by Divine Power; third, Raphael's depiction of Christ's transfiguring, important only because of its subject matter.

But for Carlyle this hierarchy can be reversed, so that the brilliance of the artist can be seen as the most important thing, lending transcendence to the heroic figure of Christ, which in turn provides evidence for the existence of Divine Power. Looking one way, God creates the hero for the artist to depict. Looking the other way, the artist creates the hero as evidence of God.[9]

Carlyle was always invoking God; but Victorians were not always sure he believed in Him. They were never sure whether

God made Carlyle or Carlyle made God. They were also worried about the character of the men Carlyle chose to make heroes of. For many Victorian writers – Dickens, George Eliot, Ruskin – Christ's transcendental nature was much less important than his human goodness. For all these writers, Christ's bodily life was important because it demonstrated the sacredness of the human body and its needs. Confronted by a need to make a synthesis out of pagan Reason and Christian faith they found that synthesis in the idea of a secularised 'Kingdom of God on earth'. What these Victorians chose to see as Christlike practical goodness was for them the stuff of heroism: a view compatible with any transcendental belief or none.

Carlyle had almost the opposite view to this. The moral qualities of the heroes of his biographies, or the nature of their practical achievements, are less significant for him than the fact of their transcendental importance. Thus, Cagliostro, whose biography Carlyle wrote in 1833, was a fraudulent alchemist and quack. But Carlyle finds him important because thanks to Carlyle's brilliant style, he can be transfigured into an emblem of the eighteenth-century spirit. John Sterling, on the other hand, whose biography Carlyle wrote in 1851, was a well-meaning and humane man who wrestled with problems of belief and duty. Carlyle's interest in him was identical to his interest in Cagliostro. Sterling mattered only because he could be transfigured into an emblem of the early nineteenth-century spirit. Moral differences between Cagliostro and Sterling matter little: both exist mainly to reveal a transcendent spirit visible beyond the human 'sham' of their lives. 'Sham' is a favourite Carlyle word. Cagliostro was a sham because he defrauded people for money. Sterling was a sham, too, because his honest philosophical bewilderment was inadequate. Pious Victorians were naturally upset by Carlyle's *Life of Sterling*.[10]

Even harder to take, for many, were Carlyle's biographies of Doctor Francia (1843) and the much longer *Frederick the Great* (1858–65). Francia was a brutal South American dictator. Frederick, in English eyes, was a megalomaniac military tyrant. But for Carlyle, both were great men because they combated anarchy, and imposed some kind of order.

While Cagliostro and Sterling were interesting, as embodying the spirit of an age, and Frederick and Francia were great because they combated a chaotic age, Carlyle's supreme hero was Oliver

Cromwell. He not only embodied the best in his own age; he also forced it – however momentarily – to surpass itself. Nevertheless, Cromwell the human being matters less to Carlyle than does the concept of Cromwell as 'transfigured', by God or by the pen of Carlyle, into a vehicle for the manifestation of transcendent truth and power.

Social commentator

Carlyle began his career as a social commentator in 1829. Francis Jeffrey invited him to review two very different books on contemporary affairs: one by the Utilitarian Alexander Mackinnon; the other by the apocalyptic Christian, Carlyle's former friend Edward Irving. Irving claimed that society would soon be abolished by Christ's personal rule on earth. His work was an extreme example of the demand of inner spiritual conviction over social responsibility. Mackinnon was equally eccentric, believing that rationalism and the imposition of efficient social machinery were all that was required to make men happy. From these two extremes Carlyle created a synthesis which was to some extent compatible with the cautious Whig individualism of the *Edinburgh Review*. Each man, he argued, must begin his own inner reformation before social efficiency could be realised. This platitude was not very startling. But it was reached at the end of an analysis that was new and challenging. It was accompanied by an affirmation of heroic individualism which was even more surprising.

Carlyle's 'Signs of the Times' of 1829 provided the groundwork for much subsequent social criticism. Its analysis was challenging. Stern and rigorous in its demands for change, it was also inspiring in its recognition of the glorious potential for change. Carlyle regarded fanaticism like Irving's or Mackinnon's as too bizarre and one-sided to be taken seriously. Both were really examples of 'dilettantism' (a favourite Carlyle hate-word). Mankind must be released from such deadly triviality, and the true 'Dynamical nature of man' brought into play with the aid of a spiritual Philosophy of Mind. At the moment there was nothing true in art or politics because there was no true spiritual leadership. Trapped in a mechanical age, every shade of opinion was alienated from regenerative action by its reverence for moribund institutions. Intelligence was exhausted in defending them, improving them, thinking about them. Truly, most of them were not even worth attacking. One new institution – newspapers – commanded Carlyle's respect. Newspaper editors had the makings of a 'true Church' in them; but as yet most journalists shared the common *malaise*. Poets, too – Byron characterised the tendency – positively worshipped 'physical, mechanical' phenomena, and had forgotten truth.

If Carlyle went further than most in his analysis of what was wrong, he also went further than many Victorians were prepared to go along the path of heroic individualism as a solution. Ultimately, Carlyle expected little from efficiency, conformity or the ideas of little men. The spread of education among the 'humblest' was welcome, but what was needed was a new dogma to inform their thought. Only then could the modern world begin to recover the 'heroic worth of our forefathers'. There were signs of renewal, but a leader was needed. When the world was ripe for a new crusade, the better part of humanity would respond again as in better days to the 'passionate voice of one man, the rapt soul looking through the eyes of one man'.[11]

Carlyle's talents for political commentary were actively encouraged by Macvey Napier, the new editor of the *Edinburgh Review*, from 1830. 'Characteristics', which appeared there in 1831, was a grander and more explicit version of 'Signs of the Times'. Grandly Carlyle invoked those noble souls who had already 'dared to say No' to conventional beliefs and could not yet 'say Yea' to the new dogmas being generated by thinkers like Carlyle. Explicitly, he urged such souls to take resolute action now. Theory must to some extent wait on practice. Let there be action to change the conditions of a world where Nations are rich and men are poor, the slaves of Mechanism, which should be our slave. Carlyle here comes near to anticipating Marxism: but his proffered solution – Emigration and Colonisation under elite captains, and the carving up of the world by 'indomitable millions, full of Saxon energy' – is a reminder that Hitler, as well as Engels, would admire Carlyle.[12]

From 1839, Carlyle's political direction became clearer. He was taken up by William Bingham Baring, inheritor of the Baring banking fortune, and his talented wife Lady Harriet. Carlyle felt more at home with their modernised Toryism than with the old-fashioned Whig 'liberalism' of Jeffrey and Napier. He began to write for the Tory *Fraser's Magazine*. Its editor, James Fraser, also published Carlyle's *Chartism* as a pamphlet in 1839. This made a great stir. Real-life politics had entered Carlyle's prose for the first time.

Baring was an active MP and opponent of Free Trade. In line with this, Carlyle lent his moral weight against '*Laissez-faire* applied to poor peasants, in a world like our Europe'. More positively, he urged that sectarian prejudices be set aside to allow at least the teaching of reading and writing to all at the state's expense.[13] The extension of the franchise – which he saw as inevitable – he regarded as an indifferent matter. Democracy was a 'self-cancelling business', the mere clearing of the ground for new trials of strength to ascertain justice, which Carlyle characterised as 'correctly articulated mights'. In the long term, he looked forward to ordered mass emigration from 'the Teutonic Countries'; in the short term he declared, 'Let the Tories be Ministry if they will: let at least some living reality be Ministry' rather than the nominally reforming Whigs.

The zenith of Carlyle's social writing is *Past and Present* of 1843. Based on the idea of a 'review' of a medieval chronicle of the St Edmundsbury monastery, it enlists the current fashion for things medieval to make a diagnosis for the contemporary world.

The sceptical eighteenth century despised everything that was medieval. The nineteenth century must pursue scepticism in a more positive spirit. There are plenty of shams which have survived the French Revolution. Plenty more are being invented every day. They must all go. But instead of allowing anarchy and revolution to rush into the void thus created, modern man must replace the void with true belief and action. The Middle Ages can supply principles for that action. It is these principles which need to be recovered in modern form. We need to distinguish the reality from the sham. We can do without the current fashion for medieval decor and medievalised Christianity. We cannot do without the true medieval principles of spiritual power, organic community and personal responsibility.

Immensely influential with other Victorian thinkers – including Emerson and Engels – *Past and Present* does what Carlyle is best at, in supplying, not specific remedies, but a powerful general challenge to initiative. Its impressive final chapter, 'The Didactic', set the terms on which much subsequent Victorian literature would be produced: combining a broad historical sense with a feeling of responsibility towards the present. *Past and Present* also put into currency a number of useful terms: 'Mammonism', 'Dilettantism', 'Windbag', 'Cash-Nexus', 'Captains of Industry', among others.[14]

It is downhill from there. Carlyle's friendship with the Barings brought him into the great world: and he flirted with political influence among Tories. He tried to forge a theoretical alliance between real-life politics and his own ideals, which under the flattery of the Barings tended to degenerate into fantasies. He selected Sir Robert Peel, the Tory leader, as a possible new Cromwell. In *Latter-Day Pamphlets* – issued serially in 1850 – he embarrassed his own Tory patrons with his contempt for constitutionalism and his violent language. Even a friendly reviewer, David Masson,[15] who honoured Carlyle's literary gifts, was offended by such prescripts as the punitive regimentation of the nine out of ten men who were 'recognizable as fools' – to Carlyle. While Carlyle was busy urging Peel to take this dictatorial stance, the Tory leader died: and any slight chance of direct political influence for Carlyle died with him.

However shocking, *Latter-Day Pamphlets* made a brisk sale – to the publisher Chapman's delight – and a similar *succès de scandale* was earned by 'Shooting Niagara: and After?', which Masson commissioned for *Macmillan's Magazine* to coincide with the Second Reform Act (August 1867). Carlyle's response to the new democracy was vitriolic. There might still be time, he wrote, for the Aristocrat of title to join his Speculative and Practical Brothers – literary sages like Carlyle and industrial heroes – in the 'simultaneous Drilling into combined rhythmic action' of the British population: but now that under the enfranchising wand of the 'Hebrew-conjuror' Disraeli 'the wild horse of a Plebs' had begun to reel out of control, the so-called ' "Governing Class" ' had better dismount and take up rat-catching. There would soon be no better game left.

Carlyle's evolving role from the compressed and suggestive thinker of 1829 through the Whig individualist of 1831, and the Conservative radical of 1839–50, to this wild Tory-anarch of 1867, found its nadir in a letter to the *Times* of 1870, gloating over Bismarck's reduction of Paris.[16] The writer whose challenge to a younger generation had already produced an abundant and varied response had himself now apparently subsided into a patriot for Prussia, right or wrong.

Sartor Resartus

Sartor Resartus, Carlyle's most successful essay in fiction, was published serially in *Fraser's Magazine*, November 1833 – August 1834. Carlyle had made a number of earlier, not very successful, fictional experiments but after *Sartor* he would write no more novels. The book makes few concessions to the nineteenth-century preference for naturalism. It is highly self-conscious, and attempts to present a world view. It deploys devices such as the unreliable narrator and long extracts from invented texts. Diverse modes of presentation are used, including elements of fairy-tale, mock history and burlesque philosophy. At the same time, it conveys a sense of seriousness, even urgency. It might be said that the principal narrator, who sometimes seems to be Carlyle, and sometimes a pose or mask adopted by Carlyle, is also the real hero. It is this narrator who compels the reader to think, not just about the story, but about the world in which narrator and reader actually find themselves, outside the book. All these aspects are probably more easily understood by twentieth-century readers who have had the opportunity to read T. S. Eliot, Brecht and Joyce. Carlyle presents a false world governed by artificial values. If the people in this world often appear to be like figures in a puppet show, this simply reinforces the reader's awareness of the hollowness and insufficiency of his own living world. Readers of Kafka, to whose work this device would be central, need not be as bewildered by *Sartor Resartus* as its original readers, many of whom were so alienated that they cancelled their subscriptions to *Fraser's Magazine*.

Sartor Resartus would seem very odd indeed in the context of the naturalistic Victorian novel. It now appears much less odd, if regarded in the much broader context of the world novel. Predecessors of Carlyle, like Cervantes and Sterne, are like him in their use of fantasy for serious purposes. In the twentieth century, writers like Beckett have often so used it. It was this apparent betrayal of 'sincerity' which alienated Victorians.

In the context of mid-Victorian fiction, the influence of *Sartor* lay rather in the realm of ideas than in such aspects as style or method. It is worth noting, however, that *Hard Times* (1854), which Dickens dedicated to Carlyle, deploys not only a number of Carlyle's ideas, but also the central fictional device of *Sartor*, which is the deliberate use of parody and burlesque to convey the falseness of the political and economic reality outside the novel.

Carlyle's title – *Sartor Resartus* – is itself a very complicated Latin joke. The whole book is full of the sort of elaborate wordplay more beloved of critics than the general reader. These things have usually been more popular in Germany than in England. Carlyle was indebted for a number of his devices to writers of German romance like Goethe and Jean-Paul Richter whom he had translated and introduced to the British public. From these German writers he borrowed such elements as unreliable narration, mock-learned commentary, and games with invented texts. He was also indebted to them for their satirical insights into European society, and their deployment of anti-naturalistic presentation of scene and character, so as to make readers think more searchingly about real scenes and characters outside the book. All of these things were quite new to British readers. Carlyle certainly overestimated the impact of his translations of *German Romance* (1827) if he thought the British public was ready for *Sartor Resartus* by 1833. *Sartor* is much more wholesale in its use of literary tricks than Goethe or Richter. Carlyle is also much more devastating in his critique of social and economic ills than his German predecessors, who remain essentially eighteenth-century in their wholesome confidence in human nature and human capacity for betterment. Carlyle's radical exposure of alienation and meaninglessness, expressed as it was in an almost excruciatingly experimental style, was bound to bewilder readers.

Modern readers may feel that the fictional experiment of *Sartor Resartus* gave Carlyle advantages which were less readily available when writing history or direct social commentary. By inventing his representative man – the wayward intellectual Diogenes Teufelsdröckh ('God-born Devil's dirt') – Carlyle could write a universal history which was also one man's biography. His tendency to resort to fantasy, so irritating in his history or social criticism, is here an advantage.

By the use of anti-naturalistic scenes and characters, Carlyle could deploy alienation as Greek tragedians had, and as Brecht would do. In all three cases, the audience begins by feeling that the remote personages represented have nothing to do with them.

But they begin to recognise information strongly relevant to their own reality. The scenes and characters are fantastic and not 'real' in themselves. They are all the more *about* reality. If skilfully done, the drama can harrow the audience with the conviction that out there on the stage are themselves. The distant pity for others is aligned with fear for themselves; and the double exposure to pity and fear can have the steadying effect of that radical readjustment Aristotle called 'catharsis'.

At the end of a Greek tragedy the audience is readjusted to the organic world of which they are part. They feel themselves at one with the realities of nature, with its seasonable pattern of death and renewal. They must take their part in that divine pattern. At the end of a Brecht play like *The Good Person of Setzuan*, the audience come to recognise that they are part of the pattern of history. They are urged to find some way of contributing to that pattern. Acceptance is not enough; they must work for tolerable change. *Sartor Resartus* may be said to come mid-way between these two kinds of feeling.

The Greek dramatists demand that we accept things as they are. Brecht demands that we change things. For him, there is no unchangeable human nature, no divine law that says that things must be so or so. For Carlyle, between the Greeks and Brecht, external changes are important *only* as a response to inner reality, which truly does not change. It is for him urgent that we renew our response to spiritual, unchanging, reality. The external changes we need would then follow.

Whether or not *Sartor* is a socialist novel, or a novel at all, remains a matter for debate. The debate was advanced in 1987 by the Oxford edition, with excellent commentary and notes. Not appreciated for some time in England, the work had its first artistic success – at no immediate financial profit to Carlyle – when, with Emerson's help, it was brought out by a Boston publisher in 1835. It is typical of Victorian culture that a provincial audience should be more adventurous than the West End of London. The first English edition did not appear till 1838.

The French Revolution

During his lifetime, Carlyle's *The French Revolution: a History* was generally regarded as his masterpiece. Its impact was enormous, and not merely among writers and intellectuals. Those who, in popular terms, referred to it as 'Carlyle's French Revolution' were in fact responding to an important aspect of Carlyle's historical theory.

For Carlyle, the chaos of temporal events could have no meaning until it was adequately written down. It was the writing which made a history out of the chaos. In particular, a muddle of violent, inexplicable doings and sayings could never, by themselves, amount to a 'Revolution': which is, by definition, an epoch-making event with far-reaching results. The 'Revolution' could not really begin to happen until it began to be comprehended. The collapse of the monarchy, the storming of the Bastille, the Reign of Terror: none of these amounted to much. Only as mankind absorbed their significance could they begin to amount to a revolution. Consciously placing himself in the Epic tradition, Carlyle provided his version of this significance, his personal engendering of the 'French Revolution'. Another writer's 'French Revolution' might well be rather different. As more and more people came to wrestle meaning out of it, the greater would be the significance and effect of the Revolution. It was not an isolated event or series of events which could be put behind us, safely in the past. It was, for Carlyle, at the same time a crisis in human affairs presenting problems which would not go away, and also an awesome manifestation of that divine presence which always underlies the universe, and which continually demands a suitable response.

Carlyle regularly uses the present tense in his descriptions of events. Historical and epic writers often resort to this 'narrative present'. Carlyle does so not merely for vividness, but in order to enforce upon his readers the awareness that the 'French Revolution', as a significant event, is happening *now* in their own minds and hearts as they read. The book is made up of approximately 1,700 paragraphs, 500 of which are taken up with direct commentary by the narrator.[17] Thus, nearly a third of 'Carlyle's French Revolution' is interpretation, without which there is no true Revolution at all, in his view.

In those other paragraphs, where events are described, Carlyle draws on his phenomenal memory of a vast range of written sources. Each source gives only a fragmented view. Sometimes there are many contradictory or partial sources for the same event. Carlyle refuses to reduce them to some neat, rational picture.

Instead, he forces them together into a vivid impressionistic scene, evoking the many viewpoints of the varied witnesses, and giving each the weight he feels appropriate. His own readers thus have the benefit of all these views and observations brought together with what would now be called 'cinematic' vividness and variety. In a single scene, the reader may look now through the eyes of a condemned aristo, now through those of a starving peasant-woman, now through those of a guard. Readers can also feel that Carlyle is not 'cheating' or inventing, but merely editing and realising the accounts of witnesses. It is always clear when Carlyle is commenting directly, and when he is editing others. In editing others, he usually lets the reader know when he is evoking eye-witnesses and when he is passing on details of official reports. The effect of all this is to display the events in all their dynamism and at the same time to involve the reader in the process of absorption and reflection to which Carlyle, along with his written sources, has contributed.

The view of history Carlyle provides in his commentary is comparable to the medieval one, which envisages a series of epochs, held together by a divine purpose which it is the function of the chronicler to explain. For Carlyle, as for Dante, 'history' is a mysterious book that can be fully read only by the light of eternity. Another epic parallel illuminates the motivation for his descriptions of events. In *Paradise Lost*, the Archangel Michael provides a panorama of history for the first man Adam. By exposure to vivid didactic scenes, Adam is morally prepared for his work of faith and renewal. In *The French Revolution*, the narrator supplies Michael's choric function. In so doing he is not recounting a vanished past, but unfolding history itself, past and future, as a single significant present.

Carlyle is equally skilful in his control of the reader's emotion. He may be said to owe something to Homer in this respect; and also to anticipate the general policy of Brecht's epic dramas, such as *Mother Courage*. Contrary to most Victorian practice, Carlyle shares with Homer and Brecht an epic outlook, which begins in alienation and leads to universal recognition. Cheap sentiments, or the glib taking of sides, are rigorously avoided. Whatever preconceptions we may have had about the events and characters, we are likely to lose them. As the drama unfolds, we become aware of a profound recognition of our own implication in the universal humanity of what is presented. Our emotional response to this must go deeper than any trivial or partial emotion.

Ruskin, who was deeply indebted to Carlyle, and whose social commentary Carlyle admired, gives the best Victorian description of the effect of this deep kind of poetic creation: 'it is the gathering and arranging of material by imagination, so as to have in it at last the harmony or helpfulness of life, and the passion or emotion of life'.[18]

An example of this effect in Carlyle is the way he handles the figure of Louis XVI himself. By the end of volume 1, we see him steadily, without sentiment. He is kept at a distance sufficient for us to see him, and his fate, clearly. He cannot, however, be absolutely distant from us, because it is all life, and our own with it, that we see in him. He is seen in relation to his three 'Paris processions', the last of which will be to the guillotine:

> Finally, the King is shown on an upper balcony, by torchlight, with a huge tricolor in his hat: 'and all the people', says Weber, 'grasped one another's hand;' – thinking *now* surely the New Era was born. Hardly till eleven at night can Royalty get to its vacant, long-deserted Palace of the Tuileries; to lodge there, somewhat in strolling-player fashion. It is Tuesday the 6th of October 1789.

> Poor Louis has Two other Paris Processions to make: one ludicrous-ignominious like this; the other not ludicrous nor ignominious, but serious, nay sublime. (I.vii.11)

This is epic writing. The key adjective is 'serious'. It is not enough to say that Carlyle is 'objective'. Ruskin's 'the emotion of life' comes nearer. When Louis dies, there is no sentimental wallowing, no cheap outrage:

> Miserablest mortals, doomed for picking pockets, have a whole five-act Tragedy in them, in that dumb pain, as they go to the gallows, unregarded; they consume the cup of trembling down to the lees. For Kings and for Beggars, for the justly doomed and the unjustly, it is a hard thing to die. Pity them all: thy utmost pity . . . (III.ii.8)

Louis's death is not made significant by his inherited position. It is not made insignificant by his personal feebleness. It is significant because it is one with all human death, and because it is part of the history of human political aspiration and failure. At this point, not only the 'emotion of life' but what Ruskin calls the 'helpfulness of life' is made manifest, in Carlyle's terms.

By pointing to 'pity' as the true response, Carlyle shows himself nearer in spirit to the Brecht of *Mother Courage* than to the Homer of the *Iliad*. Homer forces us to accept what he shows us. His text was used, throughout Greek history, as an education for the warrior. Young men learnt it by heart, and learnt to 'do likewise': to put pity and fear behind them and face up to their predestined fighting role. Clearly, Carlyle's moral is different from this. He intends his readers to put fear behind them sufficiently to embrace pity for human life, in all its implications. His explicit moral guideline to his departing audience is 'to understand . . . and do *otherwise*' (III.vii.6). Carlyle sees no escape from evil in evil, from stupidity in stupidity, from war in war. At the end of the book, he bequeathes responsibility to the reader for implementing the Revolution he has written: 'Man, by the nature of him, is definable as "an incarnated word" ' (III.vii.8).

Christ, the Word of God Incarnate, was by this time no longer a figure of unique sanctity for Carlyle. It was quite clear to him, however, that it was Christ's life and death that had separated his own mind forever from Homer's mind.[19] 'Peaceful change' and 'moral progress', were for him not pious inanities, but the only real hope for the world. That is why unlike other Victorians who were fond of referring to these things, Carlyle could never be sentimental or facile about them. In his biographies of Dr Francia and Frederick the Great, Carlyle would outrage Victorian sensibility by seeming to set them up as special idols for worship, almost as Antichrists. *The French Revolution* corrects this view, because it succeeds in presenting a universal image of the seriousness and sanctity of human life itself. It is this whole life, not Louis, or Robespierre, or Charlotte Corday alone, which is significant. Carlyle's writing would not attain this universality again. Readers of 'Carlyle's French Revolution', however, are spared the embarrassment of having to react to the idolisation of any one hero. The heroism, and the heroic agony, to which Carlyle commits them, must be enacted in their own lives.

On Heroes

Carlyle's *On Heroes, Hero-Worship and the Heroic in History* was published in 1841. In some respects, it marks a high tide in his career. As a volume of lectures, it represents not only a new departure but also the last of the sequence of literary guises in which Carlyle chose to appear before the public. Its publication was meant to prepare them for what was to have been Carlyle's *chef d'oeuvre*: a full-scale biography of Oliver Cromwell. In the event, Carlyle would issue only *Oliver Cromwell's Letters and Speeches: with Elucidations* (1845). For the first time since his apprenticeship years, Carlyle fell short of his intentions. Moreover, he was duped into accepting for publication a group of letters – supposed copies of burnt originals – which the newer scientific historians of Carlyle's day and since have universally rejected as fakes.[20] None of this diminishes Carlyle's achievements, but it highlights the early 1840s as Carlyle's period of consolidation and retrenchment.

In retrospect, it may be said that there is more excitement in following Carlyle's progress from *genre* to *genre* in his earlier years, and in reading his supreme piece of social criticism *Past and Present* (1843), than in surveying the works he reared on that foundation. His *History of Friedrich II of Prussia, called Frederick the Great* occupied him from 1852 to 1865, and his *Early Kings of Norway* appeared in 1875.

From the time when he decided against the ministry or teaching, Carlyle built his literary career piece by piece, moving on from one *genre* to another as opportunity and inspiration arose. He was passed over for at least two university professorships in the late 1820s, and turned down editorships. Choice and circumstance conspired to make him stake everything on success as an isolated literary professional. Translator, reviewer, biographer, social commentator, novelist, historian: he scaled these heights in turn, climbing steadily towards recognition. April 1837 saw the publication of *The French Revolution*, to public and critical acclaim. Carlyle had written *the* book on *the* historical problem that most obsessed his age.

His next logical step was to consolidate his public image and earn some money by appearing as a lecturer. This he did from May 1837, with six lectures on German Literature, timed to coincide with the fashionable London season. Harriet Martineau and other Liberal intellectuals were responsible for the arrangements. Carlyle earned a welcome £120. He repeated the experiment the next season with twelve lectures on European literature before another 'well-dressed London crowd'. For these he received £300. In 1839 came six lectures on 'Revolution' (£200). Carlyle was now a fashionable performer. He moved among the political and social elite. Spring Rice, Chancellor of the Exchequer, John Marshall the Leeds millionaire, sought him out. His friendship with the Barings also dates from this time.[21]

None of the above lectures was published. They had all been on themes extensively treated by Carlyle elsewhere. The last series was a new departure, in effect a manifesto for future work. Delivered in 1840, and as successful as the others, they were published the following year as *On Heroes, Hero-Worship and the Heroic in History*. Carlyle had arrived.

This success represented another kind of turning-point for Carlyle. His long financial worries were now over. He was a respected figure in England and America, and winning more and more readers on the continent, particularly in Germany. His mother-in-law's death had eased family finances, giving Carlyle and his wife a modest sufficiency, even if he never wrote again. Then, from 1856, a collected edition of his works would begin to be published, and in due course cheap editions would emerge, giving Carlyle the equivalent of 'paperback' popularity.

Less satisfactory than Carlyle's new financial security, and more painful than the recognition that he must now consolidate rather that continue to experiment, was the growing perception of the public that Carlyle was hardening into an authoritarian writer. As was the case with *The French Revolution: a History*, the new book's title was often contracted in newspaper references. In this instance, the contraction was a disservice to Carlyle. For the rest of his life, journalists would refer to 'Carlyle's Heroes and Hero-Worship' or even (particularly if they were Liberals) to 'Carlyle's Hero-Worship'. Many people who had never opened Carlyle came to associate him almost exclusively with dictatorial views.

Unfortunately, Carlyle would provide ammunition for those Liberal journalists who were in any case determined to destroy his reputation. He publicly supported the kind of dictatorial behaviour the Liberals loathed.

The outstanding occasion was in 1865–66, following an insurrection in Jamaica. The transition from slave economy to capitalist wage economy had produced an explosive situation not improved by the vagueness of colonial law. The man nominally in charge was E. J. Eyre, a humanitarian lightweight and bureaucrat. He was not invested with regular powers, but was only 'temporary acting Governor'. When armed revolt erupted in October 1865, he reacted in a mixture of dithering and panic, declaring martial law while exempting Kingston, the capital. His behaviour led to the death of 439 people, by hanging or shooting. Worst of all, in Liberal eyes, he transported a ring-leader from the safety of Kingston to an area where he could be 'lawfully' executed under martial law.

This caused a great reaction of English Liberal opinion. J. S. Mill, MP for Westminster, who had grown further and further away from Carlyle since the late 1830s, was elected chairman of a Jamaica Committee pledged to impeach Eyre. Carlyle – equally foolishly – headed an Eyre Defence Fund Committee to provide funds for Eyre's defence. The Liberal press erupted. Eyre was pilloried as a 'Carlylean Hero', one of the 'Strongmen' beloved of the author of 'Hero-Worship'. This was all nonsense, but reputations are made and broken by such nonsense. As far as the Liberal press was concerned, Carlyle's reputation was destroyed by his involvement on Eyre's behalf.

In the event, the matter became a quarrel between the judiciary and the legislature as to the nature and applicability of martial law. Mill, in Parliament, could do little to prevent politicians fudging the issue, at least for the moment. Eyre was dismissed without pension and ruined, but there was no impeachment. Ruskin, who had joined the Defence Committee at Carlyle's insistence, gratefully resigned. Its purpose was clearly ended. Carlyle appeared more exposed than ever, and under the strain of bereavement (his wife Jane died in April 1866) he blustered and used unmannerly racist language, exposing himself to further taunts from the Liberal press. The same writers covered Mill in glory. Ruskin got off fairly lightly. He had exploited the issue to attack the unjust economic situation in Jamaica. Eyre, he argued, was merely the policeman of an evil system. It was hardly fair to make him its scapegoat as well. This gave the Liberal press the opportunity to treat Ruskin as a foil to Carlyle; honourably misled, but with some thought-provoking things to say. He had spoken in favour of Mill's election to Parliament, and was careful to remind people of this. His apparently ambiguous remarks on Jamaica were taken as proof that, with the best will in the world, no one who believed in constitutional government could *honestly* support Carlyle.[22]

On Heroes, Hero-Worship and the Heroic in History is itself
the best answer to this Liberal distortion of Carlyle. As its actual
title suggests, Carlyle is careful to distinguish between 'Heroes'
and 'Hero-Worship', and to view the 'Heroic' as a phenomenon
that evolves and changes with the pattern of 'History'.

Sincerity is the keynote and theme of Carlyle's volume. Its
origin as a series of lectures shows itself to advantage in a style
that is much more accessible than usual. Carlyle begins with the
deified Scandinavian hero, Odin, and ends with Napoleon, 'our last
Great Man!' He distinguishes between true 'heroes', all human and
none perfect, and mere 'worshippers', some of them misguided
and many of them now incomprehensible. It is the ability to discern
new truths which distinguishes a 'hero' from a mere 'worshipper'.
True hero-worship is the recognition of this truth-discerning quality in others. It reverences their discoveries, while remaining free
to advance beyond them. Any true hero-worshipper may himself
become a hero. History is always moving on, yet divine law remains
transcendent. What gives history its significance is the ability to
articulate the divine truths shadowed forth by heroes, to act on
those truths, and so to discover new truths and new forms of
'heroism', which in all its forms is definable as the 'genuine'. Sincerity shows itself in different forms in different epochs, yet is
always distinct from sham. Anyone who acts sincerely by the light
of the best truth he can know, is a person worthy of compassion
and admiration. Heroism is thus progressive. It perpetually renews
itself by abjuring dead truths no longer capable of being sincerely
believed. Yet it is also tolerant. It refuses to cause unnecessary
disruption by insisting on things that are not essential.

With their wide historical perspective, these lectures act as
a corrective to the inevitable distortions of works in which Carlyle
concentrates on one 'hero' only, such as Cromwell or Frederick
the Great. Heroes as different as Dante and Luther, Robert Burns
and Mahomet are included.

On the other hand, *On Heroes* places a very high value on
order, and on submission to the divine law. Carlyle has little room
for heroic martyrs, for men and women actually destroyed by the
powers and conventions of their day, who turn out after their death
to have had something valuable in them. Socrates and Christ, the
obvious examples of this kind of 'hero' are not considered, although
Carlyle draws on Platonic and Christian writings to further his

arguments. He is thus somewhat guilty of emphasising the value of truth while playing down its tragic cost. Mahomet, Knox, Cromwell and other battlers against convention are dealt with at length. Each was rewarded with a measure of success in his life-time. Carlyle plays down the cost to other people of this success. It is as though he wishes to remain true to his Calvinist and Burgher upbringing, with its emphasis on success as the reward for piety and obedience.

The theme of progression, the playing down of tragedy, and the special status Carlyle gives to Teutonic heroes: all this may be seen as the price of the new truth Carlyle wants to impress on his upper-class English audience. In the context of 1840, it is a startling one. This truth is democracy and the authority of ideas. Carlyle brings forward the 'writers of Newspapers, Pamphlets, Poems, Books', as guardians of this new truth. It is these people who '*are* the real working effective Church of a modern country'. In large measure, the 'true University of these days is a Collection of Books'. Alongside the Hero as Divinity, Prophet, Poet, Priest and King, Carlyle makes one startling innovation in his list of heroes: 'The Hero as Man of Letters'. He instances Dr Johnson, Rousseau and Robert Burns. Lacking the old glamour, high genius or physical power, this new kind of heroism will become ever more widespread and ever more significant. Having himself attained success in the profession of letters, and making the last public appearances he will ever make for a fee, Carlyle feels entitled to demand, on behalf of his successors, that their contribution to the state, which cannot for the future thrive without them, be recognised and supported.[23]

Carlyle's audience are given the alternative of moving forward with this new kind of heroism or of succumbing to the 'charlatan-element' that destroyed Napoleon, a man who survived his useful-ness in the world and indeed betrayed his own insights. Napoleon's greatest insight was this:

> That this new enormous Democracy asserting itself here in the French Revolution is an unsuppressible Fact, which the whole world, with its old forces and institutions, cannot put down; this was a true insight of his, and took his conscience and enthusiasm along with it, – a *faith*. And did he not interpret the dim purport of it well? *La carrière ouverte aux talents*. The implements to him who can handle them: this actually is the truth, and even the whole

truth; it includes whatever the French Revolution, or any Revolution, could mean.

Napoleon betrayed this insight by acting as a tyrant instead of a true hero, for a true hero is responsive to his age. Napoleon saw the need for authority as well as democracy, but in locating authority more and more exclusively in his own person, he subverted democracy instead of securing it. Carlyle makes Napoleon's greatest criminal mistake that of killing a German bookseller.[24]

For Carlyle, the defeat of Napoleon gave England, and the world at large, the opportunity to learn from his mistakes. Despite his impatience with his own age, Carlyle did believe that it was finding its way towards a significant new truth. Self-importance was losing its claim to be considered as heroic. Great 'heroes' of the old kind, either religious or military – and here Carlyle was a little regretful – were ceasing to be possible. The new kind of heroism – and here Carlyle found much to encourage him – was to be found in the dissemination of ideas through the printed word. Democracy would thus beget its own authority.

Notes

1 *Sartor Resartus*, p. 127. Kaplan, *Thomas Carlyle*, p. 82.

2 See Alan Shelston's discussion, *Thomas Carlyle: Selected Writings*, p. 8.

3 John Stuart Mill, unsigned review of *The French Revolution*, *London and Westminster Review*, July 1837, xxvii, 17–53, reprinted *Critical Heritage*, p. 53: 'These transcendentalisms . . . excepted, we pronounce the style of this book to be . . . excelled, in its kind, only by the great masters of epic poetry.'

John Ruskin to Charles Eliot Norton, 10 March 1883, *The Correspondence of John Ruskin and Charles Eliot Norton*, edited by John Lewis Bradley and Ian Ousby, Cambridge, 1987, p. 460: '[Carlyle's] Reminscences . . . are to me full of his strong insight . . . far more pathetic than those howlings of his earlier life about Cromwell.'

4 James Gardner, *The Faiths of the World*, London and Edinburgh, n.d., I.215–31.

5 *Collected Letters of Thomas and Jane Welsh Carlyle*, I.21.

6 *Ibid.*, IV.423.

7 *Critical and Miscellaneous Essays*, I.575 (Preface to 'German Romance', 1827), 48–9, 68–70 ('State of German Literature', 1827).

8 *Works*, XXV.197, 202.

9 *Critical and Miscellaneous Essays*, II.248–9.

10 *The Critical Heritage*, pp. 380–426.

11 *Thomas Carlyle: Selected Writings*, p. 74.

12 *Critical and Miscellaneous Essays*, II.224. Engels praised *Past and Present* in his 'Attitude of the Bourgeoisie towards the Proletariat', Ch. XI of *The Condition of the Working Class in England in 1844*. Hitler consoled himself with Carlyle's *Frederick the Great* during his final days: A. Bullock, *Hitler: A Study in Tyranny*, London, 1969, p. 702.

13 *Thomas Carlyle: Selected Writings*, p. 227.

14 Other important Carlyle coinages are 'industrialism', and 'genetic' and 'environment' in their modern senses. See Rosenberg, *Carlyle*, pp. 35–6.

15 *Critical Heritage*, pp. 334–67.

16 *Critical and Miscellaneous Essays*, III.631–9.

17 Charles F. Harrold, 'Carlyle's General Method in *The French Revolution*', *PMLA* 43 (1928), 51–66. See also Rosenberg, *Carlyle*, p. 63.

18 John Ruskin, *Modern Painters*, Pt. VIII, Ch. 1, 20. *Works*, VII.215. Ruskin's 'philanthropic' tone, which Carlyle disliked, is apparent in this general acount of poetic creation.

19 Rosenberg, *Carlyle*, p. 3.

20 Clyde de L. Ryals, 'Thomas Carlyle and the Squire Forgeries', *Victorian Studies*, 30, 4 (Summer 1987), p. 495.

21 Kaplan, *Thomas Carlyle*, pp. 239, 243–9, 252–4.

22 Malcolm Hardman, *Ruskin and Bradford*, Manchester, 1986, pp. 288–91.

23 *Thomas Carlyle: Selected Writings*, pp. 242–3.

24 'The Hero as King', *On Heroes*, Lecture 6. There is a contradiction between the apparent bias of the last six paragraphs (discussed here) in favour of articulating and fulfilling the 'Message' of democracy, and the sheer bulk of encomium on Cromwell as true king (Paras. 16–63).

Books

Paperbacks

Thomas Carlyle: Selected Writings, edited with an introduction by Alan Shelston, Harmondsworth, 1971. Includes *Signs of the Times* and *Chartism* and extracts from *Sartor, French Revolution, On Heroes, Past and Present, Latter-Day Pamphlets, Frederick the Great* and *Reminiscences*.

Thomas Carlyle, *Sartor Resartus*, edited by Kerry McSweeney and Peter Sabor, Oxford and New York, 1987.

Life

Thomas Carlyle, *Reminiscences*, edited by J. A. Froude, London, 1881.

Fred Kaplan, *Thomas Carlyle: a Biography*, Cambridge, 1983.

Bernard Semmel, *The Governor Eyre Controversy*, London, 1962.

Letters

Collected Letters of Thomas and Jane Welsh Carlyle, edited by C. R. Sanders and K. J. Fielding, Durham, North Carolina, 1970–81.

Letters of Thomas Carlyle to John Stuart Mill, John Sterling and Robert

Browning, edited by Alexander Carlyle (1923), republished, New York, 1970.

The Correspondence of Thomas Carlyle and John Ruskin, edited by George Allan Cate, Stanford, 1982.

The Correspondence of Emerson and Carlyle, edited by Joseph Slater, New York, 1964.

Works

Thomas Carlyle, *Critical and Miscellaneous Essays*, 3 volumes, London, 1869.

Thomas Carlyle, *Works*, Centenary Edition, edited by H. D. Traill, 30 volumes, London, 1896–1901.

Criticism and commentary

Thomas Carlyle: The Critical Heritage, edited by J. P. Seigel, London, 1971.

Carlyle and His Contemporaries. Essays in honor of Charles Richard Sanders, edited by John Clubbe, Durham, North Carolina, 1976.

Thomas Carlyle 1981. Papers given at the International Thomas Carlyle Centenary Symposium, edited by Horst W. Drescher, Frankfurt, 1983.

Mark Cumming, *A disemprisoned epic: form and vision in Carlyle's 'French Revolution'*, Philadelphia, 1988.

Kenneth Marc Harris, *Carlyle and Emerson: their long debate*, Harvard U.P., Cambridge, Massachusetts, 1978.

John D. Rosenberg, *Carlyle and the Burden of History*, Oxford, 1985.

G. B. Tennyson, *Sartor called Resartus*, Princeton, New Jersey, 1965.

CHAPTER THREE

John Ruskin and fine art

Introduction

Read some of Carlyle's lectures. Bombast, I think; altogether
approves of Mahomet, and talks like a girl of his 'black eyes'.

Diaries, I, 199

Such was Ruskin's private reaction to Carlyle's work *On Heroes*.
Past and Present impressed him much more favourably. It was,
however, his own first-hand experience of Paris during the Revolution of 1848 which drew him nearer to Carlyle. The suffering,
degradation and violence Ruskin saw in France were all very different from the scenes of natural and architectural beauty which he
preferred to visit.

Ruskin began to feel a need for the companionship of a mind
equal to his own, capable of making him think about the hard
facts of European and British politics. In turning to Carlyle for
inspiration, he was doing what many thinking people were doing.
His own much narrower circle of readers knew him mainly as the
author of the first volume of *Modern Painters* (1843), a work which
held no interest for Carlyle. Yet while still an undergraduate,
Ruskin had written articles on 'The Poetry of Architecture' which
were in some ways more characteristic of his deeper self than
the rather theoretical and snappishly moralistic early volumes of
Modern Painters. 'The Poetry of Architecture' (1837) paid tribute
to vernacular architecture in its environmental and cultural context.
This regard for the living and developing context, and for crafts-
manship and social being in relation to architecture and fine art,
would prove to be Ruskin's main subject for the rest of his life.
The word 'environment', in its modern sense, was first used by
Carlyle in his 'Goethe' essay of 1828. Ruskin himself did not take

up the word. But it would be Ruskin who became, as far as England went, a fountainhead of what is now called 'environmental' thinking.

Partly in response to Carlyle, Ruskin's *The Seven Lamps of Architecture* (1849) attempted to combine high aesthetics with moral and social awareness. A rather precious book – though brilliant and suggestive – it would be associated with Ruskin's name in a rather disabling way. The 'Seven Lamps', with their slightly contrived symbolism, would be dragged up whenever Ruskin's name was mentioned, rather as 'Hero-Worship' was associated with Carlyle. These public images – of a repulsively authoritarian Carlyle and a repellently sugary and moralistic Ruskin – have to some extent survived. Unfair, even as judgements of those particular books, these images are dissipated in the light of the writers' relationship with each other.

The earliest record of their meeting dates from 1850. Ruskin would always suspect Carlyle's bombast and false sentimentality, just as Carlyle never ceased to disapprove of Ruskin's 'high moral small-beer', as he called it. But as a reading of their *Correspondence* shows, Ruskin and Carlyle came to respect each other. Too optimistic, too philanthropic, Ruskin was nevertheless 'sincere', in Carlyle's view, and had an intellect of 'tenfold vivacity'. Ruskin would eventually acknowledge Carlyle as 'the man who has urged me to all chief labour'.

Mrs Carlyle noted how cleverly Ruskin 'managed' her husband. The 'managing' of Carlyle would become a motive for much of Ruskin's later writing. He was quite capable of redeploying Carlyle's ideas to ends which suited himself. Thus, he came to see the leaders of the Trade Union movement, not the old aristocracy, as the future power in politics. He 'managed' Carlyle's notions about heroes into a theory of leaders chosen by free election, having fixed salaries, and whose accounting should at all times be open to public inspection. In his *Fors Clavigera* pamphlet for January 1877 (*Works*, XXIX. 18–19) he went so far as to present Sheffield – which he knew from talking to working people there to be a hotbed of communist ideas – as a microcosm for the future of England. Where Carlyle would have invoked martial law with some bombastic rhetoric whose humorous exaggeration might have alienated the reader, Ruskin strove to woo the reader with a whimsical and domestic approach with serious undertones. It would be a good idea, would it not, for Sheffield to set up a commissariat, presided over by 'a couple of honest and well-meaning married souls', elected on a popular mandate to put down 'hunger and cold'? The methods he suggested might now be called 'Trotskyite'.

The dialectic between the voluntary, corporate principle of unionism and the need for centralised state planning was suggestively explored in Ruskin's social writing. In addition, he wanted to retain elements of the free economy. The catchphrase of the 1980s – 'share-owning democracy' – is latent in *Fors Clavigera*, but for Ruskin the phrase would be empty without the other elements: unionism, co-operative ventures, state intervention. A lover of Gothic architecture for its capacity to harmonise many elements, Ruskin wanted the same sort of harmonious variety in society.

He was more optimistic of peaceful change than Carlyle, less obsessed with the stark alternatives of Aristocracy or Anarchy. Evangelical and nicely reared, Ruskin had none of Carlyle's peasant Calvinism, and very little Scottish blood. Only his paternal grandmother was Scottish, and she was partly of 'gentle' birth. Otherwise, he belonged, as he said, 'to the middle (even to the lower side of the middle) class'. He could afford to address the governing classes rather cockily, as a lower middle-class Londoner, but wellheeled, and with an Oxford degree. Lecturing army officers or capitalists, he urged them to look to their own best interests and the public welfare. If they could not do both, the public would manage without them. The tone was often playful, but the fierceness of Ruskin's intention always came through, and so did the basic pattern of his demands. Never for a moment did he forget that it was his own privileged economic position which allowed him this boldness.

Carlyle had no such position. If Ruskin 'managed' Carlylean ideas into new forms which the author of *On Heroes* would hardly recognise, it is also true that, to some extent, Carlyle relied on the younger, more socially fortunate man to carry on the battle he himself had begun. Thus, when *The Stones of Venice* appeared, with its interweaving of social and architectural criticism, Carlyle wrote to Ruskin calling it a 'most true and excellent *Sermon* in stones . . . a singular sign of the times to me'. The allusion to Carlyle's own earliest piece of social commentary would not have been lost on Ruskin. His friendship with Carlyle may be said to date from this letter of March 1851, containing as it does this hint that Carlyle might regard him as a successor.

Emboldened by Carlyle's encouragement, Ruskin put more of his own heart and mind into later volumes of *Modern Painters*. The work began to emerge as the extraordinary epic of a sensibility: part biography of Turner, part autobiography of Ruskin himself, an empirical series of discoveries about art in its task of re-creating the world. In 1856 Carlyle told Ruskin he had become 'the most eloquent Preacher I have heard these twenty years, and who does mean wholly what he says'.

Modern Painters, like *The French Revolution*, ended with biblical allusions, but also with allusions to *Past and Present*. Where Carlyle had called for an Incarnation of his own words, Ruskin invoked a material Resurrection of the whole earth and its people. The difference is significant. Carlyle wanted to see abstract concepts made flesh. Ruskin wanted the already existing physical world to achieve its best potential. He had 'managed' Carlyle's pagan German transcendentalism into an English Christian materialism. Carlyle was outmanoeuvred, and reconciled to the main current of Victorian thought.

When Ruskin attacked *laissez-faire* economics in his next piece, *Unto This Last* (1860), Carlyle was jubilant. He continued to encourage Ruskin on the appearance of *Munera Pulveris* (1862) and *Ethics of the Dust* (1865) and other works. *The Queen of the Air* (1869) on Greek myths and their modern relevance 'went into my heart like arrows', Carlyle confided to another friend. The early numbers, at least, of *Fors Clavigera* were always 'eagerly read' by Carlyle, who found the fifth number, particularly, 'incomparable . . . piercing as lightning'. Most important of all – and the key to Ruskin's relationship with Carlyle – 'Continue,' the older man wrote on 30 April 1871, 'while you still have such utterances in you.' This moral support, regardless of private reservations, was Carlyle's real gift to Ruskin.

As early as 1854, John Stuart Mill and his wife Harriet had come to the conclusion that Carlyle had written himself out. However unfair this might be as a judgement, it is understandable that Carlyle, currently pursuing research for his multi-volumed tribute to Frederick the Great, should have ceased to interest the Utilitarian Mills. Ruskin, on the other hand, Mill confided to his diary, was one of the very few living writers 'who seem to draw out what they say from a source within themselves'. Charlotte Brontë, similarly impressed, called Ruskin 'one of the few genuine writers, as distinguished from book-makers of the age'.

Both these opinions require modification. It is true that Ruskin's prose juvenilia, some of it as yet unpublished, show him to have been a 'genuine writer' from boyhood and to have had a complex, questioning 'source within' from which to articulate. Carlyle and other contemporary influences only helped to stimulate what was already latent in him. But when he came to publish, he found that he had to be a 'book-maker' as well as a 'writer'. He could offer only what the market would stand; and his 'book-making' was further constrained by the fact that his kind of book was the expensive art book. Ruskin would never be read by more than a minority, but after he began to solve the publishing problem, his 'minority' readership came to be drawn from a much wider social range. As Brian Maidment has shown, in his final years he could no longer regulate the supply of his own books, and his dependants, for motives of their own, dumped them and his reputation on the market.

Ruskin's battle with publishers was only one of a series of contests. Much more actively a member of the 'Establishment' than Carlyle, Ruskin can nevertheless be seen as an eccentric determined to articulate, despite all odds, the true 'Message' of democracy as Carlyle saw it – fairness with efficiency – and this is apparent even when he is viewed, as in the following pages, solely in terms of his reactions to the world of Victorian fine art.

He disliked the South Kensington system of centralised warehouse-museums and over-regulated and meanly subsidised design schools, more concerned with grading and labelling art than with encouraging it or conserving it. Like Dickens in *Hard Times*, he saw this mean and bureaucratic apparatus as one more form of oppression.

It was by stimulating maverick individuals – William Morris among them – that Ruskin found his true influence. This influence broadened after his election as Professor of Art at Oxford. It was typical of Ruskin's career – and not untypical of Victorian careers in general – that this election and his subsequent achievements as professor owed more to personal contacts than to official recognition or support.

Art publishing

A typical conviction of Ruskin's was that all who wished should be able to 'devote some leisure to the attainment of liberal education and to the other objects of free life'.[1] Yet his platform for arguing such a case was usually an 'art book'. Essential to his argument were engraved illustrations which were expensive and incapable of being reproduced beyond a few thousand impressions. There was thus a contradiction between the quality he insisted on, and the accessibility he desired. His theoretical solution was to insist on fairly priced and durable editions, and to argue for the provision of public reference libraries.[2] Many of those who could afford to buy his early books did not share these views. Then as now, a fine art book in a 'limited edition' was regarded as an investment whose value depended on its rarity. Moreover, an early Victorian 'art book' *could* reach only an exclusive audience, and that audience had every intention of remaining exclusive. Art, therefore, seemed an unlikely platform from which to argue for a less divided culture. Yet, should Ruskin attempt to argue from a different platform, he risked alienating any converts to his ideas about art and society he might have made by writing about art.

His first decisive move on to a new platform was made in *Unto This Last*, published initially as a series of articles in *The Cornhill Magazine*, a new venture of his publishers. Here for the first time he stated unambiguously political and economic views which, though always part of his work, could be more easily ignored by readers of *Modern Painters*. Reviews were disastrous, and the series was cut short.

Ruskin had been at the mercy of publishers and their views of the market from the beginning. He had been working towards a book on Turner since 1836, but the publisher John Murray, when approached, insisted Turner was out of fashion; and that a book on the sickly neo-medieval German school of 'Nazarene'[3] painters (loathed by Ruskin) was what the market demanded. Ruskin put himself in the hands of Smith, Elder & Co. Their policy was to make his first major book – *Modern Painters* – into a contentious and 'topical' work praising the modern English school – particularly Turner – at the expense of the seventeenth-century Dutch and other 'Old Masters'. The first volume was thus a rather uncomfortable compromise between Ruskin and his publishers, but it 'caught on'. From this somewhat ambiguous platform Ruskin was able to launch four further volumes. *Modern Painters* is an artistic whole; but cannot be seen as such without reference to Ruskin's dialectic with the very process of its publishing.

He completed *Modern Painters* in 1860, and began work on *Unto This Last* for the *Cornhill*. His action led to further difficulties with market forces. Many who could afford his art books now hated him. Those who liked the *Cornhill* articles were often unable to afford his art books. His publishers decided it was time to dismember their author. They compiled, in 1861, a volume of safe *Selections* from *Modern Painters* and seven other expensive works. This publisher's 'mince-pie'[4] as Ruskin called it, cost 6s, and went through several reprints. A full edition of *Modern Painters* alone cost £8 0s 6d. This move by his publishers was the price Ruskin paid for their consent to issue *Unto This Last* in book form in 1862, at 3s 6d. In eleven years they disposed of only 898 copies. Clearly, Ruskin had to find a new kind of audience and write a new kind of book. He began to give lectures in industrial towns like Manchester and Bradford, and to form books out of the lectures.

Eventually, he made his own platform. Ruskin's own thinking was becoming more compatible with the cultural aspirations of a broader public. Yet, under old systems of publishing, they still could not afford his books. Fortunately, Ruskin had a private income. He would use it to invest in new talent, forging an alliance between his middle-class sensibilities and working-class aspiration, in an attempt to free both from the dominance of a culturally moribund elite. Gradually, from 1871, and then finally, he broke with Smith, Elder & Co. George Allen, a former pupil at the Working Men's College, was set up by Ruskin with an interest-free loan as his publisher, employing a pioneering system which came to be known as the 'Net Book System'. Under this system, the customer paid the same price for any given edition of a book wherever it was bought, and booksellers received a fixed discount. By 1906 the Publishers' Association, which had at first derided Ruskin's efforts, acknowledged that the Net Book System had raised the trade from the 'disastrous condition to which the undercutting of prices among themselves had reduced the business'.[5]

Though he would never compromise on the quality of his product, Ruskin took the favoured Victorian option of issuing books in serial parts. The beautifully illustrated work on engraving,

Ariadne Florentina, for instance, appeared in seven parts from George Allen, between 1873 and 1875. Unfortunately, though he began by issuing parts at 1*s* each, Ruskin found that he could not maintain the quality at this price, and raised it to 2*s* 6*d*. The work came out in volume form in 1876, at 27*s* 6*d*. By keeping to Ruskin's policy, however, George Allen was able by 1890 to issue an edition at 7*s* 6*d*. Ruskin's improving popularity, and new technical advances, shared in this success. *Fors Clavigera* was a well-printed production by George Allen, with occasional fine illustrations, at 7*d* per issue. It was dedicated to the 'Workmen and Labourers of Great Britain'. There is evidence that some actual workmen read and approved of it,[6] but, ironically, its quality would also make it a collector's item.

Aside from the question of illustrations, Ruskin's books needed good printing, with adequate spacing and margins. These relatively costly 'aids to reading' are required by the way he writes. As Elizabeth Helsinger has shown, Ruskin demands active readers, prepared to 'read between the lines', to reflect on what they read, to check their own reactions by referring to several passages of a work at once. Whereas Carlyle requires a reader to be comparatively passive, merely accepting and registering the sequence of stimuli Carlyle provides, Ruskin's complex but precise style demands a book that can be objectively handled and examined. A cheap Victorian edition, with its tiny print, or a collapsible modern paperback, do not have this facility. Ruskin insisted on numbered paragraphs, respectable printing, layout and binding. All this costs money.

Nevertheless, Ruskin's short books of the 1860s, particularly *Sesame and Lilies*, a calculated popular success, brought him nearer to a broader public and further away from Smith, Elder & Co. They took what they could for themselves when the break came, in 1873, by reissuing *Modern Painters* at 8 guineas, using up the old plates. When George Allen brought out a new edition, in 1888, many of the plates had to be re-engraved. His price was 6 guineas. By maintaining sales and standards, he eventually achieved a good edition at 37*s*. Following the same policy with *Unto This Last*, Allen achieved an edition at 1*s* 6*d* by 1900 (the 'Thirty-second Thousand'). In 1887 the book had had its first major breakthrough among the working classes in a pamphlet of telling extracts at 1*d*.

Things were different in America, where British copyright

was not acknowledged, and pirate presses churned out shoddy editions of most of Ruskin's works: a travesty of *Modern Painters*, for example, at about 8*s*. In 1891, America admitted copyright, and an authorised edition of Ruskin appeared: but without *Unto This Last*.

A pioneer of the 'Net Book System', Ruskin did better than survive. He earned the respect that made *Unto This Last* viable in England; and by the early 1880s he was earning £4,000 a year as a result of his own publishing innovations.

Ruskin's private income had enabled him to make the investment in new production methods which alone made possible the dissemination of new ideas. He could claim to have become one of Carlyle's 'men of letters', articulating ideas of fairness and efficiency through publishing and selling methods that were also fairer and more efficient. It was fortunate that Ruskin's middle-class background gave him not only the financial capacity, but also the business acumen for beginning to achieve some aspects of peaceful change. Carlyle's upper-class heroes would not, and Marx's proletariat could not replace Ruskin in the most characteristic aspects of his catalytic function.

The Royal Academy

At the centre of the Victorian art establishment was the Royal Academy. The pattern of Ruskin's relationship with this body is important, and revealing.

While wishing to be on good terms with its members and partisans as far as possible, Ruskin found it necessary, and sometimes'entertaining, to outrage them. He paid a price for this in their antagonism. The President of the Royal Academy was Sir Charles Eastlake, a painter whose work Ruskin could not admire. Moreover, Sir Charles's wife, known by her maiden name of Elizabeth Rigby, was an influential writer on art who took any opportunity she could to attack Ruskin.

Among the reviews of *Modern Painters* which appeared in 1856 were two sharply contrasting ones.[7] The radical *Westminster Review* offered eight pages of measured but glowing and serious praise; the Tory *Quarterly Review* published forty pages of ranting denigration. Both were anonymous. The first was by George Eliot; the second by Elizabeth Rigby.

Eliot found in Ruskin a sense of 'substantial reality', and a dislike of 'vague forms, bred by imagination on the mists of feeling'. Sound painterly techniques could be learned from studying the Old Masters, but the actual seeing of the natural world must be done by Victorians with Victorian eyes. 'The thorough acceptance of this doctrine,' Eliot commented, 'would remould our life.'

Elizabeth Rigby's attack on Ruskin was motivated not merely by his lack of reverence for her husband's paintings, but by her awareness that his revolutionary notions of taste were a threat to the establishment she represented.

Ruskin had been drawn into art criticism in response to attacks on Turner's later Academy pictures. For Ruskin a good painting was fundamentally interesting for what might now be called 'abstract' values: the interest of arrangements of brush strokes on canvas. Side by side with this was the picture's interest as an *interpretation* of visible forms. Turner's later pictures were for Ruskin supreme examples of these qualities. What they did not provide was the illusion[8] that by looking into their frames the onlooker was looking through a window at an *idealised or prettified reality*: a substitute reality that could be preferred to actual sunlight, landscape, people. It was precisely this window into a prettified substitute reality that most Victorians wanted from art.

Portraits of notable persons were a staple of Academy exhibitions. They were perfect examples of 'window' art: so flattering, yet so lifelike. Sir Francis Grant, President of the Royal Academy 1866–78, excelled at these windows. Ruskin made a point of never mentioning them. Sir Charles Eastlake, President 1850–65, was an expert in the technical methods of the Old Masters. Ruskin wrote in praise of his expertise. But his pictures showed no awareness of the 'substantial reality' actually visible to Victorians. They were 'imitation of the Venetians, on the supposition that the essence of Venetian painting consisted in method . . . Sir Charles Eastlake has power of rendering expression, if he would watch it in human beings – and power of drawing form, if he would look at the form to be drawn'. But he preferred 'imitation'.[9]

Most critics – including Dickens – were shocked when the Pre-Raphaelites assaulted respectable taste with a series of aggressively un-pretty renderings of biblical subjects. Ruskin defended what he called their 'sternly materialistic, though deeply reverent veracity'.[10] Here was a group of young, highly talented artists, who promised to have a wider appeal than the old academic suppliers of flattering portraits and sentimental fantasies. Their work was bought by the new commercial classes – Carlyle's 'Working Aristocracy' – rather than the old landed gentry. Moreover, through engravings and travelling exhibitions they were accessible to many who could never have afforded original paintings, or visited the Royal Academy. They seemed to offer an opportunity for a synthesis between art of the highest quality and social awareness.

As *Modern Painters*, and the Pre-Raphaelite movement, gathered respect, Ruskin enjoyed a brief heyday as an arbiter of taste. His *Academy Notes*, 1855–59, provided his own view of Academy exhibitions. He made sure they were sold as near the doors of the Academy as possible: in effect as rivals to the official Catalogues. These *Notes* were eminently quotable, and extracts found their way into newspapers all over the country. The official Catalogues could not compete. Ruskin became widely associated in the public mind with the Pre-Raphaelites, and when fashion passed them by, his reputation suffered.

Three of the painters Ruskin was popularly linked with were Rossetti, Millais, and Ford Madox Brown. Rossetti never exhibited at the Academy. After his wife's suicide in 1862, he moved away from the vital little early watercolours Ruskin admired, and began fabricating his own 'windows' into a morbid fantasy 'reality'. Millais took the opposite route. The promise of the 'shocking' *Christ in the House of his Parents* (1850) was not fulfilled. Millais preferred to paint conventional and sentimental pictures, and to become, in due course, President of the Royal Academy (1896). Brown took the middle course: he had a row with the Academy over the positioning of his pictures and refused to darken its doors again. He could neither conform, like Millais, nor revolt, like Rossetti: only repeat his resentment against 'good taste' in pictures ugly in colour and sadistic in subject. Ruskin never mentioned them.

A major painter who came close to the 'substantial reality' Eliot admired was Holman Hunt. A minor one was John Brett. Yet Ruskin had to regret in Hunt a tendency to be 'blinded by his sentiment to the real weakness of the pictorial expression'. Sentiment is fine, but 'a painter's business is first to *paint*'. Brett, on the other hand, though devoted and skilful, offered no interpretation. His work seemed like 'Mirror's work, not Man's'.[11]

Though Ruskin helped to make Pre-Raphaelite work acceptable at the Academy for a while, he refused to praise it in a partisan spirit. Fashionable trends at the Academy moved on from the Pre-Raphaelites, and at the same time Ruskin became disillusioned with their failure to retain their early technical freshness and commitment to new ideas. By 1860 he was taking a more direct interest in the social and educational questions that lay behind the artistic questions. This emerges in his evidence before the Royal Academy Commission of 1863. He suggested that Academicians should become, in effect, the governing body of an artists' trade union, elected by artists *outside* the Academy to represent the claims of art within the state. A broader public might be involved in art in various ways. Art ought to form part of any general education, up to and including university level. The Academy could be a centre for encouraging and financing rising artists, liberating them from slavery to rich patrons; it could set standards of manufacture for the materials of art; it could underwrite public commissions.[12]

Ruskin wrote no *Academy Notes* between 1859 and 1875.

Pursuing economic fundamentals, Ruskin's influence on passing art fashions became weaker. Lord Leighton and Sir Edward Poynter, Presidents of the Royal Academy during Ruskin's later years, encouraged a new type of large-scale 'window' into luscious historical or mythological fantasy worlds. The most successful perpetrator of these was Alma-Tadema, who was 'discovered' by the dealer Gambart and aggressively promoted. In *Academy Notes* for 1875 Ruskin wrote some witty condemnation of these arrangements of 'imitation-Greek articles of virtu'; but could not stop rich patrons buying them. He alerted more discerning eyes to a battle picture by Elizabeth Thompson: full of 'resolution to paint things as they really are . . . not as . . . poetically fancied'. Her art was 'wrought, through all the truth of its frantic passion, with gradations of colour and shade which I have not seen the like of since Turner's death'. Here was something worth looking at; and thinking about: not a window into dreams.[13]

Art dealers

Ruskin was unusual among art critics in abstaining from the role of market tipster. Though regularly asked, he never took fees for evaluating pictures. In later years he had an arrangement with Sewening of St James's, a dealer he trusted, and to whom he would occasionally send pictures sent to him for valuing. If owners also wanted his own opinion, they were asked to contribute to the funds of St George's Guild. But Ruskin discouraged such approaches from strangers: though he supplied patient and particular advice to friends like Ellen Heaton, a small collector of Turner vignettes and early Rossetti watercolours.

Ruskin was never the hired man of any dealer. But the influence of dealers among the art-buying public was such that Ruskin's own influence was limited. He was never an 'art-dictator', though satirists called him one.

Ruskin lectured at Manchester in 1857 on 'The Political Economy of Art'. As published, the lectures confirmed Ruskin's status as a 'reformer' in matters of picture-buying. In art as in other businesses his concern was for the producer as well as the purchaser; and for ways to bring the best produce 'in some degree within the reach of the multitude'. But as originally planned, 'The Political Economy of Art' had confronted Victorian capitalism much more radically than any 'reformer'. A passage of the original text, suppressed by his publishers, survives in a Ruskin letter of 1864: 'As yet the rise in prices has merely made the fortunes of a larger tribe of dealers . . . all sales of works of art should be under government control'. The artist should get most of the initial price, which should be registered. If and as subsequent bargaining raised the price, the surplus 'should go to the government, to be employed in the form of art galleries for the nation, and support of schools. This would put an end to the dealer's trade . . . and to the purchases of art as an "investment" by people who merely keep it out of sight and use.'[14]

It was only after *Unto This Last* that Ruskin was able to be so radical as that in public. A notable instance from 1877 is his jibe at Messrs Agnew, the Manchester dealers who 'covered the walls of that metropolis with "exchangeable property" on the exchanges of which the dealer always made his commission, and of which perhaps one canvas in a hundred is of some intrinsic value'. The solution was that 'Manchester men *should* . . . "choose for themselves" ' work they could honestly enjoy, buying direct from the artist, and ignoring the pretensions of mere fashion or a large price-tag.[15]

Pre-eminent among Victorian art-dealers was the Belgian Ernest Gambart. His method was to puff his 'discoveries' as Hollywood studios would puff their sequence of 'stars'. Novelty and profit were the criteria; luxury and escapism set the tone. By the late 1850s, Ruskin's opposition to these things was becoming known. It was time for Gambart to make some sort of pact with him. Ruskin turned out to be more than a match for the dealer.

In 1856 there appeared *The Harbours of England*, a series of twelve Turner plates, published for the first time by Ernest Gambart, with commentary by Ruskin. The book was a collector's item at two guineas. The text was uncontroversial: the nearest of Ruskin's works to the ordinary art criticism of exposition and aesthetic commentary. As Ruskin's father said, it was 'more likely . . . to be received without cavil than anything he had written'.[16]

Jeremy Maas writes that Gambart was 'the first fully to understand and apply the dealer-critic system'. For a short while Ruskin began to be applied by the Gambart 'system'. Between 1856 and 1859 he appended notices of the French Gallery – an investment of Gambart's – to his annual *Academy Notes*. Unfortunately for Gambart, Ruskin limited his praise to the quiet genre paintings of Edouard Frère (1819–86). Less congenial pictures of more academic pretension were liable to be dismissed as 'dusty insensibilities'.[17]

Ruskin had now co-operated on a book for Gambart, and less enthusiastically, had helped to advertise Gambart's gallery. The next step in Gambart's game was to stage-manage a Ruskin tour of northern towns, in order to recruit new patrons for Gambart's wares. Gambart accompanied Ruskin to Manchester to make sure he performed in the 'Harbours of England' vein, with no recurrence of the radical eccentricities of the 'Political Economy of Art'. Gambart's system worked fairly successfully as far as this Manchester 'appearance' went.

But the next scheduled stop was Bradford. This was a much rougher town. It utterly lacked the niceties essential to Gambart's luxurious lifestyle. Moreoever, there was hardly such a thing as a Tory in the place.

Ruskin called on Mrs Gaskell after the Manchester lecture. She knew Bradford and its surroundings well, thanks to her friendship with the Brontës, whose father was a curate in Bradford parish. Mrs Gaskell must have made clear to Ruskin what he might have guessed from his own knowledge of Bradfordians and the Bradford landscape: that Bradford would not tolerate anything approaching the ordinary dilettante art-lecture. This was a challenge, which Ruskin turned into an opportunity.

Due to go on with Gambart almost immediately from Manchester to Bradford, he resorted to the favoured Victorian ploy for getting one's own way. He fell ill. The Bradford lecture was postponed for one week. Gambart had other business, and returned to London. The invalid spent a strenuous week in Yorkshire writing a completely new lecture which for the first time heralded unambiguously the social concerns of *Unto This Last*. The topic was 'Modern Manufacture and Design', not 'Old Masters' as it had been at Manchester.

This lecture, and Ruskin's personal relations with Bradford, helped to inspire a new school of design teaching there, which was publicised at the International Exhibition of 1862; and it earned Ruskin respect among some of the hard-headed businessmen of the town: so that when *Unto This Last* appeared in 1860, it was only in Bradford that the press received it with respect. Ruskin had shown that critics as well as dealers could exploit the 'dealer-critic system'.

Ruskin returned to lecture in Bradford in 1864. A superficial result of his appearance was a new interest in art-buying. Gambart, as Rossetti noted, quickly 'hauled in' £5,000 worth of business there. But a deeper result was that Ruskin's social ideas helped to enlarge and sharpen the political debate in the town. His interventions there remained a source of inspiration and ideas to a number of the members of the Independent Labour Party, formed in Bradford in 1893.[18]

Art education

In April 1883, Ruskin was approached by two separate groups of educators having similar aims. He accepted the invitation of Mary Christie, and T. C. Horsfall, the Manchester philanthropist and author, to become the first President of their new Art for Schools Association. However, he was already making himself ill with overwork at Oxford, and had to decline the almost simultaneous request to become President of the Salt Schools, which included night classes for adults, in Titus Salt's model village, Saltaire, near Bradford.[19] The fact that he was receiving such invitations is significant. His name had become a password for many groups who wanted to combine political and social reform with campaigns to make artistic culture broader and more accessible; and who saw education as a way to this end. The fact that the requests came from Manchester and Bradford points to the presence of small but enthusiastic groups of influential people in those towns who had warmed to Ruskin personally as a result of his lectures there (1857–64).

Such respect for Ruskin's personality and ideas had been earned by a lifetime's association with art education. A typical example was his involvement with T. D. Acland (later Sir Thomas) in furthering the cause of the Oxford Local Examinations: a pioneering initiative of 1858 to extend higher education to students outside the universities. As adviser on art education, Ruskin advocated a good general education for trainee artists, including literature, history, music and some sciences.

Aside from the inspiration provided by his books, Ruskin's influence was exerted partly through pupils, and partly by lectures and other contact with various groups, in London and the provinces. Such contact helped him to enhance cultural debate at local levels.

Although some of his pupils became professional artists, Ruskin's main concern and influence lay in promoting art as an element in general cultural training. He was sure that, by learning to see the natural world in a relaxed but attentive way, 'pupils' (in both senses) could help dispel some of the moral and political consequences of carelessness, prejudice, or inappropriate anxiety. From the Reformation English culture had been largely a verbal matter. Education was intended mainly to train students to handle the abstract concepts codified in words. Ruskin was foremost among Victorian thinkers in advocating visual awareness.

In 1870, Ruskin began work as Slade Professor of Art at Oxford: the first appointment of its kind ever made in England. Prior to that official recognition, Ruskin's art teaching was divided between classes for men in very modest circumstances, and individual work with ladies of higher social standing.

It was not unusual for a Victorian drawing master to give private lessons to ladies, while acting as evening tutor at a Mechanics' Institute, for instance. Such a man, often of lower middle-class background, might thus be meeting those above and below him in the social scale. To a limited extent, he might act as a bridge between such groups. Ruskin's family background and teaching function were similar, but with important differences. Well-to-do, and with an Oxford education, he was placed above the need to charge for his services. His personality enabled him to exploit the privileged status this gave him to further his chosen career as a catalyst of social ideas. Refusing to become a gentleman, or to remain a tradesman like his father, Ruskin acted as a kind of secular clergyman whose medium was art.

Some of his most influential art teaching was done at the London Working Men's College, founded in 1854 as a co-operative venture by F. D. Maurice and others. Timothy Hilton locates the informal contact fostered at this college between 'artisans who loved art' and 'men who made art' as 'the central moment of Pre-Raphaelitism'.[20] The leaders of the movement – Ruskin, Rossetti, Madox Brown, Burne-Jones – were all involved. Ruskin taught the landscape class, Rossetti the life school. Ruskin acknowledged that he learnt much; and if his pupils had a criticism it was that he tended to over-praise them. His enthusiasm and generosity bubbled over into political talk as well as tactful personal help of many kinds. But the most consistent impression was Ruskin's ability to communicate delight. He taught each 'separately, studying the capacities of each student', providing natural objects and art from his own collection for study in the dingy rooms in Red Lion Square, talking 'much to the class, discursively, but radiantly', and organising sketching parties. His artisan pupils recorded that it was 'not too much to say that the whole of our following lives have been enriched by these hours we spent with him'.[21]

In a similar way, Ruskin's contact with his lady drawing pupils took him and them into areas normally beyond the art lesson. The Marchioness of Waterford was a kind of correspondence pupil of his. He also made suggestions for the model village she was building. Mrs Pattison, later the wife of the maverick Liberal MP Sir Charles Dilke, sharpened her powers as a critic by arguing with Ruskin on several topics.[22] She was a friend of George Eliot, and the main inspiration for Dorothea, of *Middlemarch*. A third pupil, Octavia Hill, Ruskin himself helped to finance and support. She joined him in an influential experiment designed to show 'what might be done by firm State action' in the matter of working-class housing.

Among the places and institutions where, by lectures and contacts, Ruskin was able to disseminate his ideas were the Bradford, Manchester and Cambridge Art Colleges, St Martin's College in London, Eton College, the Arundel Society, the Architectural Photographic Society, the Architectural Association, and many others. At Coniston in later years he was frequently in the village school, to which he gave pictures, and where he might be found showing the children plants or joining them in handbell ringing. His postbag was heavy with drawings sent by individuals and institutions, and he was prodigal of help. At Sheffield and Oxford he went further, using his patrimony to found a museum at Sheffield and a drawing school at Oxford. Both are still in existence. He gave the pick of his Turner drawings to Oxford and Cambridge, and made lesser gifts to numerous places.

The local traditions Ruskin helped stimulate at Manchester were strengthened when his admirer Walter Crane became Director of Design there in 1893; and this legacy helped nurture the thought and feeling of Sylvia Pankhurst, for example, the socialist and feminist, a student at the local art college. A Bradfordian admirer, William Rothenstein, began study at his local college, and later helped the early career of Henry Moore. Both men would be influential Principals of the Royal College of Art, Crane at the turn of the century, Rothenstein in the 1920s.

Opening doors to music, art and nature study for working-class people was an aim of Ruskin's experimental St George's Guild, of which Sir Thomas Acland was the first trustee. This was an example of Ruskin's acting as a bridge between upper and lower classes, past and future. The Aclands were landed gentry. Carlyle had lamented the breaking of the power of such families, and angrily urged them to reassume authority. Ruskin, who had made friends among them at Oxford, was subtler in approach. As Carlyle dourly noted, he tended to be 'optimistic'. The gentry were going, Ruskin thought, but their departure need not be a catastrophe. There was need for urgency, for the opportunity offered to his own generation would not be repeated. There was no need, however, to despair. If the gentry allied themselves with the people while there was still time to take the initiative, they might fade away gracefully, or even be reborn in less expensive and more useful forms.

It was Sir Thomas's son, the Rt Hon. A. H. D. Acland, who as Minister of Education in 1894 brought some of Ruskin's influence to fruition in the New Code for education, pledging himself to the conviction that 'no more . . . than liberty itself, should art be for the few'.[23] None but a bankrupt successor, whatever his social origins, would wish to renege on Acland's pledge.

Art museums and galleries

Ruskin published no lengthy treatise on museums and galleries. But throughout his career the subject was of close interest to him. In pamphlets; in public and private letters; in lectures; and in giving evidence to official committees, he provided a rich source of theory, some of it influential, to curators and architects. And in practical ways: in conserving and distributing his own collection; in his capacity as Slade Professor; and by founding the museum at Sheffield that still bears his name, Ruskin provided an example that helped to form twentieth-century museum practice. It is typical of his legacy that his own house at Brantwood, in Cumbria, remains a centre of lively activity of many kinds: in no sense a dead shrine to vanished genius.

At first sight there seems to be a contradiction between Ruskin's interest in museums and his organic view of art. The paintings and architectural sculpture of any region were for him the testimony of the continuing historical life of that region. Art rose from, and belonged to, this living context. How then could museums be necessary? In particular, why should the British nation use its economic power to extort from more artistic nations the dead mementos of a vanished power for art: a power whose very prestige might stifle any revival of the native arts of Britain?

This kind of anxiety lies behind much of Ruskin's writing on museums. He was typically Victorian in concentrating as much as possible on the positive aspects of the case.

Among the negative aspects was the common practice, all over Europe at this time, for carvings, mosaics, paintings, to be obliterated in the process of 'restoration': the new work being substituted for the old. Ruskin was among the most vocal to advocate 'preservation' rather than such 'restoration'. If old work had to be replaced, at least let what remained of it be cared for in a public museum, not destroyed or – nearly as bad (and a common practice) – sold off to private collectors by fraudulent 'restoration' enterprises.

Ruskin was sure the best art was accessible and fixed, not portable and hidden: part of a public environment, not a private investment. Thus he set a very high value on the frescos of the Town Hall in Siena; and rather a low value on small Dutch landscapes, produced to a formula for middle-class dining rooms.

Art belonged to its particular place; therefore at the head of Ruskin's priorities for conserving it was the conviction that, whenever possible, it should remain where it was. What was healthy for people was good for art: an unpolluted environment was a priority for both. While campaigning for that, the conservers of art must do as much as possible to protect and preserve their treasures: from the weather, the vandal – military or casual – and above all, the unscrupulous 'restorer'.

Up to a point, art of various kinds could, and should, be conserved in the place for which it was originally designed. Medieval town hall, or church, or piazza; even Renaissance palace or formal garden – though here Ruskin's sympathies were much less strong – were living entities to be conserved, not collections of loot. But conservation was not always possible; and there was also much art, from the Renaissance on, actually designed to be 'collected' in palace galleries or private houses. Ruskin violently regretted this tendency: but nevertheless recognised the value of such work.

While art could remain alive in its place, it should be conserved there. When this was no longer possible, or perhaps desirable, art might be said to die. The museum was the place for it then. But the museum – and this is one of Ruskin's most characteristic and enabling convictions – should be, not a dead and deadening shrine; but an Easter Sepulchre: a place of Resurrection, a powerhouse for the renewal of the 'arts of life'. It is this conviction that has made Ruskin a beneficial influence on museums, and it has a number of practical implications.

A first principle would be to promote public munificence at the expense of private hoarding. Turner left his pictures to the nation on condition that a public gallery be built to house them. In 1867 Ruskin lectured the British Institution on a dream of his for a great gallery stretching from Westminster to Vauxhall along the Thames, to house this Turner collection and other works:[24] a dream only very partially realised thirty years later in the Tate Gallery and – ninety years later still – the adjoining Clore Gallery.

Ruskin hoped for many kinds of museum and gallery. Some for conserving rare or fragile treasures might need to be accessible only to serious students. But, if only to increase the supply of serious students, there should be free libraries and museums of popular education open all day and till late at night. There should be local town museums and village museums: not as tourist 'investment' or a preening-ground for snobs. Lounges, coffee rooms, restaurants, may be useful annexes to museums, in Ruskin's view, but a museum itself is none of these things. Children should have their own environment, with 'plenty of room for running about, plenty of flowers . . . a cheap alphabetical catalogue'.[25] Drama and music should play their part in a live museum.

Ruskin's pet plan for a gallery was a spiral, lit from above:[26] a suggestion eventually carried out by one of his readers, Frank Lloyd Wright, in the Guggenheim Gallery in New York.

Again, rather than engulf visitors with room after room of masterpieces, arranged in 'schools', it might be advisable, Ruskin thought, to arrange an 'epitome' or small exhibition of sample works designed as an introduction to the larger galleries. Such an 'epitome' could become known and loved by regular visitors in the way an overpowering Warehouse of Culture never could. As visitors got to feel their way round the 'epitome' exhibition, they could sally forth with more confidence and benefit to themselves into the galleries beyond.

All galleries should be pleasantly, but not richly, decorated. A gallery was for clarity and visibility, not for 'showing how many rich things can be got together'. This principle would be an inspiration to Ruskin's admirer Sidney Cockerell at the Fitzwilliam Museum, Cambridge. Sculpture should be in the same building, but preferably not in the same room as pictures, Ruskin thought. For the general public and the scholar, the significance of art as a clue to the deepest feelings and preferences of historical periods should be kept in mind when arranging a gallery. Artists had different needs: often arbitrary and obsessive. Each needed access to the 'very few pictures of the class which that particular artist wished to study' and this should be kept in mind at art schools. As part of their broader educational function, some galleries might show furniture, needlework, and even 'pots and pans, and salt cellars, and knives' as well as the work of 'minor' masters. There was truly no absolute division between the value of such things and the value of greater works.[27]

On a small scale, at Sheffield, during the 1870s and 1880s,

Ruskin was able to provide a practical experiment in some of these ideas. The municipal authorities could not, or would not, provide an adequate town-centre gallery – this was not realised till a century later – and the Georgian house they did provide was cramped and suburban. But the museum – whose contents were Ruskin's gift – functioned partly as an educational 'outing' for schools and the public, partly as a focus for more serious students. There were debates and lectures, and the resident curator supplied a personal and domestic element missing in more formal places. Minerals (a Victorian preoccupation) were included; also casts of sculpture – some of them taken from architectural work threatened with 'restoration' – coins, drawings and prints, books and illuminated manuscripts, and specially commissioned photographs and studies of buildings and of paintings. The copies of masters were made on a new educational principle under Ruskin's direction: he ensured they were 'descriptions' rather than substitutes for the original. Unlike common copies, they did 'not pretend to the same excellence in the same way'. Formerly slighted, these 'interpretations' of painting and architecture are now rightly valued as an education for the eye. The architectural studies particularly – a field in which Ruskin himself excelled – do what no photograph can do (in many instances the subject is no longer there to be photographed): they entrain the eye of the beholder to look and look again with fresh delight at the features or environment depicted. The 'copies' of pictures, too – which can now be studied side by side with modern photographs – allure the eye into patient appreciation of the original masters. In such ways Ruskin still fulfils his own definition of himself as a 'village showman' whose whole message is ' "Look – and you shall see".'[28]

The latest in a historical series of imperial nations, Britain, in Ruskin's view, had a great opportunity before her. She could choose to follow Rome and Venice in looting other cultures, and bury herself under the loot, producing feebler and feebler travesties of her plunder. Or she could use her moment as leading figure on the world stage to initiate conservation instead of looting, and respect for the past and for variety of cultural tradition instead of exploitation and despoilment. 'Whatever is good or great in Egypt, and Syria, and India,' he said, 'is just good or great for the same reasons as the buildings on our side of the Bosphorus.'[29] In her brief time of hegemony beyond the Bosphorus, Britain dare not forget her 'debt to the future'.[30]

The Slade Professorship

Ruskin's functions as Slade Professor might be divided under four headings: to research; to lecture; to write books; to arrange means for the practical study of his subject. Geology and natural history formed part of his research, and so did new intellectual and aesthetic experiences at Assisi and in Sicily. His lectures were, in a word, spectacular; and he published six volumes of them; the means for practical study he had not only to arrange, but to finance, himself. Art was not a subject for examination at Oxford; the professorship was financed by private bequest; and the authorities provided no grant.

Ruskin's election as Professor, and the terms under which he was able to function on his return to Oxford, are explicable from his earlier experience there.

Ruskin inherited some £120,000 in 1864, as well as valuable pictures. In 1836 his father had bought for him a place as gentleman-commoner at Christ Church, an undergraduate status the most prestigious in the world. At Oxford, Ruskin was judged to be such a bad examinee – anxiety over examinations, combined with a consumptive cough, kept him away from university for two years – that he was not entered for honours at all; but he performed so well in the pass degree examinations that the authorities awarded him a 'complimentary double-fourth' to register his anomalous brilliance. He learned to communicate with the upper classes; and gained two important friends: H. G. Liddell, the future Dean of Christ Church; and Henry Acland, the future Professor of Medicine. Ruskin's own father, however, was a wine-merchant: and some of his mother's relatives kept a public house. He made a point of announcing himself as lower middle class. Already, as an undergraduate, he had begun to establish himself as a writer on art.

All these elements were important when Ruskin returned to Oxford as the first Slade Professor in 1870. Liddell and Acland were among the group who elected him. He would pay his assistants from his own pocket; and organise a drawing school with petty-bourgeois thoroughness. He would be controversial, stimulating:

but always – in the words of one who heard him – 'benign and betwitching'.[31] Self-doubts remained; and the professorship would be interrupted by illness. His anomalous brilliance would enhance Oxford life: but he would not be able to smuggle Art into its degree structure.

The authorities were reconciled to having an art professor provided he did not actively promote his subject. Thus they supplied no money, and viewed any attempt by Ruskin to spend his own as empire-building. Nevertheless, he spent £2,000 on examples of art specially chosen for a new drawing school; and gave others in his possession. The University allowed him the use of the west wing of the Taylorian building; but the furnishings and fittings – £400 – came out of the Professor's pocket; as did £5,000 towards a mastership of drawing. His ambition was for a school where 'the grammar of all the arts may be taught to young persons in Oxford or its neighbourhood' – whether they were the children of 'gentlemen' or 'artisans' whether they were members of the University or not. He hoped for proper provision for an elementary drawing class, and workshops for modelling, metalwork and other crafts. But the University had no intention of making art one of its school subjects, or extending artistic illumination much beyond its own members; and in these circumstances, as Ruskin wrote to the Vice-Chancellor, a 'competent' professor would degenerate into a drawing master for casual study; an 'incompetent' would merely give formal lectures which 'no one would attend'. Ruskin needed all his genius, energy, and money, to make any headway. Fifteen or twenty male undergraduates might turn up for drawing classes when the Professor was present: only two or three when classes were taken by his assistant Alexander MacDonald. There was much more success in attracting women students: but as women were not officially members of the University at this time, this success amounted to an indictment in the eyes of conservative dons. A final blow came in 1883 when Ruskin's offer of an adequate new building enriched with the pick of his valuable collection was rejected: the University would not make land available. The authorities apparently succeeded, however, in hanging on to some of the works of art Ruskin had merely placed in the School but not made over to the University.[32]

These frustrations did not improve Ruskin's mental well-being. Environmental and humanitarian concerns were always part of his own research; and during his Oxford professorship his mind was becoming progressively more radical in these areas. He had promised the University authorities in 1869 that he would not be politically controversial; and such political points as he made at Oxford (often to undergraduate applause and donnish disapproval) tended to be in the paternalistic and philanthropic tradition. But to compensate for this, he simultaneously began a series of pamphlets – *Fors Clavigera* – aimed at intelligent workmen. In these pamphlets, he made hits against the Established Church, the landed gentry, and other institutions dear to Oxford.

The conservative and radical elements were both genuinely part of Ruskin's mind – he called himself both a Tory and a Communist – but the strain of simultaneously producing Oxford lectures and sevenpenny pamphlets that would complement each other, while remaining acceptable to their diverse audiences, was one of the causes that led him into irritability and exhaustion. This culminated in a bad-tempered attack – in *Fors Clavigera* in 1877[33] – on the American painter Whistler, who sued him for libel. Ruskin's mistake was to suggest that a painting by Whistler was not worth the asking price. The price of paintings was a conflagration-point for Ruskin the art professor and economic thinker. Whistler won the case; and was awarded damages of one farthing. Disgruntled and worn out, Ruskin resigned from the Slade Professorship.

By 1880, in *Fors Clavigera* Letter 89, Ruskin was propagandising his theory that the trade unions would soon replace 'the upper classes, so called' as the determining power in British politics.[34] In this and other ways he was becoming less and less acceptable to conservative academics. But his prestige was still so great that in 1883 William Richmond, his replacement as Slade Professor, resigned in his favour. Ruskin returned to Oxford and continued as Professor till March 1885, when he finally resigned. This time the causes were partly exhaustion, partly frustration at the University's refusal to make any financial contribution to his work, partly anger at their funding of a new laboratory for vivisection. This was another conflagration-point for him as both aesthete and conservationist.

During his Oxford years, Ruskin's mind was further burdened and excited by new discoveries and campaigns. His thinking about society and his explorations in art always went hand in hand. In his social thinking he was currently attempting to achieve a synthesis between Oxford's ancient ideals and the new aspirations of the trade unions. In similar vein, his new artistic explorations were reaching out further than ever before beyond the Protestant middle-class English taste of his youth. A visit to Sicily opened up pagan Greek architecture for him as never before. A stay at Assisi gave him new respect for the Catholic tradition he had been brought up to despise. His students were just catching up with his taste for Botticelli and Carpaccio: but their Professor had moved on – at Assisi – to Cimabue; and confronted there also an unsolvable enigma: close study suggested that little or nothing of Giotto's original handiwork remained on the frescoed walls – yet also revealed that Giotto was a far greater artist than Ruskin had ever appreciated.

Social and artistic commitment were united in concern for the urban environment. This concern was not limited to street-scenes admired by lovers of the picturesque. Thus, at Venice he contributed to the successful campaign to prevent the dismantling and 'restoration' of the facade of St Mark's. Simultaneously, in the East End of London, he employed a contingent of much needed street sweepers at his own expense.

These tensions were increasingly at play in his lectures, which sometimes commanded such large audiences that they had to be given twice. A performer who could not repeat himself, Ruskin made alterations that doubled the strain. His later lectures, particularly, were frequented by reporters from the national press: who added to his troubles by sensationalising, or simply misquoting, his remarks. There was plenty to report. Lectures were often dramas for three performers. Ruskin, his drawing master, and his manservant each enjoyed his moments of theatre. Large-scale illustrations, specially prepared, were manoeuvred, unveiled; given exits and entrances. Dramatic tension and timing were in full evidence, as Ruskin deployed his cap and gown and other 'props'. His sense of his own absurdity worked in poignant conspiracy with a sincere and passionate delivery that grew 'more and more wonderful and tender' as the lecture advanced. Girls resident in Oxford often came; and Ruskin's charm of manner seems to have enhanced the lecture hall's potential as a trysting place: a phenomenon he would sometimes allude to, and even appropriate into his theme. Traditional dons were righteously indignant. On the other hand, when Ruskin pioneered cultural history in a series of carefully composed lectures on Florence, which he read out, students found them difficult, and many stayed away.

The books Ruskin founded on these Oxford lectures demonstrate the breadth of his initiatives. The *Lectures on Art* embrace 'religion', 'morality' and 'practical use' as well as 'colour', 'line' and 'light'. *The Eagle's Nest* pleads for a unified consciousness, with scientific observation and social and environmental responsibility as inseparable from aesthetic perceptions. *Love's Meinie* compels respect as well as delight and accuracy in our observation of living creatures. *Aratra Pentelici* opens up the thought-world of the Greeks as well as their bequest of economic line. *Ariadne Florentina* performs a similar task for Florentine engraving. *The Art of England* shows Ruskin's skill in providing telling criticism which nevertheless is helpful, not destructive, to living artists. Professors who cannot draw have not always been so charitable. And *Val d'Arno* (which undergraduates found difficult) is foundational in its attempt to see art deeply rooted in its environmental and cultural context.

But the Professor was perhaps at his best in his personal influence with undergraduates. He had himself learnt to appreciate the art of bricklaying after endeavouring (unsuccessfully) to build a brick pillar in the Oxford Museum. He not only employed street-sweepers, but came to respect them after trying his hand at sweeping. He remained convinced that practical attempts – however brief and incompetent – at undertaking manual labour were a useful way of breaking down the Oxford habit of preferring theory to practice, of delighting in gentlemanly ignorance and superiority at the expense of the kind of knowledge that comes only from doing. He was astonished, however, at the enthusiasm with which students took up his suggestion of practical road-making at Hincksey, where carts were destroying the village green. The amateur foreman there became 1st Viscount Milner, Secretary of State for the Colonies. His right-hand man was Arnold Toynbee, the future social reformer and inspiration behind the University Settlement Movement in the East End of London. Oscar Wilde, who learnt much from Ruskin's meticulous prose, went along to supply conversation.

A different type who found Ruskin equally fascinating was W. H. Grenfell. Rowing in the open sea as the Venetians did would be a good way, suggested the Professor, of learning through practical experience to appreciate the fundamental realities of Venetian culture. Grenfell got a crew together and rowed from Dover to Calais.

Michael Sadler, a future Professor of Education and Director of Special Inquiries in the Education Department, never forgot Ruskin's extempore support of William Morris in the hall of University College in 1883. The socialist Morris spoke on 'art under a plutocracy', with sharp reference to Oxford. Dons began noisily to leave the hall. Ruskin rose from his place in the front row and – in Sadler's memory – stopped them in their tracks with a sublime defence which drew storms of undergraduate applause.[35]

Unrepentant, Ruskin exploited the issue in the peroration of his *Art of England* lectures. It may serve as his last word as Slade Professor:

> The changes [Morris] so deeply deplored . . . in this once loveliest city, are due wholly to the deadly fact that her power is now dependent on the Plutocracy of Knowledge . . . There never . . . can be any other law respecting . . . wisdom . . . than 'Buy the Truth, and sell it not.' It is to be costly to you – of labour and patience; and you are never to sell it, but to guard, and to give.
>
> Much of the enlargement, though none of the defacement, of old Oxford is owing to the real life and the honest seeking of extended knowledge. But more is owing to the supposed money value of that knowledge; and exactly so far forth, her enlargement is purely injurious to the University and to her scholars.[36]

Those who applauded that may have felt what Tolstoy would write: 'John Ruskin . . . is one of those rare men who think with their hearts . . . he thinks and says . . . what everyone will think and say in the future.'[37]

Notes

1 *Time and Tide*, para. 2.
2 *Sesame and Lilies*, para. 49.
3 Mr Casaubon sits to such an artist in *Middlemarch*, Ch. 22.
4 *Works*, XVII.li.
5 Cook, *Life of Ruskin*, II.332.
6 Hardman, *Ruskin and Bradford*, pp. 300, 311–14.
7 Bradley, ed., *The Critical Heritage*, pp. 179–95.
8 *Modern Painters*, III, Ch. 10, 'Of the Use of Pictures'.
9 *Works*, XIV. 13–14.
10 Evans, ed., *Lamp of Beauty*, pp. 159, 162. See also *Works*, XII. 319–23.
11 Evans, ed., *Lamp of Beauty*, pp. 77–8, 108.

12 *Works*, XIV. 476–89.
13 *Works*, XIV. 272, 308–9.
14 Hardman, *Ruskin and Bradford*, p. 253.
15 *Fors Clavigera*, Letter 79, para. 8 (g).
16 *Works*, XII.xx.
17 *Works*, XIV. 142, 181.
18 Hardman, *Ruskin and Bradford*, pp. 7, 36–7, 86, 123–4, 232, 311–12.
19 *Works*, XXVII.lxix; XXXIV. 563.
20 Hilton, *The Pre-Raphaelites*, p. 211.
21 *Works*, V. 40.
22 *Works*, XX. xxx, 7, n. Emilia Strong, successively married to Mark Pattison, Rector of Lincoln College, Oxford, and Sir Charles Dilke: Bradley, ed., *Critical Heritage*, pp. 316–18.
23 Cook, *Life of Ruskin*, II. 368.
24 *Works*, XIX. 227.
25 *Works*, XIX. 218. See also Evans, ed., *Lamp of Beauty*, Index, under 'Art galleries'.
26 *Works*, XIII.xxviii, 176–9.
27 *Works*, XIII. 541–50.
28 *Works*, XXVI. 333. *Works*, XXX tells the story of the Sheffield Museum, which since 1985 has been housed at 101 Norfolk Street, Sheffield.
29 *Unto This Last and other writings*, p. 240.
30 *Works*, XIX. 164: 'the faculty of art is not one which we can separately cultivate [without] true joy in the treasures of the past or any true sense of our debt to the future – that debt and pledge, under which we are bound to those who come after us'.
31 *Works*, XXVI.xliii.
32 *Works*, XXI. Introduction outlines the story of Ruskin's Slade Professorship.
33 *Works*, XXIX. 160.
34 Hardman, *Ruskin and Bradford*, pp. 314–17.
35 Alfred, 1st Viscount Milner, 1854–1925. Secretary of State for the Colonies, 1919–21. Arnold Toynbee, 1852–83, land reformer and democratic radical. Toynbee Hall, the University Settlement in Whitechapel, was named after him. Oscar Wilde, 1854–1900, describes Ruskin's prose in *The Critic as Artist*, Part I (1891). W. H. Grenfell, 1st Lord Desborough. His son Julian (1888–1915) hymned the family ideology in his poem *Into Battle*. Michael Ernest Sadler, 1861–1943, Director of Special Inquiries in the Education Department, 1895–1903; Professor of Education, Manchester University, 1903–11. His reminiscence of Ruskin forms the Introduction to Edith Hope Scott, *Ruskin's Guild of St. George*, n.d.
36 *Works*, XXXIII. 390–1.
37 Leo Tolstoy, 'An Introduction to Ruskin's Works' (1899), *Recollections and Essays*, translated by Aylmer Maude, 1937, p. 188.

Books

Paperbacks

John Ruskin, *Unto This Last and other writings*, edited with an introduction by Clive Wilmer, Harmondsworth, 1985. Includes *Unto This Last*, *The King of the Golden River* and extracts from *The Stones of Venice*, *The Two Paths*, *Modern Painters*, *The Crown of Wild Olive*, *Sesame and Lilies* and *Fors Clavigera*.

The Lamp of Beauty: Writings on Art by John Ruskin, selected and edited by Joan Evans, Oxford, 1959, reprinted 1980. Illustrated.

Ruskin Today. Kenneth Clark's interpretative anthology is currently (1989) available as a Penguin book.

Timothy Hilton, *The Pre-Raphaelites*, 157 illustrations, London, 1970.

Marcia Pointon (editor), *Pre-Raphaelites re-viewed*, Manchester, 1989, (paperback).

Life

E. T. Cook, *The Life of Ruskin*, London, 1911.

Tim Hilton, *John Ruskin: the Early Years*, London, 1985.

Derrick Leon, *Ruskin: The Great Victorian*, London, 1949, reprinted 1969.

Helen Gill Viljoen, *Ruskin's Scottish Heritage*, Urbana, Illinois, 1956.

Diaries

The Diaries of John Ruskin, edited by J. Evans and J. H. Whitehouse, Oxford, 1956–59.

The Brantwood Diary of John Ruskin, edited by Helen Gill Viljoen, New Haven and London, 1971.

Letters

John Lewis Bradley, editor, *Ruskin's Letters from Venice 1851–2*, New Haven, Connecticut, 1955.

John Lewis Bradley and Ian Ousby, editors, *The Correspondence of John Ruskin and Charles Eliot Norton*, Cambridge, 1987.

Van Akin Burd, editor, *The Ruskin Family Letters: 1801–1843*, Ithaca, New York, 1973.

Van Akin Burd, editor, *The Winnington Letters of John Ruskin*, London, 1969.

C. E. Maurice, editor, *The Life of Octavia Hill from her Letters*, London, 1913. Much interesting material on Ruskin.

Harold I. Shapiro, editor, *Ruskin in Italy: John Ruskin's Letters to his father from Italy, 1845*, Oxford, 1972.

Virginia Surtees, editor, *Sublime and Instructive: Letters from John Ruskin to Louisa, Marchioness of Waterford, Anna Blunden and Ellen Heaton*, London, 1972.

Works

The Works of John Ruskin, edited by E. T. Cook and Alexander Wedderburn, London 1903–12.

John Ruskin, *Unto This Last: Four Essays on the First Principles of Political Economy*, edited by P. M. Yarker, London, 1970.

Criticism and commentary

Ruskin: The Critical Heritage, edited by J. L. Bradley, London, 1984.

P. D. Anthony, *John Ruskin's labour: a study of Ruskin's social theory*, Cambridge, 1983.

Patricia M. Ball, *The Science of Aspects: the changing role of fact in the work of Coleridge, Ruskin and Hopkins*, London, 1971.

David R. Ellison, *The Reading of Proust*, Baltimore and London, 1984.

Raymond E. Fitch, *The Poison Sky: Myth and Apocalypse in Ruskin*, Athens, Ohio, 1982.

Malcolm Hardman, *Ruskin and Bradford*, Manchester, 1986.

Elizabeth K. Helsinger, *Ruskin and the Art of the Beholder*, Cambridge, Massachusetts, and London, 1982.

Luke Herrmann, *Ruskin and Turner*, London, 1968.

John Dixon Hunt and Faith M. Holland, editors, *The Ruskin Polygon: essays on the imagination of John Ruskin*, Manchester, 1982.

Brian Maidment, 'Ruskin, *Fors Clavigera* and Ruskinism, 1870–1900', in *New Approaches to Ruskin*, edited by R. Hewison, London, 1981, pp. 194–213.

J. D. Rosenberg, *The Darkening Glass: A Portrait of Ruskin's Genius*, London, 1963.

John Unrau, *Looking at architecture with Ruskin*, 101 illustrations, London, 1978.

John Unrau, *Ruskin and St. Mark's*, London, 1984.

Victorian painting

Royal Academy of Arts Bicentenary Exhibition, 14 December 1968 – 2 March 1969, *Catalogue*, with Introduction by Graham Reynolds, and accompanying volume of *Illustrations*, London.

Jeremy Maas, *Victorian Painters*, London, 1969.

Jeremy Maas, *Gambart*, London, 1975.

Graham Reynolds, *Victorian Painting*, revised edition, London, 1987.

CHAPTER FOUR

Harriet Taylor

Introduction

The continuing ambiguity of women's position is reflected in the difficulty writers still have in choosing a name for Harriet, successively Mrs John Taylor and Mrs John Stuart Mill, née Hardy (1807–58). Her intellectual friendship with Mill dates from 1830.

Carlyle's 'Signs of the Times' of 1829 goes some way towards characterising Harriet's own intellectual mood. Scepticism was everywhere, wrote Carlyle. It was a symptom of disease, yet also the beginning of cure. Let us cease to pay lip-service to institutions, and respond to the 'dynamical nature of man'.

Carlyle grew less dynamic, and more authoritarian. He tended to see man's nature (he had very little to say about women) in generalised and absolutist terms. Ruskin's love of particularity and individuation made him much more radical than Carlyle. To some extent, as far as his own experience allowed him, Ruskin operated as a responsive catalyst, and even enabled some women to do so. Octavia Hill records how Ruskin enlarged her ambition as a typical Victorian woman hoping to do good by working for 'changes in individuals'. 'No!' was Ruskin's reply. 'You can't alter natures . . . I think we may live to see some great changes in society.'[1] With his financial and moral support, Octavia became an internationally respected housing reformer, pressing for state action on housing.

Whereas Octavia warmed to Ruskin's 'strange mixture of the childlike and the manly', she found Mill much less sympathetic. 'Mill would never win my heart,' she wrote, 'but he is decidedly an able man, and I liked watching him, as one would a finely contrived machine.'[2]

Harriet, as true to her unique self as Ruskin to his, could see beneath the 'machine' to which Mill's authoritarian rationalist father had apparently reduced him. He entered her world of art and poetry. Much more unexpectedly, she began to enter more and more into his world of politics and economics. They found a common love in Plato, with his idea of an elite formed equally of men and women. But, like Plato, Mill tended to see intelligent women as substitute men. Harriet had to resist this simplification.

In collaborating with a man who was less radical in his economic ideas than she was, Harriet faced a typical dilemma for women: how to enter the economic world without compromising her radicalism. Ruskin never met either of them, but his insights into Mill's work help to clarify Harriet's difficulty. Commenting on a passage of Mill's *Political Economy* which is now known to have been written under Harriet's influence, Ruskin lamented that by advocating further career opportunities for women in the current world of *laissez-faire* economics, Mill was simply abandoning women to 'Rationalism and commercial competition',[3] and denying their right to change the world. Ruskin's own formula for woman as catalyst was most sharply defined in his *Lilies* lecture. It goes as far as most men would have wished. Women must take their full part in society, but primarily – like Octavia Hill – in women's roles like teaching and social work. Their influence on commerce and politics must be exerted through moral pressure on men.

In a world where even 'advanced' men had such ideas, Harriet had in practice to compromise. Her daughter Helen was given a broad general education to equip her to influence an important man: John Stuart Mill. Helen would succeed her mother as Mill's inspiration and helpmeet. Mill seems to have accepted this. His picture of Harriet in his *Autobiography* is absurdly fulsome. When Mill remembered that Harriet was not a substitute man, he flew to the opposite extreme and idealised her, like Ruskin's imaginary women in *Lilies*.[4]

Towards the end of his writing career, Ruskin reached the point from which Harriet had begun fifty years before. His outline for the education of young children of 1884[5] is very similar to Harriet's fragment on 'Toleration' of 1832. The 'total exclusion of the stimulus of competition' was Ruskin's formula. Harriet's was identical: 'our strongest effort must be to prevent individual emulation'.[6] Both Harriet and Ruskin were more passionately dedicated than Mill ever was to the idea that the Victorian spirit of competition was merely a device for repressing the individual and providing slaves for the *laissez-faire* system.

Ruskin's comment in *Unto This Last* (1860) about Mill's *Political Economy* (1848) was more perceptive than he could have realised. The value of the work, he noted, was in its 'inconsistencies'.[7] Elsewhere, he exemplified Mill's failure to reconcile liberal economics with radical demands for social justice and corporate action. Thus, Mill denies the right of a landed proprietor to own land if he is not using it for the public good; but then 'retreats from this perilous admission' and reaffirms the landlord's absolute right to rent and profit from his land, regardless of social obligations.[8] What Ruskin could not know was that this 'inconsistency' between commercial competition and social obligation reflected a dialogue between that hater of competition Harriet Taylor and the cautious liberal economist John Stuart Mill.

A paper by Ruskin on the 'Basis of Social Policy' (1875) shows him retreating from a feminist position in much the same way as Mill retreats from a radical economic position. Referring to his drawing pupil Bertha Patmore,[9] Ruskin ironically notes that with her talents and his tuition she might become a professional painter and be liberated from the 'vulgar career of wives and mothers' which current fashion condemns on 'Mr. Mill's authority'. Changing his tone, however, Ruskin goes on to say that 'the automatic instincts of equity in us . . . revolt' against unfairness between the sexes, as against any other unfairness. But he retreats from what he calls 'speculations in extreme' lest they disturb 'the serene confidence of daily action'. In other words, the same Ruskin who claimed to be demanding radical changes in economics is content, in the case of women, to rely on piecemeal individual action. After all, he adds, Darwin has shown us that Nature is unfair. Ruskin is usually a harsh critic of social Darwinism, with its crude application of the doctrine of the 'survival of the fittest'. But, in the case of women, he retreats into social Darwinism.[10]

There is no major male Victorian writer apart from Mill who comes any nearer to Harriet's feminism than Ruskin does here. There is no major Victorian writer who comes as near to Ruskin's ideas for co-operation and state intervention in economics as Mill does, with Harriet's encouragement. She anticipated Ruskin, and informed Mill. Moreover, where they retreated, she advanced. It is understandable that Mill should regard Ruskin as the only truly creative English thinker apart from himself and Harriet.[11] But it is Harriet alone who can claim the credit of insisting that economic justice and justice for women must go hand in hand, and that both, together, make radical demands for worldwide *human* liberation.

Harriet was a Unitarian. The martyr–heroine of Unitarian feminist women was Mary Wollstonecraft, author of *A Vindication of the Rights of Women*. After her death in childbirth in 1797, her reputation and influence were unwittingly destroyed by her rationalist husband William Godwin, who revealed the 'improper' secrets of her private life. In a much more prurient age, Harriet not only needed Mill's friendship and public reputation to further her ideas, she needed to protect that friendship and reputation from the gossip that could destroy her life's work. If she occasionally emerges as over-anxious, she had good cause.

Background

Harriet Hardy was born at 18 Beckford Row, Walworth, South London, on 10 October 1807. Walworth was largely a lower middle-class area, rapidly filling up with new housing. Harriet's parents were Unitarians, a sect which had long been subject to political disabilities. Only in 1813 were Unitarians placed on a footing with other Protestant dissenters; and it was not until 1828 that such dissenters were permitted to hold public office.

Unitarians had been persecuted because they denied the godhead of Christ, while revering him as an historical figure uniquely appointed by God to lead all humanity to truth and virtue. Equating Christian regeneration with the liberation of individual energies, Unitarians believed in universal redemption, in the right of individual congregations to define doctrine, and in access to communion for all without test.

As their political disabilities were removed, the respectable element among Unitarians tended to prevail over the rebel element. This was already happening in Harriet's girlhood, but she never lost their early passion for the idea of the radical liberation of humanity in history. With a sectarian background virtually the opposite of Carlyle's, Harriet remained as strong-minded as Carlyle in clinging to the full implications of that background. She would never accept that the political 'emancipation' of Unitarians was the last word in human progress. It was the first word of a new chapter of progress. It was an opportunity to promote progress in an area specially connected with Unitarianism: the liberation of women. In particular, now that male radicals like James Mill were pressing for manhood suffrage as the key to peaceful change, there was a need for a Unitarian woman capable of forming an alliance with some male radical to promote a strategy to bring votes to women.

Such was the logic of Harriet's alliance with John Stuart Mill. In upbringing and personality they were natural complements of each other. Both were trained in the path of duty. Both felt the force of the challenge that was being articulated by Carlyle. In a world where thought and feeling had come adrift from action and been reduced to 'dilettantism', they longed to have some real work to do. George Eliot, who also responded to Carlyle's challenge, would describe what many felt: 'Our sense of duty must often wait for some work which shall take the place of dilettantism – make us feel that the quality of our action is not a matter of indifference.'[12]

In finding each other, John and Harriet were released from indifference into meaningful action.

'Most valuable friendship'

The relationship between Harriet Taylor and J. S. Mill dates from the late summer or early autumn of 1830, when he was twenty four and she was twenty two. It has always been a source of puzzlement. Harriet described herself as Mill's *Seelenfreundin*,[13] or 'soul-friend'. There was, and remains, no English equivalent.

In some respects, a comparison might be made with the continental tradition of a great lady taking under her wing a promising writer, in no sense a rival to her husband, and acting as his social ally, confidante or nurse. Such a tradition was not unknown in Victorian England. The relationships between Carlyle and Lady Harriet Baring, Ruskin and Lady Trevelyan, Arnold and Lady de Rothschild, might be said to belong in this tradition. They have rarely been a source of prurient speculation. Social convention raised these ladies above tittle-tattle. The problem with Harriet – and what makes her friendship with Mill so innovative and important – is that she dared to act with the freedom society reserved only for great ladies. British hypocrisy was puzzled.

Harriet was no *grande dame*. Nor, on the other hand, could

she pass as a *petite amie*. It was acceptable for a middle-class Bohemian like Rossetti to 'keep' a poor girl like Lizzie Siddal. Respectable people like Ruskin's mother could be told (they did not have to believe) that Lizzie was merely Rossetti's artistic inspiration and that he was helping her financially. Gossips could speculate all they wished.

Harriet called the bluff on the hypocrites and bewildered the gossips. The problem was that she was entirely suitable by background to be Mill's wife. She was his social equal. She was also, however, a married woman with (by the summer of 1831) three children.[14] Yet her relationship with Mill gave no indication to onlookers of being adulterous. What could they see in each other? Then and since, it has been this failure to conform even to a reprehensible category that has fuelled resentment against Harriet.

Very few letters from Harriet to Mill survive. She asked him to destroy them. The same fear of exposure seems to have made her delay publication of the few pieces she did publish, and to insist on anonymity. Her relationship with Mill was so simple, and so necessary to both of them, that it was always likely to be misunderstood – occasionally, even by Mill.

Mill told his father he needed Harriet for his work, as he might need a congenial male friend. This was a half-truth. The very fact that she was a woman daring to think as a woman – the living reality behind the theory of women's liberation that was in Mill's head before he met her – made her irresistible to him. Harriet had a genius for putting searching questions, for insisting on fundamentals, for opening vistas: for editing, in short. The fact that Mill was a man comparatively willing and able to assimilate her thoughts without the almost invariable male condescensions and revisions, and that he was in a position to incorporate her ideas into acceptable 'masculine' literary works, made him necessary to her.

As Harriet's surviving letters show, Mill was in no sense a rival to her husband. She made this very clear to him when she was nursing her husband as he lay dying, in 1849. Mill suggested she distract her mind by thinking about other topics. 'Good God,' she wrote, 'should you think it was a relief to think of somebody else while *I* was dying?' She also wrote, 'I feel as if he [Taylor] beside you is the only life I value in this wretched world.'[15] Harriet would not deny her feelings for her husband, nor flaunt convention at the expense of her own family and Mill's civil-service career in order to pander to Mill's ego. Mill sometimes wondered about his own usefulness. Harriet told him that his usefulness as a thinker was 'certainly not' like her usefulness as a wife and mother 'marked out as a duty'. Men might always put their own inclinations first. A woman, in Harriet's view, could rarely do that. Men of genius could behave as though they had no ties. Harriet did not accept their right to do so, but was equally clear that to fulfil the duties imposed on her by marriage was 'my only earthly opportunity of "usefulness" '. [16] In Utopia, of course, things might be otherwise.

It is insights such as these which make Harriet important. She never pretended – as Mill sometimes did – that high-flown theories were an excuse for bad behaviour in the real world. This difference applied even after their marriage. Mill tried to use Harriet as an excuse to cut himself off from his family, with whom he felt he no longer had anything in common. To his disgrace, his new status as a Victorian husband enabled him to succeed. But his sister, who had met Harriet, was not deceived. 'Do not imagine that I attribute to the influence of your wife this conduct of yours', she wrote.[17] No wonder that, despite her love for him, and despite his eagerness to make a theoretical equality part of their marriage contract, Harriet was in no hurry to marry Mill. She was, and is, a constant reminder of the responsibilities and embarrassments male theorists dump on to women in their own pursuit of the ideal.

If Harriet was always reminding Mill of practical actuality, she was also more radical than he tended to be. A pair of essays they wrote for each other in 1832 shows this. John tinkered with rules for easier divorce and better economic status for women, but gallantly forbade women to strive to compete with men in the labour market. Woman's 'occupation should rather be to adorn and beautify'. Such sentiments would be much modified, though not to vanishing point, by the time Mill wrote *On the Subjection of Women* in 1861, three years after Harriet's death. In 1832 his education had hardly begun. 'What evil can be caused,' Harriet wrote, 'by, first placing women on the most entire equality with men . . . and then doing away with all laws whatever relating to marriage?'[18] He had, after all, asked for her opinion.

Harriet's essay on Toleration, also of 1832, holds the beginnings of a critique of a society dominated by male competition. Suppression of women is only part of the male herd-instinct for aggressive conformity. The nineteenth-century creed of rugged individualism emerges as a poor thing. It actually stunts individuals, and replaces natural happiness with anxious 'oneupmanship'. Men are deformed by 'the spirit of Emulation in childhood and of competition in manhood'. The social pressures which instil these vices are 'part of the conformity plan, making each person's idea of goodness and happiness a thing of comparison'.[19]

Such defiant individuality, together with a longing for genuine reconciliation based on respect for differences, would be part of Harriet's contribution to works published under Mill's name.

When Mill came to write his *Autobiography*, he would call his relationship with Harriet 'the most valuable friendship' of his life. His praise of Harriet has been found excessive and unconvincing by some, but even supposing he exaggerated the *weight* of that influence, his rigid analytical training and lifelong habit of intellectual honesty make it unlikely that his account of the *shape* of that influence is radically inaccurate.

His praise of Harriet was designed as her monument, to be unveiled only after both their deaths. Mill asked her to look through it and comment, as he did with most of his work. She has been censured for accepting this tribute without comment. But what kind of mother criticises the bouquet lovingly gathered for her by her favourite and most sensitive son? The maternal element was always a strong part of her feeling for him. She could be usefully brisk with Mill in urging him to his proper work, and in keeping him from wasting his talents on what she called the 'gentility' class. But she seems not to have had the heart to put the pencil through his hymn of love to her. It is possible she concealed this embarrassment along with lesser ones.

If its florid excesses are ignored, Mill's tribute to Harriet may be regarded as indicative. Assigning to himself the role of theorist, he acknowledged a double debt to her. She insisted that theory be directed towards the practically obtainable. At the same time, she quickened his imagination towards more generous ultimate aims. In his own words, she exalted his 'conceptions of the highest worth of a human being'.

Yet her greatest gift, he says, was scepticism: in particular, the awareness that societies do not embrace measures merely – or at all – because they can be proved to be reasonable. She went to the 'marrow of the matter', undeflected by 'verbal sophistry'. In the matter of women's disabilities, she helped him to know from her side how they 'intertwine themselves with all the evils of existing society'.[20]

Surviving letters and writings of Harriet support Mill's analysis, and there is no need to belittle Harriet because Mill pretties up the analysis with fulsome additions. Fulsomeness was not what she wanted. Indeed, she had written to him with quite different advice for the *Autobiography*:

> Should there not be a summary of our relationship from its commencement in 1830 – I mean given in a dozen lines – so as to preclude other and different versions . . . This ought to be done in its genuine simplicity and truth – strong affection, intimacy of friendship, and no impropriety. It seems to me an edifying picture for those poor wretches who cannot conceive friendship but in sex . . . But that of course is not my reason for wishing it done. *It is that every ground should be occupied by ourselves on our own subject.*[21]

The last phrase, 'our own subject', is interesting. At one level, Harriet has slipped into a French form of expression, natural to someone whose happiest hours were spent with Mill in France. We might 'translate' her words as meaning 'on the subject of ourselves'. But at a deeper level she is saying something more important than anything in Mill's analysis of her intellect, wrapped up as that is in puerile excrescences. She is going to 'the marrow of the matter' with her implication that their real 'subject' was precisely 'our relationship from its commencement in 1830'. The Mills' attempt to articulate the implications of their innovative friendship is indeed their true 'subject'; and it is this which makes the work they did together so interesting and significant.

'The Enfranchisement of Women'

Harriet Taylor met John Stuart Mill through their shared interest in the *Monthly Repository*, a journal edited by Harriet's Unitarian minister W. J. Fox. Harriet wrote some verses and reviews for this journal, in the amateurish 'ladylike' style natural to her background. Mill was already established as a political writer working in the exclusively rationalist style which was at that time natural to him.

Their coming together educated both of them, and followed a natural progression right up to Harriet's death in 1858, and even beyond, for Mill continued to be supported by her memory and ideas.

In the first stage, Mill came over to Harriet's world, producing articles on poetry and other artistic questions, with Harriet's help. The next stage came when Mill published some translations of Plato in the *Monthly Repository* in 1834. He had made the translations in 1828, but had since read Plato's dialogues again with Harriet. His new comments of 1834 show that his discussions with Harriet about Plato had awakened in him an inspiring sense that truth was not to be found in rationally coherent theories, isolated from reality, but in the open process of dialogue itself.[22] From this discovery, which Mill and Harriet made together, they embarked on their next stage.

Harriet came over to Mill's world, and made increasing contributions to his writings on politics and economics. Among the most important would be her insistence on the inclusion of a chapter on 'the probable future of the labouring classes' in his *Principles of Political Economy* (1848 – Harriet's points were strengthened in later editions). She was able to bring a more outspoken element of socialism into Mill's rather cautious views about property. She considered there could be little security for the community or for property until legislation was passed favouring 'the diffusion instead of the concentration of wealth'.[23] Mill's eminence guaranteed that this and other important ideas of Harriet received wide circulation, an outcome that could never have been achieved by Harriet alone.

The high point of their collaboration would be *On Liberty*, not published till after Harriet's death. This deserves separate treatment, but meanwhile it might be described as a conspectus of their years of Platonic dialogue with each other on the subject dearest to them both. It has been called the most 'moving' of the works issued under Mill's name.[24]

As Mill came more and more into Harriet's early world of poetry, art and music, and Harriet entered more fully into Mill's world of politics and economics, their dialogue was progressively enriched. None of this could have happened, however, without Mill's sympathy with the issue that concerned Harriet most: the position of women and their political future. Despite his sympathy, this was an area that Harriet had to explore largely alone.

She did so in two connected areas. The fact that they were connected was her own significant insight.

First, in a series of anonymous newspaper articles of 1846 and 1849–51, fifteen in all, she explored ways in which male oppression, based ultimately on brute force, lay at the root of a whole range of injustices.[25] Secondly, in an article on the 'Enfranchisement of Women' (1851), she collated arguments for women's right to full political citizenship. Mill helped with both, but just as the *Political Economy* was principally his subject, so this double 'protest against the aristocracy of sex'[26] was principally hers.

Male reformers saw the need to extend political rights to lower-class men in order to avoid outbreaks of intolerable violence. In her articles on violence Harriet went to the marrow of the matter. She located and publicised examples of the kind of intolerable violence which operated already at every level of society as a permanent expression of men's brutalisation by the power all men had over women. Like Mill and other Utilitarians, Harriet believed that nothing would ever really be done for the oppressed until they got a fair say in politics. Mill was in a minority of male Utilitarians in thinking that women deserved the vote, but even he was more interested in the right of intelligent women to make their contribution to political debate: almost as honorary men. It was Harriet who insisted that the security of society itself, and its continued capacity for peaceful and humane development, depended on women achieving political rights *as women*, and using them as such. A whole array of consequences followed for education, employment, for religion and the arts; and these consequences are hinted at in works appearing under Mill's name. But it is Harriet's 'Enfranchisement of Women' which most cogently addresses the central issue of political enfranchisement for women.

The article appeared in the *Westminster Review* for July 1851. Much of it was written in 1848–49, but despite Mill's urgings, Harriet delayed publication till after their marriage. This was partly for reasons of security: it was very difficult for a woman to gain a hearing for anything controversial, doubly so if her marital status was at all dubious. The article was anonymous, and Mill fussily insisted on protecting Harriet further by allowing it to be believed that it was by him. But Charlotte Brontë, and perhaps others, spotted that it was a woman's work.[27] Harriet might want to write more. It was as well to begin from a respectable base.

Harriet's timing had a more important strategic aspect, however. Coming out when it did, the article was able to appear within a frame provided by other women, not in a context of male patronage. Harriet begins by discussing the 'Women's Rights Convention' held in Massachusetts the previous October, and ends with news of a similar meeting at Sheffield in February 1851.

A further advantage to the timing was the general mood of 1851. It was the summer of the Great Exhibition, a time of confidence and taking stock. England was flooded with new ideas from all over the world. Even Prince Albert was reminding public meetings that this was a time of 'transition'. Humanity, it was generally agreed, must move forward to greater tolerance and freedom. One example of the beginnings of improvement in women's affairs came that same year with the publication of Herbert Spencer's *Social Statics*, which included a plea for the legal emancipation of women. Another was the appointment of Mary Ann Evans ('George Eliot') as the effective, though anonymous, editor of the *Westminster Review*.

Harriet's article fitted the mood of the time in America, also, where it was made the basis of resolutions on women's rights, and continued to be read and discussed among members of the women's enfranchisement movement there. Harriet's ideas were of course powerful in themselves, but the trick was to get them into the prestigious *Westminster Review* at a seasonal moment.

In England, men got in on the act. The radical George Jacob Holyoake, to whom Mill had given financial help at Harriet's intervention, reissued extracts from the article in 1856 as a pamphlet under the eye-catching title: 'Are Women Fit for Politics?' Mill quarrelled with Holyoake about the vulgarity of his behaviour, but did not find time to record, or perhaps even fully discover, Harriet's own reaction.[28] Mill could sometimes be a surprisingly conventional Victorian husband.

The whole tenor of Harriet's thinking had been to stress that the 'votes for women' issue, though vital, was only part of *human* liberation.[29] This point would become obscured in the debate conducted by Mill and other men in Parliament, but at least Harriet's article, in its pristine entirety, was brought out by Mill's election committee in 1865, and helped to create interest in his candidature. He insisted it appear under Harriet's name. There were other reasons than gallantry, or even honesty, for this.

Despite his sympathy, Mill never followed Harriet very far in certain directions that she considered essential. Foremost among these was her desire to see married women set free to take on truly challenging employment. Unlike Mill, she was prepared to welcome the consequences of this: 'High mental powers in women will be but an exceptional accident, until every career is open to them and until they as well as men, are educated for themselves and for the world, not one sex for another.'[30]

In this and other demands for human liberation, Harriet remained ahead of the cautious political economist John Stuart Mill. She contributed much to his enlightenment, but emancipation comes most truly from within. The 'Enfranchisement of Women' has been edited by Alice S. Rossi, and is best read in its entirety in the context of that edition.

Towards liberty

In 1853 Harriet suffered a lung haemorrhage at Nice. Mill, too, was gravely ill with consumption at this time. Under the shadow of death, the Mills drew up a list of topics on which to concentrate whatever time remained to them. As J. M. Robson comments, this 'programme adumbrates . . . most of Mill's later writings, but of its detailed working out in the years before Harriet's death not a great deal is known'.[31] Essays on Utility and Justice formed a basis for *Utilitarianism*, published in 1861. *On Liberty*, which Mill described as 'more directly and literally our joint production than anything else which bears my name', originated as an essay of 1854, but was published only in 1859, after Harriet's death at Avignon the previous November, and dedicated to her.

Given their deep interest in Greek thought and history, it is useful to draw on the examples of Aristotle and Plato to clarify the way the Mills faced their own moment of opportunity. Aristotle gave advanced seminars in the mornings and popular lectures in the afternoons. His popular books, drawn from those lectures, were much admired, but have since almost entirely vanished. Aristotle's surviving works – which have nourished thinkers ever since – are compressed and difficult abstracts of the discussions in the advanced seminars. The Mills looked ahead to a time not far distant when the life of England, like that of Athens, would be overtaken by newer and more ruthless powers – not least America. Using an idea from the indigenous life of North America which had already been swept away by the almighty dollar, they considered preparing what they called a 'pemican': an American Indian word for the concentrated food carried by travellers. Like the works of Aristotle which survive the wreck of his civilisation, such a 'concentrate' might nourish the pilgrimage of future thinkers displaced by the servile conformity of the foreseeable future. Such thinkers might then mediate the ideas in the 'pemican' to a broader public, as Aristotle has been mediated by commentators.

This notion has every mark of being a 'poetic' idea of the defiantly independent Harriet. Mill's idea was to produce a popular work which would make their thoughts immediately and widely accessible. But how soon would it fall out of fashion, like the vanished popular works of Aristotle? Like Ruskin, they took the Victorian 'debt to the future' with great seriousness.

In the end, they took the middle ground. There was a popular Anglo-American idea which was also Harriet's most defiant principle: Liberty. The work on Liberty 'was probably the only essay of this period that was entirely written, both in its original and revised versions, while they were together'.[32] It is nearer in spirit to Plato than to his pupil Aristotle. Like Plato's later dialogues, it takes the form of a synthesis in which the different voices co-operate to discuss a topic within an atmosphere of broad agreement. Though not set out in dialogue form, *On Liberty* has the atmosphere of sympathetic but partly divergent minds concentrated on a topic of perennial importance.

Like Plato's dialogues, *On Liberty* is neither 'popular' nor 'academic', but aimed at the intelligent general reader prepared to engage with the debate as it proceeds. There is a tragic tension between the occasional feebleness of its pleas and the vibrant conviction of its pleading. It concludes no case, achieves no definition, but rather affirms a value. In the words of the essay 'On Genius' which Mill wrote in 1832 under the joint influence of Harriet and Carlyle, *On Liberty* allows the reader to *discover* 'truths which he thought he had known for years'. Each fresh reading renews the impression that 'the truths which we *know* we can discover again and again'.[33]

It was Harriet, not Carlyle, who won the battle for the mind of Mill. Freedom of speech, the widest freedom of conscience: these values are unforgettably affirmed in *On Liberty*. The Mills do not conceal the difficulties which arise in their attempt to define the limits which it is right for society to impose on individuals in order to guarantee a measure of fairness to each and so a tolerable security to all. This irresolvable theoretic difficulty is part of the book, not because of any failure of intellect by the Mills, but because it is only by informed practice that any real-life solution can start to happen. As Gertrude Himmelfarb has written, the book provides a 'functional ideal . . . a means of recalling us to first principles'.[34]

Because the book is not in dialogue form, it is not possible to be clear which phrases can be assigned to Harriet and which to Mill. It is in a sense their joint autobiography, the book they wrote together about what Harriet called 'our subject'. This subject is truly their own relationship itself, a relationship of co-operation and discovery.

On Liberty is the argument for the right to pursue this kind of relationship, and for the extension of that right to more and more of the human race. It is about 'the nature and limits of the power which can be legitimately exerted by society over the individual'.[35] Community and freedom were not alternative values for the Mills. As Ruskin saw in a sympathetic note about the book, the implied meaning of ' "Individual" ' in the 'essay on *Liberty*' is a double one: 'distinct and separate in character, though joined in purpose'.[36]

That distinctness of character, with unanimity of purpose, make the Mills significant, and their most famous 'joint production' a true classic.

Notes

1 C. E. Maurice, *The Life of Octavia Hill from her Letters*, p. 176.
2 E. S. Maurice, *Early Ideals: the Letters of Octavia Hill*, London, 1928, p. 100.
3 *Works*, XXIII.332, with reference to Mill's *Principles of Political Economy*, book iv, ch. vii, para. 3.
4 Mill wrote flowery letters to Harriet in French, and Ruskin's *Lilies* is improved in Marcel Proust's translation, *Sésame et les Lys*, Paris, 1906.
5 *Fors Clavigera*, 95. *Works*, XXIX.496.
6 Hayek, *John Stuart Mill*, p. 279.
7 *Unto This Last and other writings*, p. 205.
8 *Time and Tide* 23, para. 156. *Works*, XVII. 442–3, with reference to *Principles of Political Economy*, book ii, ch. ii, para. 6.
9 The daughter of Coventry Patmore, author of *The Angel in the House*.
10 *Works*, XVI. 166–8. Herbert Spencer (1820–1903), the main theorist

of Social Darwinism, helped to educate and finance Beatrice Webb (1858–1943). He supported women's emancipation from a right-wing standpoint. Like Harriet Taylor, Beatrice Webb combined women's emancipation with economic objectives similar to Ruskin's. She formed the Fabian Society with her husband Sidney Webb (1859–1947).

11 Diary for 21 January 1854, in *Letters of John Stuart Mill*, 1910, II. 361: 'in England (ourselves excepted) I can think only of Ruskin'.

12 *Middlemarch*, Chapter 46 (of Ladislaw).

13 *Collected Works of John Stuart Mill*, XIV. xxvi. She told Theodor Gomperz this some years after her marriage to Mill.

14 Herbert, b. 1827; Algernon, b. 1830, and Helen, b. 1831. Kamm gives details.

15 Kamm, *John Stuart Mill*, p. 79.

16 Kamm, *John Stuart Mill*, p. 42.

17 Kamm, *John Stuart Mill*, p. 96. John Taylor died in July 1849 and Harriet married Mill in April 1851.

18 Rossi, ed., *Essays*, pp. 75, 86.

19 Hayek, *John Stuart Mill*, p. 279.

20 *Collected Works of John Stuart Mill*, I. 192–7.

21 *Collected Works of John Stuart Mill*, XIV. xxiv, 166, n.

22 *Collected Works*, XI. xx.

23 *Collected Works*, I. 255, 257, n.; II. 208.

24 Mary Warnock (ed.), J. S. Mill, *Utilitarianism, On Liberty, Essay on Bentham*, 1962, p. 19.

25 *Collected Works*, XXIV. 303, 305, 307, 318, 329, 350, 383, 389, 390, 392–6, 400. Topics include wife-beating, flogging in the army, cruelty to animals, disputes over children, corporal punishment and the law of assault. The police, the magistrates and the Church of England are exposed, and reforms are suggested for prisons, education, and marriage law.

26 Rossi, ed., *Essays*, p. 96.

27 Gaskell, *Life of Charlotte Brontë*, Chapter 24: 'I thought it was the work of a powerful-minded, clear-headed woman.'

28 Kamm, *John Stuart Mill*, p. 90.

29 Rossi, ed., *Essays*, p. 46.

30 Rossi, ed., *Essays*, p. 43.

31 *Collected Works*, X. cxxiii.

32 Himmelfarb, *On Liberty*, pp. 248, 250–3.

33 *Collected Works*, I. 332.

34 Pp. xii-xiii.

35 Mill, *Utilitarianism, On Liberty and Considerations on Representative Government*, ed. Acton, p. 69.

36 Ruskin, *Modern Painters*, V, part viii, ch. 2 (1860). *Works*, VII. 229. The chapter, which begins with the thesis that 'the *minutest* portion of a great composition is helpful to the whole', implies many subtle corrections to the individualism of *On Liberty*. Ruskin described chapter 2 – 'Of the Liberty of Thought and Discussion' – as 'beautifully expressed', an unwitting tribute to Harriet's gift for the vivid phrase.

Books

Paperbacks

George Eliot, *Middlemarch* (1872), Harmondsworth, 1988.

E. C. Gaskell, *The Life of Charlotte Brontë* (1857), Harmondsworth, 1975.

Harriet Martineau, *Autobiography* (1877), 2 volumes, London, 1983.

John Stuart Mill, Harriet Taylor Mill, *The Subjection of Women and Enfranchisement of Women*, with an introduction by Kate Soper, London, 1983.

J. S. Mill, *Utilitarianism, On Liberty* and *Considerations on Representative Government*, edited by H. B. Acton, London, 1972.

Alice S. Rossi, editor, *Essays on Sex Equality: John Stuart Mill and Harriet Taylor Mill*, Chicago and London, 1970.

Mary Wollstonecraft, *A Vindication of the Rights of Woman* (2nd edition 1792), edited with an introduction and notes by Miriam Brody Krammick, Harmondsworth, 1975.

Mary Wollstonecraft, *Mary* and *The Wrongs of Woman*, edited and with an introduction by Gary Kelly, London, 1987.

Life and letters

F. A. Hayek, *John Stuart Mill and Harriet Taylor: their Correspondence and Subsequent Marriage*, London, 1951.

J. Kamm, *John Stuart Mill in Love*, London, 1977.

Background and commentary

Elizabeth K. Helsinger, Robin Lauterbach Sheets and William Veeder, editors, *The Woman Question: society and literature in Britain and America 1837–1883*, Manchester, 1983.

Gertrude Himmelfarb, *On Liberty and Liberalism: the case of John Stuart Mill*, New York, 1974.

Philippa Levine, *Victorian Feminism*, London 1987.

Jane Rendall, *Equal or Different: Women's Politics 1800–1914*, Oxford, 1987.

Mary Lyndon Shanley, ' "One must ride behind": married women's rights and the Divorce Act of 1857', *Victorian Studies*, 25, 3 (Spring 1982), pp. 355–76.

Jack Stillinger, 'Who wrote J. S. Mill's Autobiography?', *Victorian Studies*, 27, 1, pp. 7–23.

CHAPTER FIVE

Mill and Parliament

Carlyle and Ruskin had high-handed views of Parliament. Both tended to despise party politics, but given the existence of class-divisions and the divergency of their personalities, it is not surprising that when Carlyle and Ruskin looked beyond contemporary political reality in search of solutions, they should do so in opposite directions. In *Latter-Day Pamphlets* of 1850, Carlyle urged a 'right-wing' solution. The kind of men capable of promoting necessary change were, he thought, unlikely to be elected into the Commons or born into the House of Lords. Very well, let prime ministers appoint unelected ministers to get the job done. This solution became a possibility in the twentieth century, with the development of life peers selected by prime ministers, and has been employed during the 1980s.[1] Ruskin took the opposite course. In 1862 he urged working men to boycott Westminster and elect their own Parliament of Trade Unions. There was no other way to pressure society into the kind of radical economical reforms which would make life bearable for the (as yet unenfranchised) working class.[2] This anticipated the first Trade Union Congress of 1868, and foreshadowed the quasi-constitutional status trade unions have sometimes enjoyed, particularly under Labour governments.

Mill was a constitutionalist to the marrow. At seventeen he was working in the offices of the East India Company, which administered India. At nineteen he was editing the Benthamite *Parliamentary History and Review*. He had the civil servant's sense of detail and the Liberal reformer's preference for gradualism. His criteria were competence and participation. His *Considerations on Representative Government* of 1861 argued that the disabling class war which must be fought in Parliament once the working classes were enfranchised must be mitigated by careful machinery which would ensure the participation of minorities through proportional representation and the politicisation of localities through regional parliaments. Competence must be ensured by the development of a more responsible civil service, and by the establishment of a Commission of Legislation which would be responsive to parliamentary debate, but not – as was currently the case – at the mercy of the tricks and quirks of such debate.

Sharing Carlyle and Ruskin's dislike of the way common sense was thwarted by parliamentary machinery, Mill typically argued for the improvement of the machinery. Carlyle wanted the masses kept at bay by a revival of aristocratic leadership. Ruskin wanted capitalists kept at bay by an advance in unionism. Mill wanted democracy moderated by constitutional safeguards. A certain dogmatism, which for Carlyle and Ruskin seemed essential to any harmonious system, was for Mill precisely the disruptive element that must be kept at bay in favour of responsiveness and dialogue.

It has been said that 'Mill never was the force in Parliament that he had been in the field of ideas.'[3] Yet Mill was convinced that only by entering the realm of practice could a thinker's ideas be tested. A similar feeling sustained Ruskin as Professor at Oxford, Newman as Rector of the Catholic University and Arnold as Inspector of Schools. In this typically mid-Victorian spirit Mill accepted the invitation to stand for the Westminster constituency as an Independent Liberal, in 1865. There was every chance that the next Parliament would see a successful Reform Bill of some kind, and Mill was determined to make his contribution.

In particular, he was determined to 'test the water' on proportional representation and – even more important – the enfranchisement of women. Harriet's article of 1851 was reprinted, and when the opportunity came for Mill to speak in Parliament on the issue, he used a number of her ideas and words. Like Ruskin, Newman and Arnold, he was drawing on inner convictions to connect with the present and to educate the future. Like them, he did not anticipate rapid success.

Whereas Carlyle and Ruskin, from different viewpoints, address the politics of crisis and confrontation, Mill presents a vision of a politicised society working peaceably and rationally towards agreed ends.

In early life Mill was a personal friend and admirer of Carlyle, fired by his spirit of intellectual reform and political urgency.

He provided many of the documents for Carlyle's *The French Revolution*.[4] He was also very much influenced by the idealistic socialism of Saint-Simon and his successors the Saint-Simonians, 'the only association of public writers,' Mill thought, 'who systematically stir up from the foundation all the great social questions'. One of these, Auguste Comte, founded his own system of Positivism. Mill never lost his sense of indebtedness to these French thinkers; but he would adjust the terms of their basic tenet: that the only recipe for political stability was to *complete* the revolution of 1789.[5]

By 1854 Mill had rejected the high-handedness of Auguste Comte along with that of Carlyle. Impressed with Ruskin – a relative newcomer to political thought – Mill nevertheless found him inadequate too.

There was a truly disruptive arrogance, Mill felt, in the Comtean notion of 'completing' a revolution; just as there was in Carlyle's notion that readers of *his* 'French Revolution' had only to 'incarnate' the words of Carlyle. Both implied that the revolution in ideas and the human liberation that went with it must go so far and no further. Comte's idea of a quasi-priestly elite indoctrinating the masses for their own good must have seemed little better than Carlyle's doctrine of 'heroes'. And now, in 1853, Ruskin had produced a much-discussed scheme for a modern national education system based on the natural sciences and extending to state responsibility for child welfare.[6] Mill shared Ruskin's objectives, but could not tolerate their totalitarian implications. Ruskin became lumped in his mind with Comte: 'to the practical doctrines and tendencies of both . . . there are the gravest objections'. Mill saw no intellectual rival to Ruskin or Comte, and Carlyle had 'written himself out'. Only two people remained to carry on the intellectual battle for peaceful change: 'ourselves': his wife Harriet and himself.[7]

Absurdly arrogant though that judgement may seem (it was recorded in a diary entry), there is a sense in which Mill's relationship with Harriet – 'ourselves' – was indeed a specially valuable source of political ideas.

The work in which Mill expressed the moral rationale of these ideas was *Utilitarianism* (1861), which had begun as essays on Utility and Justice written with Harriet's help. It was a personal and more humane version of the radical tradition Mill had inherited from Bentham and his own father, James Mill. Read together with

On Liberty, it provides a social context for Mill and Harriet's championship of the individual.

Like many Victorians, Mill was an idealist who deliberately sought contact with reality. He entered the point-scoring, chauvinist, unfair world of parliamentary debate on behalf of a different kind of discourse: the kind of debate of sympathetic minds in pursuit of workable values to which he and Harriet had devoted their lives and which they had celebrated in *On Liberty*. Such a debate could hardly begin at the political level until women were free to enter it on equal terms with men. In Mill's eyes, the enfranchisement of women was not an 'optional extra' for parliamentary democracy. It was the basis for that continuing revolution towards ever fuller human liberation without which neither democracy nor stability could survive. The case for this was made in Mill's *The Subjection of Women*. It was published in 1869, when he had himself ceased to be a Member of Parliament. As he intended, it became a textbook and rallying-point for political movements by women themselves in pursuit of the franchise.

Utilitarianism

Mill's *Utilitarianism* appeared as three articles in *Fraser's Magazine* between October and December 1861. More measured, less inspirational, than *On Liberty*, it is evidence that Mill had begun to recover, not only from Harriet's death, but from the creative stress of their relationship. Yet he wrote that her memory remained 'a religion' to him:[8] and some of the unresolved difficulties of *Utilitarianism*, as well as the credal affirmations with which they are met, seem to reflect her spirit. The product of half a lifetime of reflection on the subject, *Utilitarianism* attempts to complete and humanise what as early as 1833 Mill called the 'basis of half-truth' on which Bentham's opinions about political questions were based.[9] This involves Mill in the search for a persuasive rationale from which to test, and as far as may be, promote, some of the ideas on the role of government which he had set out in his *Principles of Political Economy*.

Mill defines the meaning of 'Utilitarianism' – a term he himself first brought into general use – as the 'creed which accepts as the foundation of morals, Utility, or the Greatest Happiness Principle'. It holds 'that actions are right as they tend to promote happiness, wrong as they tend to promote the reverse of happiness. By happiness is intended pleasure, and the absence of pain; by unhappiness, pain, and the privation of pleasure.'[10] To this general end, Bentham had set about reducing the law to 'a simple piece of practical business'. While he never lost faith with Bentham's reformism, Mill had long perceived that the lawyer's genius for simplification looked more like idiocy when applied undiluted to politics and morals. Whereas Bentham urged the aristocratic government of the 1790s to cure the woes of society by erecting the perfect prison – the notorious, unbuilt Panopticon – Mill's *Political Economy* is notable for its insistence on the need to develop an 'unauthoritative' sphere of government for 'giving advice and promulgating information'. Indeed, this 'unauthoritative' – or enabling – sphere should be radically expanded precisely in order to minimise the need for 'authoritative' or coercive measures. Coercion is at best a necessary evil. State schools, colleges, hospitals; a national bank; government factories and technical services: such institutions of government might supplement penal and civil law on the one hand and corporate and private enterprise on the other. They might limit the socially corrosive effects of *laissez-faire*, yet not impede private or co-operative initiative.[11]

Here, Mill seems to correct his father, James Mill, whose essay *On Government* of 1820 had advocated 'universal male suffrage', while naively hoping that the mere social influence of the middle classes could permanently be relied on to leaven the self-interest of the masses and the peerage. Mill the son saw middle-class hegemony as a transitional stage only towards a wider democracy that must be buttressed by enabling laws which it was the task of his own generation to encode.

John Stuart Mill's *Political Economy* insisted that a 'democratic constitution, not supported by democratic institutions in detail, but confined to the central government, not only is not political freedom, but often creates a spirit precisely the reverse'. The government should encourage people 'to manage as many as possible of their joint concerns by voluntary co-operation'.[12] Such a measure of freedom and co-operation would be possible only where there was trust between government and governed. That trust could not be manufactured by relying on the old radical cure-all of 'universal male suffrage'. In the first place, the exclusion of women was not only a wasteful injustice but also helped to perpetuate the Benthamite 'half-truth' that man, as a political animal, was infallibly and rationally motivated by a quantifiable self-interest. The existence of woman contradicted this fantasy: not because women were 'irrational' but because the world which included two human sexes also included human emotion, and memory, and hope; and (at however primitive a level) a measure of altruism. It was no longer Bentham's world of the clever boy, predictable and sterile.

In the second place, 'universal suffrage' needed detailed adjustment if it were truly to promote happiness. *Thoughts on Parliamentary Reform*, Mill's pamphlet of 1859, predicted the politics of the 1980s. The mathematics of the matter were such that an electorate, each of whom had a single non-transferable vote, could produce a government having only a minority of the votes but with a commanding majority in the House of Commons.[13] In some fantasy world of rationalism, such a government could be rational and beneficial. In the real world of relationships, and checks and balances, it could only be deleterious. Trust and co-operation are impossible without discussion, and discussion is meaningless under a representative democracy if the wishes of most people can be permanently disregarded. Mill's solution was proportional representation.

Such is the background to *Utilitarianism*: the fruit of years of theorising, and the preparation for Mill's own entry into Parliament. The old anti-reforming Whig Lord Palmerston was still prime minister. No radical had succeeded in educating him. Once he died (which happened in 1865) there would be a scramble between rival claimants for the political patronage of the working classes, to whom the vote could not much longer be denied. *Utilitarianism* is Mill's attempt to educate in general principles some of the would-be patrons, and some of those about to be patronised.

A difficulty that has confronted philosophers who desire the improvement of society is that the ordinary motivations of their lives may not be the ordinary motivations of society. Common ground may be looked for in the idea of pleasure; and philosophers may argue for educational arrangements that would increase the number of those sharing their kinds of pleasure. The classic discussion of this dilemma, familiar to Mill from an early age, is in Aristotle's *Ethics*. Noting that happiness is 'the end to be sought in human life', and that pleasures are the rewards of active (rather than contemplative) life, Aristotle suggests arguments favouring higher pleasures like music and science over lower pleasures like eating and sex. But he denies that these arguments are likely to affect the practice of average people; urges philosophic minds to withdraw to the contemplative life – as free as possible from the distractions of pleasure and pain – and postpones the improvement of society to the arrival of some state system of compulsory education.[14]

Mill faces similar problems to Aristotle: but in keeping with his Benthamite legacy actively desires the reform of society, not his own withdrawal into transcendency. Unlike Bentham, however, he cannot resort to the device of denying that pleasures are qualitatively different. For the puerile Bentham, push-pin and poetry were equivalents in that both could provide pleasure. Since the human race derives more pleasure from childish games like push-pin than from the *Iliad*, the legislator certainly had no business to be promoting poetry at the expense of push-pin, in Bentham's view.

Mill, who agrees with Aristotle that some pleasures develop human capabilities more than others, sees Bentham's infantile theory of pleasure as malign, since it would discourage the governed from acquiring responsibility. What does not improve deteriorates, and it is the duty of government to promote improvement. Here is a role for its 'unauthoritative' function. Pleasure, like self-interest, involves questions of quality as well as quantity. Enlightened self-interest pursues pleasures that promote the good of society, in Mill's view. A benevolent government would thus wish to maximise opportunities for higher pleasures: if necessary, at the expense of lower pleasures. Those who have experienced both kinds are the fit judges of which pleasures are (in an almost esoteric sense) 'desirable': a word which Mill seems to use in the sense of 'desired by those entitled by capacity and experience to discriminate for themselves and others'. This conviction pushes Mill to the very edge of the democratic camp, and seriously limits his enthusiasm for *laissez-faire*. Yet Mill still believes that Bentham, with his broad definition of the aim of government as 'the greatest happiness of the greatest number' is the founding father of the *science* of legislation. He resolves the problem by a credal affirmation of the progressive potential of human society, once established on such a scientific basis. He believes that, given the opportunity, more and more people will prefer the *Iliad* to push-pin. They will never be in a majority, but they have as much right to their better preference as others to their worse preference. And since their preference is better (and less popular) it should receive more support from the state.

A serious difficulty to this view is that it depends ultimately on Plato's assumption that the mind is 'higher' than the body. The condition of Mill's relationship with Mrs Taylor made this assumption advisable, but what lies behind it is the Greek male intellectual's view that physical pleasure is inferior because its most distracting source (for most males) is women: uneducated, and perhaps uneducable.[15] This view continued to be dominant among imperial elites, down to and including Mill's father, head of foreign correspondence at India House.

John Stuart Mill's rationale of pleasure is thus at root a theory devised for superior male intellectuals supported by the work of underlings and women. His own credal affirmation of 'progress' – the liberation of underlings and women into the higher pleasures – owes some of its temperature to Harriet: 'A great number of progressive changes are constantly going forward in human affairs and ideas . . . it is only by looking at a long series of generations that they are seen to be, in reality, always moving, and always in the same direction.'[16] That impassioned spirit sustained Mill's own conviction, but contributed to its ambiguity.

Utilitarianism is Mill's synthesis of elitist male morality and the new pressures for democracy and human liberation. Like Carlyle's Old Testament morality or Ruskin's New Testament ethic, Mill's Aristotelian view of pleasure contributes to creative tensions in his text, and to more general tensions between theory and practice.

Considerations on Representative Government

Political responsibility is Mill's central consideration in this work. Two editions were issued in 1861, and a third in 1865; with frequent reimpressions.

Whereas *Utilitarianism* argued for the moral principles behind Mill's vision of democracy, *Representative Government* attempted to propagate that vision, and to provide practical guidelines towards its realisation. The ideal MP would have some intelligent grasp of principle as well as practical experience of politics, but plenty of MPs had neither. There was room in Parliament, Mill thought, for those like himself 'who, though untried practically, have been tried speculatively; who in public speech or in print, have discussed public affairs in a manner which proves that they have given serious study to them'.[17]

To Mill's central consideration of *responsibility* must be added this corollary of *intelligence*, for him equally important.

The idea of responsibility implies for Mill that representatives, once elected, be empowered to take responsibility *for* their own decisions. They are not mere mouthpieces of those who elect them. At the same time, they remain responsible, or answerable, *to* the sovereign authority; which is, for Mill, nothing less than the 'entire aggregate of the community'.[18]

For such responsibility to be effective, however, democracy requires not only the fullest, but also the best, intelligence. Freedom of information and discussion is essential, but at the same time guidance is required from those whose experience or serious study in any matter give them a special right to be heard. Some of these would be permanent civil servants, irremovable except for personal misconduct; who enter their profession by competitive examination and whose views ministers should be obliged at least to hear.

Parliament is for Mill the focus of information to and pressure upon governments. Since elections are the main (though not the only) machinery for making governments answerable, the electoral machinery needs to be regulated so that it can provide such information. Mill wants the information to be as broad, as specific, and as informed as possible. These three principles determine his suggestions for the electoral machinery. First, the electorate should as far as possible be universal: of all adults, including women. Second, its elected representatives should represent all the people, not merely the most blinkered or most apathetic majorities. This implies proportional representation, so that Parliament, from which ministers are drawn and which is the main debating chamber of the nation, should as far as possible typify the whole people, including 'minorities' with their special experiences and knowledges. Everyone is in a minority of some kind. Thirdly – and this is a serious matter for Mill, but less essential than the first two principles – electoral machinery should be designed to ensure that special intellectual capacity is given due weight. It may be advisable to allow 'plural voting which may assign to education, as such, the degree of superior influence due to it'.[19] On the negative side, it may be advisable to withhold the vote from those unable to pass simple tests of numeracy or literacy. A vote is a trust held on behalf of others, not a personal right. Such a position demands qualifications, however minimal.

For Mill, the people *are* the 'machinery' of a democracy. Under any system that falls short of his principles, he fears that the machinery – and the people – will be manipulated by the rich more or less secretly; or by class warriors from left or right whose equally secret machinations will be conducted under cover of deceptively popular slogans.

Though less riskily so than *On Liberty*, *Representative Government* also is an impassioned work: less an analysis of the likely outcome of moves towards wider electoral reform than an intervention in favour of what Mill saw as desirable electoral reform. If one defines 'desirable' in this context in the same terms as appear to apply to Mill's use of the word in *Utilitarianism*, one might infer that the reforms he advocates in *Representative Government* are reforms which, like the 'desirable' pleasures of *Utilitarianism*, are desired by those entitled by capacity and experience to discriminate for themselves and others. The discrimination, in *Utilitarianism*, was between 'lower' and 'higher' pleasures. Those qualified to discriminate between pleasures in *Utilitarianism*, were those who had experience of both kinds. When it came to discriminating between forms of government, Mill could claim special qualification. He had participated in the volatile 'freedom' of middle-class democracy in England; and had also risen through the bureaucracy of the East India Company which, at a distance, governed India. A striking feature of such a government was its alienation from the people governed. Mill uses India as an analogue of alienation in his first chapter, and spends his last chapter lamenting that, with the abolition of the East India Company, the alienation will be more complete. It would be a mistake to assume that Mill's anger about India has distorted a book on British representative government. India is surely an analogue of what Mill's own country, in decadence, might become. Alienation and irresponsibility would increase with the increase of the people's sense of powerlessness. For Carlyle, decadence became certain with the passing of the second Reform Act in 1867. Mill, too, envisaged this merely nominal broadening of the democratic base of government as a step into decadence: not, however, like Carlyle, because it deprived the elite of their just power: but because it betrayed the people with a pretence of power. Mill felt that centuries of oppression under succeeding empires had made Indians 'unfit for more than a limited . . . freedom' and incapable of 'co-operating actively with the law and public authority'. This was true, he felt, even when India was governed by the zealous bureaucracy of the East India Company. Now the sub-continent would be handed over to the lowest politicians and entrepreneurs. That a similar fate awaited the United Kingdom should alienation become endemic was the clear inference. Hence Mill's passionate aim of 'educating the mind of the nation not only for accepting or claiming, but also for working, the institution' of representative democracy. Still close to Harriet's spirit, he affirms the benign ruthlessness of his task: 'One person with a belief is a social power equal to ninety-nine who have only interests.'[20] More subtle and passionate in his Utilitarian beliefs than his father, Mill affirms the need for all sectors of society to influence government, yet claims his own special duty to advocate machinery of a quality fit to achieve and maintain the vulnerable treasure of representative government. Between the waning of aristocratic power and the rise of democracy, there is room and need for the 'didactic' middle class Carlyle appealed to in *Past and Present*. Mill rises to the occasion with at least some of Carlyle's authoritarianism intact.

This involves Mill in defining Parliament's role more usefully. Parliament supplies information to government as to the will of the people. There is an urgent need, however, for a Commission of Legislation to supply the means to define that will and to pre-scribe for its effectiveness. Parliament should cease to fiddle with piecemeal amendments -- the British way of ruining laws -- and confine itself to accepting, rejecting, or referring laws back for reconsideration by the Commission. A Code of Laws -- rather than a rag-bag of precedents from which upper-class judges have the picking -- might eventually be achieved by such means. Again, a Prime Minister should not do the work of his own ministers. He should appoint them, as Parliament appoints the Legislative Commission. Then he should give them responsibility. Their decisions should be informed by an intelligent Civil Service; and a code of conduct should ensure they listen to the experts inside the service, and where necessary, outside. Politicians cease to be useful when they pretend to expertise they do not possess. Greater openness in high-level discussions is needed if expertise is not to be thrown away. Greater openness is also required in all the broader discussions that surround government. The decision-makers of Mill's day, such as Lord Palmerston, were quite often both privileged and incompetent, in his view. A broader electoral system, however well adjusted, would not produce perfectly competent decision-makers, nor could it separate privilege from power. The inevitable incompetence of decision-makers must therefore be made to respect expert advice; and their privilege must be exposed to the scrutiny of all sections of society. Otherwise there would be no substance to democracy.

Mill argued for local seats of government – with local parliaments – operating on the same principles. In both areas, the 'unauthoritative' role of government would be vital for educating the sovereign people to be a match for those who represented them.

The ideal relationship between local and centralised government had already been defined in *On Liberty*: 'the greatest dissemination of power consistent with efficiency: the greatest possible centralisation of information, and diffusion of it from the centre'.[21] It was because the Victorian House of Commons already operated as a prime focus for the diffusion of information that Mill was persuaded to accept nomination for Westminster, and thus to pursue the path that led from theory into practice.

Member of Parliament

Mill was a candidate for Westminster at the General Election of July 1865. At this date, uncontested elections were still quite common. A vacancy had been created by the retirement of George de Lacy Evans, who had first been elected to Westminster in 1833. Robert Wellesley Grosvenor, a representative of the family of the Duke of Westminster, who owned much of the constituency, proposed to slip into the vacancy as of right, without a contest. The other Westminster seat was held by a third highly connected Liberal of little personal distinction, Sir John Villiers Shelley, MP since 1852. Some local Liberals were dissatisfied; and moreover sensed the efficiency of the threat represented by the Tory candidate W. H. Smith, the bookseller, a new kind of Conservative entrepreneur.

Mill had not put himself forward as candidate: and had refused other such invitations. He accepted nomination for Westminster only after a respectable local revolt by a group of Liberal electors, meeting in February 1865. They were determined to obtain as candidate some man of national eminence and proven integrity. Mill's name was one of those proposed: and eventually a Committee selected him, and invited him to stand. Such a method of selection did not match Mill's theory of democracy. He urged the Committee to persevere with an earlier plan which had been dropped at the Committee stage: to solicit names of candidates from the Liberal electors at large. Accordingly, a circular letter was drafted inviting voters to submit 'the names of two persons for whom, without any personal solicitation, you would be willing to vote'.[22] The stated aim of this letter – in agreement with Mill's published opinions – was to emancipate voters from the undue pressures of wealth and family influence, while maintaining the principle of the openly cast vote. There was no satisfactory law at the time limiting the amount of election 'expenses' (often bribery under a politer name); and tenants and tradesmen, particularly, were at all times at a disadvantage.

A common outcome, in constituencies having two representatives, was for electors to record one of their two votes for a 'moderate' Tory, and the other for a 'moderate' Liberal: helping to ensure that Parliament remained the preserve of privileged nullity. This pattern would appear at Westminster in the General Election of November 1868, when Mill was ousted, and Grosvenor and Smith returned. Meanwhile the open letter to electors from Mill's Committee of 1865 – from which other candidates held aloof – brought in the hoped-for result. Grosvenor was outflanked: and became Mill's successful 'colleague'; Shelley retired before the election; and Smith, for the present, was sent back to his shop. Mill's addresses and replies at election meetings were conducted in a simplified form of his most popular newspaper style: his forthrightness and modesty were a bonus. Harriet's daughter Helen was his untiring secretary and catalyst, particularly on women's issues.

It was ironic that Mill, who regarded himself as an Independent, and who had attacked the House of Lords more than once, should be helped into Parliament by an electoral alliance with a

Whig–Liberal aristocrat which had been stage-managed for him by others. His religious views were also suspect. Here again, he was lucky in 1865. Charges of atheism that had been made against him were eloquently rebutted by Connop Thirlwall, Bishop of St Davids, and other Established Churchmen.[23] Popular editions of Mill's works which appeared at this time completed the case for Mill as an important radical thinker who could simultaneously be shown to be respectable, and to have won important friends.

The House of Commons into which Mill was elected has been described as 'perplexed but malleable'.[24] It was an appropriate setting for Mill's exertions; for the apparent failure of his efforts; for the sounding of new ideas which, in the longer term, had important consequences. Mill's election as MP was as unlikely an event as Ruskin's election as Oxford Professor of Art, four years later. In each case, the maverick entered the establishment just long enough to make it a focus for his own ideas, and the establishment tolerated him until it could take no more.

Tactless to the last, the anti-reforming octogenarian Whig-Liberal prime minister Lord Palmerston died shortly after the election of 1865 had given his cohorts a majority in the House of Commons. In October, his Foreign Secretary, Lord Russell, septuagenarian relic of the first Reform Act of 1832, became prime minister, with Gladstone as Chancellor of the Exchequer and Leader of the Commons. Their Representation of the People Bill, which would have added some 400,000 names to the electoral register, was thrown out on 18 June 1866, thanks largely to the opposition of anti-reforming 'Liberals' such as Robert Lowe and the Grosvenors. Russell resigned; but did not call an election. Instead, the Tory Lord Derby took office. He had no majority in the House of Commons. Benjamin Disraeli, Chancellor of the Exchequer, manipulated the lower house on his behalf, aided by Derby's son, Lord Stanley, who was Foreign Secretary. This unelected, minority Tory government introduced its own Reform Bill which eventually added a million new voters to the franchise. Just because it was a Tory measure, it achieved what the more modest Liberal measure could never have done: safe passage through the House of Lords. It became law in 1867.

In such a setting, Mill's pleas for proportional representation and for women's suffrage became to some extent distractions which Disraeli was able to exploit for his own ends. But the extraordinary conditions of an unelected minority government out-bidding the opposition to stage-manage an epoch-making reform provided just that concentration of volatility – of earnestness and flippancy – in which Mill's extraordinary ideas could find their seed-bed.

Mill had no intention of being a 'good local MP', in the sense of acting as go-between for local pressure on Parliament: and made this clear from the outset.[25] Nor was he capable of being the mouthpiece of any party line. Such functions virtually complete the role of the 'mere' MP; and Mill's refusal suggests his intention of using Parliament to publicise a broader debate, with few illusions about realising major reforms in his lifetime. He was not naive about Parliament. His first original pieces had been for the Benthamite *Parliamentary History and Review*, from 1825. He had given evidence before Parliamentary Committees in the 1850s and early 1860s, mainly on taxation, banking, and other financial matters. His testimony had a radical tendency, notably in the direction of facilitating much wider access to capital and land: but his real achievements were necessarily no more than the 'groundwork for later reform'.[26]

Two reforms dear to Mill were proportional representation and the liberation of women. The first turned out a painful and absolute failure. For the second, he had a surprising amount of support.

The destruction of Mill's Amendment in favour of proportional representation took place on 30 May 1867. The main beneficiary has been the Tory party. With the coming enfranchisement of the working classes, Liberalism could have had no better defence and Toryism no more effective adversary than the proportional representation of intelligent minorities. The alternative – according to *Representative Government* – was irresolvable class war between capital and labour. In that work, Mill had strongly advocated Thomas Hare's scheme for proportional representation, and once in Parliament, remained loyal to its main ideas. Unfortunately, Hare's scheme, though logically elegant, was liable to grave difficulties in practice. Moreover, it seemed to threaten the status of MPs as local representatives:

> According to this plan, the unit of representation, the quota of electors who would be entitled to have a member to themselves, would be ascertained by the ordinary process of taking averages, the number of voters being divided by the number of seats in the

House: and every candidate who obtained that quota would be returned, from however great a number of local constituencies it might be gathered. The votes would, as at present, be given locally, but any elector would be at liberty to vote for any candidate in whatever part of the country he presented himself.[27]

The rational Mill saw this as a small but saving adjustment of the electoral machinery. For most Members, it was a 'Hare-brained scheme', of devastating import, but fortunately unworkable. Disraeli had no difficulty in manipulating the business of the House to give it the worst possible reception; Mill was politely damned as an alien from 'the world of letters'; and the Amendment was, by leave, withdrawn without a vote.[28]

On the matter of legislation affecting women, Mill was among the most radical of a substantial group. The Married Women's Property Bill passed its second reading in 1868 by the Speaker's casting vote, though no further action was taken for the moment. *Hansard* for 10 June 1868 shows Mill's more comfortable alienation in this context: as a brainy mascot of the Liberal party. Jacob Bright spoke forcefully, claiming the support of 'a large portion of the population of Manchester', and rehearsing a relentless series of effective arguments, stroke after stroke cracking smartly to the boundary in the best Lancashire manner. Robert Lowe added some manly sentiment. 'We ought to put ourselves *in loco parentis*', he urged, extending to defenceless working wives that right over their income which family lawyers provided for the daughters of the rich. Mill spoke third. He began with a broken-backed sentence dragging in the extraneous question of women's suffrage; passed on to some old-maidish jokes; to some further irrelevancies about the need for a Select Committee of lawyers to replace the practice of *ad hoc* Amendment. It was not very impressive: but the Liberal oracle had spoken; and Bright was able to summarise the gist for sleepier members. Mill could never have forced through an unpopular measure with such an incomprehensible speech. But in this case, issues were finely balanced, and he could act as the scruple that tipped the scales.[29]

More impressive was Mill's speech of 20 May 1867, proposing an Amendment to the Representation of the People Bill, Clause 4, on the Occupation Franchise for Voters in Counties, whereby the word 'man' would be replaced by 'person'; thus opening the way to a limited enfranchisement for women: in effect for spinsters and widows who were moderately prosperous householders (and taxpayers) in their own right. Not surprisingly, the subsequent motion, 'That the word "man" stand part of the clause', was nevertheless passed. But the vote: 196 for the motion, 73 against, was in the circumstances encouraging. Mill's speech, which incorporated many of Harriet's ideas, was published as a pamphlet that same year, and helped to foster a nation-wide campaign, in which Mill and Helen shared. Even more encouraging – in retrospect – was the bad comedy of the opposing 'arguments', which really had nothing more decent to offer than the charge of effeminacy against American men (due to the uncharming energy of their womenfolk) and the contention that any boy bred at a public school would have had unmasculine ideas such as Mill's thrashed out of him 'under the influence of the birch': a complete vindication of Harriet's notion that male political supremacy was part of a perverse class-led collusion of violence and unreason.[30]

Crippled by gout, Derby presented Disraeli with the premiership in February 1868. Gladstone, now leader of the Liberals, made much of a new issue: the Disestablishment of the Church of Ireland; and achieved the downfall of the government that November. The election was a Liberal triumph – a majority of 112 under the new franchise – but Mill was not among those returned. The outspoken manner which had gained Mill votes in 1865 did not go down well with the new electorate. He had also forfeited respectability by his support of the candidature of the atheist Bradlaugh. The author of *Representative Government* was ousted by W. H. Smith. But during his thirty months in Parliament he had made a number of good protests, with mixed success.

On some issues – he was against the secret ballot for elections and against the abolition of capital punishment, for instance – Mill was a puzzle to other radicals. He lectured the House on the need to reduce the National Debt, not always to its enlightenment. His 'attempt to obtain a Municipal Government for the Metropolis' met with indifference in Parliament, though he was giving voice to a formidable body of opinion outside; and lived to see Parliament change its mind. He found ample opportunity for 'denouncing . . . the English mode of governing Ireland'[31] and was one of a group who prevailed on Derby not to make a martyr of the Fenian General Burke. He was the House's leading radical voice on the Irish land question. Ruskin was among those outside Parliament who thoroughly agreed with Mill on this issue; but very moderate bills by both Liberal and Tory ministries for improving conditions of tenure in Ireland failed to get beyond the second reading. He supported Gladstone's moves to disestablish the Church of Ireland; and to repeal the remaining disabilities of non-Anglicans.

After the fall of Russell's ministry, and the apparent defeat of Parliamentary Reform, there were scuffles between police and working-class crowds wishing to hold a rally in Hyde Park. The incident would be discussed at length by Arnold in *Culture and Anarchy*. Mill used his influence outside Parliament to help allay tension; but made a determined and successful effort inside to kill a Tory bill to ban meetings in the Royal Parks. Trade unionists had supported his election; and he spoke in Parliament for fairer legal treatment for unions. Ruskin, who had urged working men to vote for Mill, would have welcomed this.

Ruskin would also have approved of Mill's efforts for conservation: for instance his protest (unfortunately unsuccessful) against the destruction of 50 acres of woodland at Hainault.[32] Over the Jamaica insurrection they came into collision with Ruskin seizing the opportunity to make socialist demands for a re-ordering of the world economy and Mill arguing for legislative security for individuals against arbitrary governments. This dialectic was obscured, in the public press, by Carlyle's intolerant heroics. In Parliament, Mill's strictures against martial law were lost in the welter of prevarication produced by those amiable opponents the Liberal W. E. Forster (Arnold's brother-in-law) and the Tory Home Secretary, Gathorne Hardy. Both were Bradford capitalists well used to keeping the options, and the power, in their own hands.[33]

Mill was more successful, in the House, and on Select Committees, in furthering an Extradition Act, which gave protection to political refugees. On the home front, Mill spoke in favour of the Tory bill to transfer jurisdiction in cases of electoral bribery from the House of Commons to the Judges, but was dismayed that his Liberal colleagues failed to press for more radical reforms.

After losing his seat in Parliament, Mill produced no more political theory. His time was divided between activities that reinforced his sense of union with his dead wife. He became a figurehead for the women's suffrage movement, in which Harriet's daughter Helen was deeply involved. With his long-term view of politics, Mill would not have been surprised that it would be another fifty years before any woman could vote. Having established his integrity by losing his parliamentary seat over support of the atheist Bradlaugh, Mill felt free to move beyond time to eternity. His essay on 'Theism' of 1869 was surprisingly orthodox: more so, perhaps, than Harriet herself had been. In the same year he published *The Subjection of Women*, which he had written eight years before.

The Subjection of Women

Mill's *The Subjection of Women* came out in May 1869, in an edition of 1500 copies. Two further British editions were called for that year; and two American editions. The book – or extended pamphlet, in four chapters – was soon translated into French, German, Italian, Polish and Russian. Mill, by now a prominent public figure, found himself the recipient of a good deal of correspondence. As usual, Mill gave thought to the timing of publication: though written as early as 1860–61, the work was not released till he had tested the issue of women's enfranchisement in the House of Commons. When it did appear, the book became propaganda for the National Society for Women's Suffrage, a movement actively prompted by Mill and his stepdaughter. Some of Helen's ideas, and 'passages of her writing', as well as 'striking and profound' insights of Harriet's, were included in the text.[34]

Mill's *System of Logic*, begun in the late 1820s and published in 1843, owed nothing to Harriet. *The Subjection of Women* derives much of its interest from the fact that it combines a narrow reliance on the mentality of the earlier work with a sense that no form of discourse, logical or otherwise, yet exists for the subject now dealt with. Consolidation and innovation run together. It is no detraction to say that what Mill consolidates remains open to question; and that what he innovates is a debate that will never finish.

Mill's *Logic* attempted to combine the associationist psychology pioneered by Locke – who insisted that all knowledge is derived from experience, and experience only – with a belief that the primitive social science of the nineteenth century would eventually establish reliable hypotheses from which practical deductions could be made: in other words, that social science would take its place as a system which like the physics of Locke's contemporary Newton could be tested and developed to promote usable results. Mill was very aware of the dangers of imagined success in this endeavour: his political radicalism made him insist that even the principles of mathematics were only generalisations from experience, not necessary truths. This permits him to envisage a social science which, on the paradigm of the 'hard' sciences, can supply usable 'knowledge'; but which – for even the 'hard' sciences, he insists, are always subject to radical revision – will not trap the social scientist and his subject matter (human lives) in a dogmatic framework of received ideas.

The Subjection of Women consolidates this pattern of thinking, or rather this mechanism for insisting on liberality of thought. The title echoes a phrase from an unpublished fragment of Harriet, which refers to the 'present legal and moral subjection of women' as 'likely to be the last remaining relic of the primitive condition of society, the tyranny of physical force'. At the same time, Mill's book never lets the reader forget that *all* our 'knowledge' as to the 'natural' behaviour and relations of the sexes may be founded on false premises: that almost no form of language or argument on this subject is usable because the subject-matter dealt with has been in itself distorted by millenia of false perceptions. Harriet had gone to the marrow of the matter with her usual demand for the right to be eccentric: 'even if the alleged differences of aptitude did exist, it would be a reason why women and men would generally occupy themselves differently but no reason why they should be forced to do so'. But Mill feels a need for some reliable hypothesis about gender, from which politically compelling arguments can be made. Harriet sweeps history into her vision: 'It is one of the aberrations of early and rude legislation to attempt to convert every supposed natural fitness into an imperative obligation.'[35] Mill knows this is not a *reliable* hypothesis: but also knows he has little chance of improving on it. He alludes to history, rather than deploying it as proof. For him, the Age of Reason to which Locke and Newton belonged has been succeeded by a reliance on Instinct 'infinitely more degrading'. Mill's faith does not flinch, however. He looks forward to the development of a 'sound psychology, laying bare the real root of much that is bowed down to as the intention of Nature and the ordinance of God'.[36] To establish his argument for women's liberation, he requires some system for understanding human personalities and private and political relationships, as they are affected by gender. There is no such system that provides the kind of reliability Newton could claim for physics. Here, Mill's feeling that the 'hard' scientific systems are not absolutely reliable either comes to his aid. With a panache that would amount to sophistry in a lesser mind, he proposes, in effect, that only by trial of the utmost legislative and social equality that can be attained will the personalities of men and women come sufficiently into the light for any usable inferences about them to be drawn. Social psychology, like physics, will be advanced by experiment.

After the manner of a lover or a theologian rather than a scientist or an entrepreneur, Mill's is a faith that seeks to understand, not a speculation in search of a new formula. Control, as essential to experiment, means less to him than freedom to experience. His convictions about sex equality connect themselves with his feelings about socialism. Both are an idea: as unrealisable, absolutely, as a triangle or any other geometrical figure. But he seems to think that, like Platonic ideas, they may inform practice as usefully as ideas about geometry inform the practical science of trigonometry: 'there is time before us for the question to work itself out on an experimental scale, by actual trial'. Neither socialism nor equality will be attained absolutely; but they are 'the guiding principles of the improvements necessary to give the present . . . system of society its best chance'.[37] In neither area was Mill a conventional 'revolutionary', for he believed that imposition from above destroys what it pretends to impose. Instead, he intended to work through the democratic system towards political power for women, which as he reminded Florence Nightingale, was 'the only security against every form of oppression'.[38]

In *The Subjection of Women*, he does not deal with the question of divorce, believing that enlightenment on the subject was impossible till women were free to speak and influence the law. This of itself highlights his and Harriet's main intent: the securing of women's suffrage, connected with which (in a system where votes were still based on property) was the gaining of full property rights for women.

It is poignant, and inevitable, that the relationship between the sexes which Mill envisages should be based on his relationship with Harriet. This has been maligned as a 'dowdy and ascetic partnership' whose 'sole gratification is the mental improvement of the parties and society at large'.[39] But there is nothing dowdy about *The Subjection of Women*: rather it is charged with a poetic vehemence which continues to be appealing: and not merely to those who, sharing Mill's personal Utilitarianism, regard the so-called 'higher' gratifications as more desirable than 'lower' ones. *The Subjection of Women* is a disappointment as an argument. Its poetic status does not deprive it of its political usefulness, however: 'One person with a belief is a social power equal to ninety-nine that have only interests'.[40] Buried with Harriet at Avignon, Mill, by virtue of his belief in her, remains controversial, and catalytic.

Notes

1 David Ivor Young, b. 1932: Lord Young of Graffham, 1984; Minister without Portfolio 1984–85; Secretary of State for Employment 1985–87; for Trade and Industry 1987–89.

2 Ruskin, *Works*, XVII. 324–7.

3 Fetter, p. 242.

4 See Chronology, above; and *Thomas Carlyle: The Critical Heritage*, edited by J. P. Seigel, London, 1971, p. 52.

5 Mill, *Collected Works*, XXII. lv–lvii.

6 *The Stones of Venice*, III (1853), Appendix 7. *Works*, XI. 258–63: 'On Modern Education'.

7 Diary entry for 21 January 1854, *Letters of John Stuart Mill*, 1910, II. 361.

8 *Collected Works*, I. 251.

9 *Collected Works*, X. 10, 17, n.

10 *Utilitarianism*, etc., ed. Acton, p. 7.

11 *Collected Works*, III. 937–8.

12 *Collected Works*, III. 944.

13 *Dissertations and Discussions*, III. 29.

14 Aristotle, *Ethics*, translated by J. A. K. Thompson, Harmondsworth, 1959, pp. 287–312. For Ruskin's 'answer' to this dilemma, see above, n. 6.

15 For an extreme view, ascribed to one Pausanias: Plato, *Symposium*, translated Walter Hamilton, Harmondsworth, 1951, p. 46. Plato's 'Solution' in the *Republic* was to eliminate the family and reduce sex to breeding festivals.

16 Harriet Taylor, fragment on 'Rights of Women', *Collected Works*, XXI. 378.

17 Mill, *Utilitarianism*, etc., ed. Acton, p. 346.

18 P. 233.

19 P. 311.

20 Pp. 192–7.

21 P. 183.

22 *Collected Works*, XXV. 1210–12.

23 *Collected Works*, XVI. 1070.

24 Philip Magnus, *Gladstone*, London, 1963, p. 185.

25 *Collected Works*, I. 274.
26 Fetter, *The Economist*, p. 131.
27 *Utilitarianism*, etc., ed. Acton, p. 283.
28 3 *Hansard*, vol. 187, cols. 1343–66. The UK and USA are at present alone among Western democracies in not employing some form of proportional representation.
29 Married women began to have security for their own earnings and property with the first Married Women's Property Act, 1870.
30 3 *Hansard*, vol. 187, cols. 817–45.
31 *Collected Works*, I. 277. Cf. Ruskin, *Works*, XVII. 444, 'Mill right at last, and attacked for being so.'
32 3 *Hansard*, vol. 182, col. 2012.
33 3 *Hansard*, vol. 188, cols. 908–14. See also M. Hardman, *Ruskin and Bradford*, Manchester, 1986, pp. 104–6.
34 *Collected Works*, I. 265.
35 Harriet Taylor, fragment on 'Women – (Rights of)', *Collected Works*, XXI. 386–8.
36 Rossi, ed., *Essays*, p. 128.
37 *Collected Works*, V. 736.
38 *Collected Works*, XXI. xxxvi.
39 Thomas, *Mill*, p. 122.
40 *Utilitarianism*, etc., ed. Acton, p. 197.

Books

Paperbacks

J. S. Mill, Utilitarianism, On Liberty *and* Considerations on Representative Government *with Selections from* Auguste Comte and Positivism, edited by H. B. Acton, London, 1987.

Alice S. Rossi, editor, *Essays on Sex Equality: John Stuart Mill and Harriet Taylor Mill*, Chicago and London, 1970.

William Thomas, *Mill*, London, 1985.

Life

Alexander Bain, *John Stuart Mill*, London, 1882.

M. St. J. Packe, *The Life of John Stuart Mill*, London, 1954.

Works

Collected Works of John Stuart Mill, edited by J. M. Robson and others, Toronto, 1963–

J. S. Mill, *Dissertations and Discussions*, 2 volumes, London, 1859; vol. 3, 1867; vol. 4, 1875.

Background

Walter Bagehot, *The English Constitution* (1867), Oxford, 1928.

Jeremy Bentham, *An Introduction to the Principles of Morals and Legislation*, New York, 1961.

F. W. Fetter, *The Economist in Parliament 1780–1868*, Durham, North Carolina, 1980.

Jack Lively and John Rees, editors, *Utilitarian Logic and Politics: James Mill's 'Essay on "Government" '*, *Macaulay's critique and the ensuing debate*, Oxford, 1978.

J. S. Mill, *Utilitarianism, On Liberty, Essay on Bentham*: together with selected writings of Jeremy Bentham and John Austin, edited with an introduction by Mary Warnock, London, 1962.

Douglas W. Rae, *The Political Consequences of Electoral Laws*, New Haven, 1967.

Eric Stokes, *The English Utilitarians and India*, Oxford, 1959.

W. Thomas, *The Philosophical Radicals: Nine Studies in Theory and Practice, 1817–1841*, Oxford, 1979.

Criticism and commentary

Graeme Duncan, *Marx and Mill: two views of social conflict and social harmony*, Cambridge, 1973.

Ronald Fletcher, editor, *John Stuart Mill, a logical critique of sociology*, London, 1971.

Samuel Hollander, *The Economics of John Stuart Mill*, 2 volumes, Oxford, 1985.

David Ritchie, *The principles of state interference: four essays on the political philosophy of Mr. Herbert Spencer, J. S. Mill and T. H. Green* (1902), reprinted Freeport, New York, 1969.

J. M. Robson, *The Improvement of Mankind: the social and political thought of John Stuart Mill*, Toronto and London, 1968.

C. L. Ten, *Mill on Liberty*, Oxford, 1980.

Dennis F. Thompson, *John Stuart Mill and Representative Government*, Princeton, 1976.

CHAPTER SIX

Newman and the university

Introduction

Despite differences, Newman shows a surprising measure of agreement with Ruskin and Mill on the subject of higher education.

For all three, the university was the place where the selfish principles of personal advancement and intellectual curiosity could be disciplined and instructed so as to become instruments for creative and communal development. All three defined 'liberal education' – what Newman called the 'idea of a University' – as not merely an optional complement to technical, academic or vocational knowledge but as essential to the informed acquirement and use of such knowledge. Mill spoke for all of them when he told students of St Andrews: 'You are to be a part of the public who are to . . . help forward the future intellectual benefactors of humanity; and you are, if possible, to furnish your contingent to the number of those benefactors.'[1] For all three thinkers, liberal education for the individual implied a criterion of 'reverence and duty' towards society. Tradition and innovation went hand in hand. All three respected the ancient classics enough to want them taught in relevant modern ways; all three believed that an adequate scientific training was in itself an induction into practical ethics; all three were confident enough of the traditional values of academic discipline to support controversial new disciplines like engineering, psychology and agricultural science.[2]

Ruskin linked his ideas about higher education to his own sociopolitical reinterpretation of the gospels. Mill's thinking about universities was part of his attempt to evolve a more civilised Utilitarianism. These personally chosen responses to their own upbringing allowed room for agreement as well as disagreement.

Newman alone, by the time he came to compile his *Idea of a University*, had embraced not merely a personal viewpoint but an institution: the Roman Catholic Church. What made Newman unique was the fact that he combined an intellectual liberalism which had much in common with Mill with a devotion to an institution denounced by Mill (and others) for its intransigent dogmatism.

The pattern of Newman's life helps to explain this apparent paradox. As Mill would in theory have approved, Newman came to his convictions through personal experience.

As an Oxford college tutor, Newman became convinced that education must be pastoral. It required an atmosphere of open dialogue which met the particular needs of each student's intellect and character. Involved in university politics as Vicar of St Mary's and leader of the Tractarian Movement, Newman learnt a further lesson. Only an institution truly independent of state control and free from the ideological manipulations of politicians could provide a field for the free development of intellect and character. Oxford, as long as it remained the exclusive preserve of the State Church, could not do this. Newman found his own freedom in the Roman Church. He was given the opportunity to act as founding Rector of a Catholic University in Ireland. This proved to be an experiment that influenced future thinking rather than a going concern in its own right. A Catholic University such as Newman envisaged it, founded on faith yet open to all[3] and promoting the fullest liberal education as a source for the renewal of faith in the modern world, could not yet be realised, he discovered. He realised more and more that he needed to encourage lively liberal thinking within the whole Church – even arguing for the laity's right to be consulted on doctrine – if the Church were truly to fulfil its task of providing light in the world. Education was not merely a matter of colleges and schools but of the life of a community.

Newman remained within an authoritarian church. He wholeheartedly shared Carlyle's belief that spiritual conviction was essential to action. Nevertheless his own view of authority was almost symmetrically opposite to Carlyle's. In *Characteristics* (1831) Carlyle had depicted the dilemma facing young intellectuals. Lacking any dogma in which they could believe, they had no principle of action. Society was essential to intellectual growth, Carlyle wrote, and without a governing spiritual principle there could be no society.

Carlyle's thinking about intellectual institutions became increasingly divided and despairing. On the one hand, he envisaged the replacement of the university by 'a collection of books' which each could consult in isolation. On the other, he grew fond of the idea of institutions – universities included – being drilled into useful work without much questioning about ultimate aims. He could assure Edinburgh University that humanity could never fall below Christianity, once having attained it. Personal honesty, therefore, and submission to due authority, were all that was required of students.[4] For Newman such a view was horribly inadequate on both counts. Humanity needed a strong church as a buttress against evil. The Church would never be strong without constant protest and reform from within. Newman's letters provide criticisms of the practice of his own hierarchy quite as scathing as anything in Mill. Catholic reactionaries practised what Carlyle preached. Newman called them 'Nihilists'. Like Carlyle, they reduced to zero the *quality* of what was done and believed, provided something was done and believed without question.

Newman's struggle for Catholic reform included a campaign to allow Catholics to attend Protestant universities. Protestants had removed the ban: but the Roman hierarchy delayed the work of reconciliation. In his own capacity, Newman was acting as Mill advised the Presbyterians of St Andrews to act: 'let all who conscientiously can, remain in the church. A church is far more easily improved from within than from without.'[5]

There is an important difference between the implications of Newman's theory and practice and those suggested by Mill's advice, however. Mill confined his generous encouragement to the 'national church': the Presbyterian Church of Scotland or episcopal Church of England. He merely denounced 'Roman Catholic Universities' for their intransigence. He could not, or would not, see the value of an international religious body capable, at least in theory, of harbouring opposition to the State.

With his dislike of confrontation, and what Ruskin called his 'deficiency of the imagination',[6] Mill was not given to acknowledging that there might be such things as irresolvable mysteries. Such questions as the individual's function in the universe, or the bonds of tradition and aspiration that go to the making of communities, were for both Ruskin and Newman not problems to be solved by reason, but mysteries to be celebrated in art (for Ruskin) or in liturgy (for Newman). For both of them, earthly life was not an intellectual puzzle but a sacrament. Armed with this conviction, Ruskin imaginatively and Newman by faith evolved principles for resistance where Mill only remained rational and bewildered. Ruskin and Newman anticipated in their own terms the existentialist affirmation of the right to say 'no' to the intolerable. This inner conviction, formed regardless of what Newman termed the 'usurpations of reason', sometimes organised into a church (such as Newman wished to see), sometimes in the shape of a trade union movement (such as Ruskin advocated) has, since Victorian times, occasionally performed a function Mill could hardly have foreseen. Faith, however embattled and ambiguous, has been as necessary a safeguard as reason for the seeds of individual liberty.

Newman thus provides an extreme example of the Victorian thinker's policy of reforming an institution from within. He chose to enter a church which has often been reactionary, and he endeavoured to impart to it the most liberal possible vision of the freedom of conscience. The university had a unique part to play in this strategy.

Tutor of Oriel

Newman managed only a Third Class in his finals examinations as a scholar of Trinity in 1820; and was awarded a fellowship at Oriel in 1822, on the strength of a prize essay. The individual nature of his intelligence had something to do with both these events: but his tutors had left him to overwork as they had left others, presumably, to do too little. It was not in Newman's nature to be content with a system that had failed him, merely because it had also rewarded him.

If England was in a state of transition, Oxford, the traditional nursery of its intellectual elite, was in the throes of a prolonged crisis which had been developing for some centuries.

National and international politics were implicated in Oxford's internal arrangements from the beginning. Its earliest period of growth was stimulated by England's quarrel with France in the twelfth century, which had closed the University of Paris to the English. The Oxford University which emerged would never be wealthy. Its system of professorial teaching would never have enough funds. The money that went into Oxford during the later Middle Ages went into semi-independent colleges, founded for graduates and to support a few clever boys – 'scholars' – to provide an intelligentsia for Church and State. Most students eked out an existence in halls of residence, which were little more than unendowed hostels.

Developments in the sixteenth century sowed the seeds of the nineteenth-century crisis. The sons of the gentry bought their way into the colleges as undergraduates. There was no parallel increase in funding for scholars. Social and political considerations prevailed over religious and scholarly concerns. Unable to compete, the halls of residence began to disappear. The University grew poorer, the colleges richer and less intellectual. Professorships became a thing of the past. 'Learning' shrank to classical literature, mathematics, and some theology. Then, with the break from Rome, Oxford became the preserve of the episcopal Church of England. Catholics – English, European and Irish – as well as all Protestant dissenters, were excluded.

The political and social changes heralded by the French Revolution were felt at Oxford, as elsewhere. But because of Oxford's peculiar history, the movement for change was coloured by a desire to renew in contemporary forms the spiritual and intellectual concerns of the Middle Ages, while at the same time meeting those financial and organisational needs of the University which the sixteenth century had betrayed.

Eventually, in 1850, a Royal Commission was appointed to begin looking into the problem. Meanwhile, a devout young intellectual like Newman, with a family background in banking and a flair for the law, was in a state of ferment.

There were theological questions, including the status of the Church of England, to be considered. How far did teaching methods promote the pastoral needs of students? How long must the vested interests of rich colleges take precedence over the national need for a well-endowed university with professors capable of establishing faculties in modern subjects? What was the prestige of Oxford worth as a finishing school for the gentry in the face of the growing desire among the middle classes (the working classes were hardly thought of in this connection) for access to the kind of higher education that would equip them for modern careers?

The young Newman could hardly imagine that he would one day inaugurate a Catholic University of Ireland which would give him the opportunity to address all these matters, at least in theory; and that his theory would help to inform Oxford's own revival. For the moment, he approached the problem at its nearest point: the pastoral and intellectual needs of the undergraduates allocated to him by his Provost, Edward Copleston.

Copleston was himself a reformer. He had supported the new Examinations Statute of 1800, which provided for Honours and Pass degrees. The almost expiring University was reborn. As Provost of Oriel, Copleston promoted two developments which, theoretically compatible, led to practical difficulties. First, he filled his Common Room with the brightest young men he could find. Self-consciously elitist, yet also reformist, these new Fellows called themselves 'Noetics' – which is Greek for 'Intellectuals'. The task Copleston required of these stars, however, was to revive an efficient system of teaching on schoolmasterly lines.

Oxford tutorial standards had slumped to the point where official classes were disorderly and inept, and serious students – if they could afford it – resorted to extra private tuition, sometimes outside their own college. Copleston discouraged this practice, and also frowned on favouritism towards the 'gentleman commoners': the social elite of the college, for whom idleness was a point of honour. Teaching at the endowed – or 'public' – schools, from which many undergraduates came, was equally at a low ebb. Well-connected boys spent just enough time in them to scrape into Oxford. Their time at Oxford was taken up with forming alliances for future life. Except for the few seeking ordination, the taking of a degree was considered rather *arriviste*.

There was no short-term solution to a problem whose origins lay in the sixteenth-century hijacking of the colleges by the gentry. Hiring brilliant original minds and giving them what amounted to a schoolmaster's job was bound to exacerbate the problem. One of Oriel's most promising 'Intellectuals' – Thomas Arnold, the poet's father – left Oriel to begin part of the solution by pioneering the reform of the endowed schools. Newman, six years younger, was ordained in 1824 and appointed tutor in 1826, just in time for a crisis in the college's power structure.

Copleston became Bishop of Llandaff in 1827, and left Oriel. Newman supported the election of the uninspired but practical

Edward Hawkins as his successor. A possible contender was John Keble, the highly regarded but unworldly leader of a new Catholic movement in the Church of England. His *Christian Year*, which versified the call for a more spiritual and disciplined kind of faith and practice, came out that year and would help to win him the Oxford Professorship of Poetry. At the moment it was being committed to memory by his godson, Matthew Arnold.

The consequences of Keble's election might have been enormous; but in the face of Newman's opposition he withdrew, and Hawkins was elected. He continued Copleston's policy without his flair for management.

Copleston's general policy had been to keep undergraduates at a distance, and this was continued with ever less rewarding results. The tutorial lectures, or 'classes', were kept subservient to the general college lectures, which were formal and unadventurous. Scripture, routine classics and some Euclidean mathematics were the principal dole. Possibly effective in the Middle Ages, when undergraduates had been much younger and there had been university lectures to go to in addition, this was no way to stimulate the minds or consciences of men who would be governing Victorian England and much of the globe. A lowly class tutor like Newman was required to be a hack who corrected exercises, explained college lectures over again to the indifferent, and obliged with the occasional pep-talk, as required by his superiors. There was an avoidance of any attempt to find the 'right' tutor for an individual student; and almost an aversion to any notion of personal development through the tutorial process: for instance, it was not regarded as necessary that a tutor should retain any class a second term, even if they were to continue with the same book. Rowdiness might be kept at bay, if also induced, by such means, and the 'diligent and clever young man' might 'obtain honours'. But issues like personal moral development within a community or individual intellectual culture under the stimulus of like minds – the issues that drew Newman to teaching – were guaranteed not to be raised under such a system.

Newman raised them. It was regarded as correct for college tutors to be clergymen of proven intelligence. At Oriel, particularly, with its High Church atmosphere, it was regarded as unChristian to discriminate in favour of 'gentlemen' at the expense of poorer children of God. Such were the formal traditions. Like other mavericks of his generation, Newman caused trouble by breathing life into formal traditions. He determined to discriminate in favour of intelligence and also to make the tutorial office a truly pastoral one. There would be different levels of intellectual discipline for different types of mind, and respect for every type of mind: mere formal 'discipline', he imagined, would soon cease to be a problem.

He inaugurated his tutorial reforms at Christmas 1828. He had the support of two younger men: Robert Wilberforce and Hurrell Froude. Ironically, it was a shared admiration for the sensitive pastoral spirit of the ousted Keble that made them conspirators with Newman.[7] The Dean and Senior Tutor, Joseph Domford, vacillated; but permitted the experiment. Hawkins was not, officially, informed. His belated decision to become aware of what was going on precipitated a major row at the end of 1829. As Provost he regarded himself as responsible to the University for efficient teaching. Newman theorised that he could appeal directly to University authority for the right to form his own policy. It was a puzzle in the medieval regulations which had once governed relations between the University and the colleges. The University had long since yielded the unequal struggle. In practice there was no university authority to appeal to. There were only the Oriel College Statutes, administered by Hawkins. University rules that protected tutors against heads of colleges – who might be of any degree of senility or incompetence – had ceased to function.

Newman was advocating something like the Oxford college tutorial system as it was later revived, when it would be complemented by university lectures by qualified experts. Such things did not then exist. It would be Benjamin Jowett, sixteen years younger and very much stolider than Newman, who would see them through, as tutor, then Master, of Balliol, as Professor of Greek and Vice-Chancellor of the University.[8]

Newman was trapped. He resorted to haranguing his Provost on the need for 'due attention to . . . private instruction' as opposed to 'mere lecturing';[9] and was abetted by Froude and Wilberforce, the latter reminding Hawkins that he too had argued for some such reform immediately before securing election. The dithering Dean reminded his juniors that innovations require unusual men of unusual oneness of spirit to carry out. The three rebels were such: but as would often be the case throughout Newman's career, his superiors saw to it that routine prevailed. He did not resign: but from June 1830 Hawkins stopped sending him pupils.

Newman turned instead to a work of research on the Arians of the fourth century. He would, however erroneously, always in future see the demands of teaching and research as incompatible.

Vicar of St Mary's

In 1828 Provost Hawkins, sensing Newman's pastoral vocation, offered him the living of St Mary's Oxford, in Oriel's gift. A parish church, though far too grand for its small and geographically fragmented parish, St Mary's had for centuries been adopted as the University Church. During the reign of the Catholic Queen Mary in the sixteenth century, it had been the scene of the show trial staged to convict and condemn the Protestant martyrs Cranmer, Ridley and Latimer.

Newman's new position provided him with important opportunities, and an important warning.

As in effect 'vicar' of Oxford, Newman had a weekly opportunity to address the University as such. His sermons provided some of the rare occasions on which the collective mind of Oxford could be invited beyond college politics into more important considerations. In addition, attendance at these sermons – unlike college chapel services – was entirely voluntary. This element of choice and consent in his listeners was central to Newman's ethical outlook. Thirdly, because St Mary's did also have a parochial function, Newman could reach beyond the academic world of the 'gown' to the life of that part of the 'town' that came within his care. Some of his happiest times were spent at Littlemore, a semi-rural segment of his parish, where he provided a chapel and won the esteem of people who would never have ventured into St Mary's.

All these elements of Newman's theory and practice would be repeated in Dublin during the 1850s, when he would build his own University Church to serve similar purposes.

Newman's oratory divided dons and undergraduates at Oxford rather as Ruskin's would do. His Sunday afternoon sermons became irresistible to many bright and earnest undergraduates – including Matthew Arnold – with their combination of clarity and risk; their uncompromising but reverent unfolding of the speaker's inner consciousness; the surprising inevitability of conclusions offered almost in parenthesis. Alarmed by the suspense that thrilled the young, conservative dons made efforts to prevent their students' attendance: an infallible stimulant. More traditional, but with some equally surprising elements, were Newman's weekday lectures, published in 1837 as *Lectures on the Prophetic Office of the Church*. The prophetic function for Newman, as for Carlyle, meant engagement with current events in the light of divine truth. Newman became engaged with others in ecclesiastical politics.

It was in this new departure that the 'warning' of St Mary's became clearer to him. The Oxford of the 1830s was still being manipulated, as it had been in the sixteenth century, by the use made by secular governments of the ecclesiastical status of the University. With less cruelty than Stalin or the Spanish Inquisition, the English state of Newman's day exerted its power to maintain at institutions of higher education the ideology which suited its political ends. A similar effect was being experienced in central Italy by the Pope's double function as head of Church and State. This could lead, in Newman's view, to the 'tyrannous use of his spiritual power'.[10] This was his opinion after becoming a devout Catholic. As a devout Anglican at Oxford he faced a different version of the same tyranny.

The position of the Church of England was currently giving concern to many. Yoked to an increasingly secular state, the Church retained embarrassing secular privileges and a social prestige which disabled its mission to the poorer classes. At the same time it was not in control of its own doctrine or the appointment of its own senior clergy, both subject to political manipulation. Keble, Pusey,[11] Froude and Newman were among those who formed a new Catholic party in the Church of England, determined to argue for the authentic voice of an independent church within the state. 'Tractarians' and the 'Oxford Movement' were names found for this group by others. Their first tract was published by Newman in September 1833. It affirmed the principle of the Apostolic Succession in the Church of England. Newman's theory was that the Church spoke, not at the bidding of secular politicians, but with the authentic voice of the Apostles bearing the mandate of Christ Himself.

In practice, political manipulation was written into Oxford's constitution. By the law of England a university was subject to the visitation of the Archbishop of Canterbury, himself a state appointment. In effect this meant that a number of university appointments were also in the gift of politicians. Thus, when in 1836 the Regius Professorship of Divinity at Oxford fell vacant, the Archbishop prepared a list from which Melbourne, the Whig prime minister, might choose. It included Keble, Newman and Pusey. Melbourne ignored it, and lulled the king into appointing the Whig Dr R. D. Hampden, who had declared in favour of secularising Oxford by removing religious tests for degrees, while still maintaining its constitution as an 'Anglican' – i.e. politically manipulated – institution. For Newman, this was the worst of all possible worlds. He became embroiled in a campaign against Hampden as heretic and rationalist:[12] a diversion from the true target, which was the Royal Supremacy over the Church, and its inevitable consequence in political abuse of universities.

Newman's conversion to Rome was gradual, but absolute. At the deepest level it was the natural sequel to his own voluntary conversion to Christianity in his teens. Unlike Carlyle or Matthew Arnold, his own family background was not strictly religious. Some converts become more intolerant than those born into a strict faith. Newman embraced faith and tolerance together. Faith for him was the guarantee for freedom of discussion, and the only valid principle for action. Once he came to see the Catholic Church as a divine institution, he began to see it as the stronghold of all true liberty. Whereas the Anglican Church was founded in the sixteenth century as an organ of secular tyranny, the Catholic Church, like the individual conscience, was of directly divine origin. Within the Catholic Church, therefore, Newman felt he could follow his own conscience with a fuller sense of ultimate security, whatever his own failures or those of other Catholics.

For a while, Newman sought ways to advocate the kind of faith and freedom he desired within the context of Anglican Oxford. To gain a degree, students had to affirm the Thirty-Nine Articles of the Church of England: a legacy from Reformation times which seriously distressed many consciences. Newman, in his famous Tract 90 of 1841, tried to argue for the Catholic status of these Articles. They were, he reasoned, an authentic version of the faith of the Universal Church: not a series of traps to keep consciences at the service of the State. Hampden had wanted the religious element removed from Oxford's constitution while retaining the State's right to control. Newman on the other hand argued for the retention of the religious element in a spirit that might foster divergence from the State. The immediate consequence for Newman was that, like Hampden before him, he found himself censured for heresy. There was a further ecclesiastical row about a professorship: this time over Keble's successor as Professor of Poetry.[13] All this came as a last straw.

Newman, whose historical researches were leading him nearer and nearer Rome, was compelled to join these to the promptings of his own personality and the irresolvable political dilemma of his position. There was no freedom for a strict Catholic faith except in a Church emancipated from State control. The termination of the Pope's temporal power (it came in 1870) seemed more likely than the disestablishment of the Church of England (which remains under parliamentary control to this day). To avoid implication in beliefs he could not share Newman must avoid further complicity in the State's tyranny over his own soul. Like his Huguenot ancestors, he fled: withdrawing from college in 1842 to Littlemore, where people knew him as pastor, not controversialist.

It was there that he was received into the Roman Church. Part of his rationale for taking this step had been made in an Anglican sermon at St Mary's in December 1831.

It was 'as absurd to argue men, as to torture them, into believing', he declared. The sermon's theme was 'The Usurpations of Reason'. Newman conceded that 'power, as well as intellectual endowments, is necessary to the maintenance of religion, in order to secure from mankind hearing for an unpleasant subject'. But the sermon continued, in its most telling phrase, to make clear that beyond the securing of that 'hearing' for the hard truths of Revelation, institutional power of any kind betrays truth itself through the 'fallacy of persecution'.[14] Browbeating, undue pressure, physical force: none of these has any power to promote the truth.

Newman would never deviate from this double programme: to secure a hearing for Christianity through the institution of the Church while at the same time renouncing the fallacy of persecution. His belief in both principles would run through all his educational theory and practice. As an Anglican, and as a Roman Catholic, he would therefore frequently be misunderstood by those among his superiors who preferred prejudice and routine.

The idea of a university

Newman was received into the Roman Church in 1845 and ordained priest in 1847 after studying at Rome. His commitment to Catholic belief would henceforth colour all his theory and practice. His personality, and educational convictions, would remain unchanged. Urged to become the Rector of the new Catholic University in Dublin in 1851, he provided a series of discourses which formed the basis of his classic work, *The Idea of a University*.

The image that is implicit in Newman's theory of a university is that of a complete 'circle' formed by the whole conspectus of human knowledge. This image goes back to Aristotle, who also made a further contribution to Newman's scheme. This is the concept of liberal knowledge or 'philosophy'. This liberal knowledge is the means of understanding the relations between the different aspects of knowledge – the segments of the circle – and the whole.

For Newman, there was room in a university not only for academic specialisms like mathematics and history, but also for technical and vocational subjects like engineering and medicine. Nevertheless, he thought that the governing 'idea' of a university – what *made* it a university – was the presence of liberal knowledge.

As a Christian and a Victorian, Newman's sense of how liberal knowledge or 'philosophy' should be institutionalised into the system was rather different from Aristotle's. Aristotle tended to see 'philosophers' as special people, set apart, to guide and arbitrate among the possessors of 'lesser' knowledges. Newman was careful to avoid this view, which was a dangerously tempting one in a Catholic context. Some of the clergy had no difficulty in identifying Aristotle's guiding principle or 'philosophy' with their own special subject of theology, and would like to have seen theologians arbitrating on what could and could not be taught in other subjects. Newman opposed this, not always with practical success.

For him, the liberal knowledge or 'philosophy' which ought to form the guiding principle or 'idea' of a Catholic university was nothing less than Christianity itself in its fullest humanism.

Newman's own essential conversion to Christianity, in his teens, was to Evangelical Christianity. He came to regard the Roman Church as the true Universal Church, but he never lost the basic convictions of nineteenth-century Evangelical Christianity. For him, these convictions were perfectly compatible with Catholic belief, though among entrenched and embittered Irish Catholics he may have been in a minority in thinking so. Evangelical belief focused on the idea of the 'talents' given to an individual by God.[15] These talents or 'personal gifts' were to be used in God's service. Since God had chosen to become man in order to do good in the world, it followed that the service of God involved Christians in using their personal gifts in the service of humanity. This view made Newman an eccentric in the eyes of the more hidebound members of the Catholic hierarchy, but it also made his 'idea of a University' accessible to many others, regardless of religious affiliation.[16] Ruskin, Mill and Arnold, in particular, had an Evangelical upbringing in childhood. It is not surprising that, in many points of principle, their educational views were not radically diverse from Newman's.

What a liberal education should do, in Newman's eyes, is to cultivate the personal gifts of students and exercise their innate *capacities*: for gaining further knowledge of a specialised kind; for joining in the cultural and political activities of later life; for making their contribution, it may be, even to the defining of the doctrines of the Church, as laymen. This latter point would involve Newman in charges of heresy; but for him it was logical and orthodox that a liberal education should equip a Catholic student for the fullest participation in life, religious as well as cultural and political. Newman's wish to see an educated *politically* aware middle class in Ireland was of course another source of annoyance for conservative critics of his theory and practice.

There was a need, he felt, for the fullest exchange of ideas, among Catholics, and across all religious and political barriers. What a Catholic university could do was to provide the context of a Catholic life and religious practice, a relatively sheltered environment within which the tools could be acquired for such an exchange. Sharing the same religion, dons and students could be all the more secure of a common purpose, and could exercise their minds uninhibited by the need always to be on the defensive against unbelievers.

Despising 'Liberalism' – which he saw as the futile pretence that principles of morality and conduct could be arrived at by empirical means – Newman was nevertheless almost heretically 'liberal' in the Catholic context.[17] Catholic doctrine, for him, was a

127

dynamic principle perpetually renewed by the minds of the whole Church and responsive to historical development. Catholic theological experts had their part to play in this, and there should be faculties of theology at any complete University: but the Church was more than theology, and theology itself needed to be renewed by alert and responsive minds, including non-experts.

The generating of such minds was the task of the essential 'liberal' core of university studies: philosophy (in its narrower sense), logic, literature and the arts, history and some principles at least of science. All students should partake of these as far as possible before specialising in 'academic' or 'vocational' subjects.

There is a remarkable measure of agreement between Newman's *Idea of a University* and J. S. Mill's Inaugural Address as Rector of St Andrews University. In practice, Mill was an opponent of denominational education, though he also believed that there would be little progress for the human race until a 'credible' religion of some kind evolved to supply a basis for ethics.[18] He agreed with Newman and most other Victorian thinkers that knowledge without ethical commitment was pernicious. While Mill worked empirically towards an 'idea of a University' quite similar to Newman's, Newman deduced his own 'idea' from his Catholic faith.

The priests and bishops with whom Newman had to deal in Ireland mostly lacked his subtlety, generosity and childlike conviction. Furthermore, the secular British State was suspicious of the whole enterprise. Newman soon found himself in the familiar, though never comfortable, position of being misunderstood.

The Catholic University of Ireland

Newman was not officially installed as Rector of the Catholic University till June 1854 – more than two years after his first journey to Dublin to deliver the inaugural Discourses. Less than three years later – in March 1857 – he gave notice of his resignation; which became *de facto* at the end of that year, and official a year later.

The difficulties facing him were enormous. Fully employed already in running an oratory in Birmingham, and required by the Holy See not to neglect that work, Newman was a gifted inspirer and theorist and a competent administrator; but his was not the personality to shoulder aside the obstructions put in his way by his ecclesiastical superiors. As an English convert, he was doubly displeasing to Irish Catholics.

Newman's dream of a modern liberal Catholic institution, devoted to developing the capacities of its members, and happy to engage in dialogue with non-Catholic institutions, was rendered impossible by the very circumstances of the Catholic University's foundation. If Catholic Irish education was repressive, this was in good measure a reaction to centuries of persecution from Anglicans, who until 1793 retained a complete monopoly of Trinity College Dublin, the country's only institution of higher education, and managed to bar non-Anglicans from its staff and scholarships till the early 1870s. Attempting to break the deadlock, Sir Robert Peel annoyed conservative Catholics still further by founding state-funded Queen's Colleges at Belfast, Cork and Galway. These were opened in 1849, and were strictly non-denominational. They were labelled 'godless colleges' by an Anglican MP, and the label caught on. Pope Pius IX's determination to found a 'Catholic University' in Ireland was largely motivated by the desire to make these 'godless colleges' unworkable: an example of the sort of Catholic intransigence Newman disliked quite as passionately, but for different reasons, as J. S. Mill. With similar ideas to Newman's as to the value of a 'liberal education', Mill was involved as MP for Westminster in the struggle to prevent diehard Catholics from ruining the Queen's Colleges.[19] Ironically, Newman faced the same enemies in defending his own institution.

Dr Cullen, prime mover of the Catholic University, became Archbishop of Dublin, while remaining Apostolic Delegate, in 1852: but he inherited a situation created by his predecessor Dr Murray, who together with a substantial number of bishops was in favour of co-operation with the British State in educational matters, and opposed to a separatist university. A new Papal Brief of April 1854 had renewed Newman's commission in terms that contradicted the public intentions of his Discourses: for it spoke only of a 'literary institution', ignoring Newman's argument for science; and to Newman's metaphysical eye at least seemed to insist on the kind of interference by theologians in other disciplines which he was determined to resist. The Pope left ultimate authority in the University to the four Archbishops. Of these, Cullen feared the encroachments of science, and really wanted a college or Lyceum whose arrangements were subject to his personal veto. Newman's lecture on *Christianity and Scientific Investigation* retains even as published the marks of this priestly scrutiny.[20] Yet its drift was so shockingly liberal to the hierarchy that Newman was prevented from delivering it at all. Archbishop MacHale of Tuam, an aggressive nationalist and Home Ruler, thwarted Cullen's attempts to act alone and made the University Committee – which was dominated by the hierarchy – virtually unworkable.

The English Cardinal Wiseman attempted to make Newman's position tenable by persuading the Pope to make him a Bishop, which would have given him a measure of free action: but this English ploy – as it was seen – was outmanoeuvred by the Irish; and Newman, in his own words, was forced to appear as an upstart 'Englishman taking upon himself to teach the Paddies what education was . . . a convert . . . feathering a nest from the pockets of the Irish'.[21] In modern parlance, Cullen intended to use Newman as a 'fall guy', who would stump through Ireland drumming up support entirely on his own responsibility. Newman's refusal to 'understand' this, and MacHale's intransigence, delayed everything for two years.

From 1854 Newman became more sympathetic to Cullen as he realised what the underlying difficulties were. Many of the laity wanted integrated education. It would be another twenty years before youths qualified for higher education were leaving Catholic secondary schools in numbers sufficient to support a Catholic university. The middle classes were not prosperous enough to provide large financial support; smaller townsfolk were too demoralised to support night classes; and the poor would give nothing without command of their bishops. The gentry wanted degrees: but even if the Catholic University felt able to grant any they would not be recognised by the British State. The upper classes had a tradition of sending their sons abroad; but they wanted Oxford; and the removal of religious tests for those graduating at Oxford, which came in 1854, seemed to make this their obvious option. In the event, Newman, apostle of separatist education, found himself pressing for a compromise whereby theological degrees and qualifications in arts for church purposes could be granted from Rome, but Catholic University students would be examined by Queen's College staff for state-recognised degrees in other areas: a proposition which by now had no chance of success, however little it might seem to differ from the original 'godless colleges' Bill of 1845, which had allowed for denominational chairs of theology, funded by churches; for halls of residence and Deans of discipline on sectarian lines; not to mention handsome endowments from the State. MacHale had rejected this Peelite compromise as giving insufficient control over subject-teaching to the hierarchy. He demanded dual professorships – Catholic and non-Catholic – in all subjects. Cullen was not such a spoiler: but he found it hard to understand the difference, so essential to Newman, between a 'godless college' and a Catholic University in which science and literature were to be taught on a basis independent from theology. And almost none of the hierarchy understood Newman's wish to give the laity real influence in running the University. He wanted a financial committee of experienced laymen; but the bishops stuck to the money. Most of it was invested in Government Stock: an inevitable compromise with a state whose endowments were refused.[22]

On Cullen's initiative, the University bought two splendid Palladian houses on St Stephen's Green, Dublin. As a former Rector of the Irish College in Rome, Cullen meant to combine central premises with a regime which would closely guard its inmates from worldly corruption. Newman was for a suburban site but reasonable access to the amenities of the town, even hoping to enhance these with a licensed theatre to bring 'town' and 'gown' together for the enjoyment of respectable plays: a scheme too far ahead of its time to be comprehensible. He was able, however, to establish his own house, where something approaching to the tutorial system he had pioneered at Oriel was established: the possible nucleus of a college.

Newman's vision of a Catholic University would never be realised. There was, however, one truly surprising success. In 1854 he managed to purchase a Medical School building. Theatre and dissecting rooms were already installed. Cunning was needed: the vendors would not willingly have sold to Catholics. W. K. Sullivan, Newman's chemistry professor and fellow-conspirator, ensured that a good chemistry laboratory was added to the facilities. A medical lodging house was opened. Students – there were fifty-nine by November 1856 – were able to qualify by taking the examinations of the Colleges of Physicians, in London or Dublin. The near monopoly of Protestants on the medical profession in Ireland was broken; and an important new outlet was provided for the ambitions of young Catholics. But Sullivan was a Young Irelander, a Fenian nationalist; and Cullen was perplexed to see Newman supporting him. MacHale resented the cost: £1,450 at the outset, with further expenditure on fittings; and £1,000 a year to run the school. He thought the Rector had exceeded his powers.[23]

A more foreseeable success was the survival, albeit in diminished form and in isolation, of the liberal studies courses which were the practical embodiment of Newman's 'idea of a University'. For Newman, higher study in medicine, law, theology, science or literature must always be based on two years' preliminary training in the department of 'Philosophy and Letters'. This would provide the initial 'liberal education' in classics, mathematics, logic, history, and elementary biblical and doctrinal study. Cullen's ambitions for the whole University really went no further than this. Thanks partly to his influence, the department of 'Philosophy and Letters' was the only one to prosper, apart from the Medical School.

By 1896, 'Philosophy and Letters' could look back on over forty years of continuous usefulness; could boast prosperous night classes, and an academic standard that compared well with the Queen's College in Belfast. Two elements guaranteed its small-scale but real success. From 1879 it was in receipt of government grants as a recognised college of the Royal University of Ireland. Also, from 1883 the college was run by Jesuits, the crack troops of the Catholic Church. Much of their work now involved mere examining of external candidates: a distortion of Newman's priorities. From 1884 till his death in 1889, G. M. Hopkins was the Professor of Classics, marking papers, teaching; and (in secret) wringing fresh pangs from the English sonnet.[24]

Law, science, and other important faculties never came to anything. But at least Newman was able to do something for Celtic literature. His one good friend in the hierarchy, Dr Moriarty, introduced him to the work of Eugene O'Curry, who with the University's financial help published one thick volume of Irish MSS. Sullivan began work on another; and Newman had a font of Irish type cast for University use. O'Curry had received some help from Trinity College Dublin, but Protestants were unwilling to risk much in support of 'superstition'. When Newman sought to rescue further Irish MSS from their 'safekeeping' in Rome, he was met by an equally entrenched obstructionism.

Law was very much a Protestant preserve: and Newman failed to persuade the Catholic lawyer O'Hagan (later Lord Chancellor) to risk his own future by supporting his co-religionists. The failure of science – outside medicine – was guaranteed by the timidity and guile of the hierarchy. In his fourth official Report – for 1857–58 – Newman highlighted the difficulties of Dr Lyons, struggling hopelessly to found a science faculty. The Report was not merely ignored: it 'disappeared'.[25]

As propaganda for science, Newman founded the *Atlantis* in 1857: but without support it faded away. The *Catholic University Gazette* was for a time more successful: but it depended on Newman. He 'wrote up' his own installation; supplied exclusives on his own Senates; attacked himself in anonymous letters. The hierarchy did nothing to support Newman's central institution of propaganda, the new University Church, a modest masterpiece by John Hungerford Pollen, built in an early Christian basilica style during 1855–56.[26]

Newman had a genius for selecting the best available men as lecturers; but a number of these were English and not welcome to Cullen; or if Irish, might be Fenians and not in love with the hierarchy. Nevertheless, Newman's foundation survived to become part of the National University of Ireland in 1908. By 1945, Dr D. J. Coffey, first President of University College Dublin (the heir of Newman's enterprise) could testify that Newman's intervention had given the Catholic struggle for university education 'a massive character'. The college's historian attests that Newman's twin ideal – a liberal education within a Catholic institution – provided a focus for reconciliation and debate. It did something towards Newman's avowed aim of increasing the political power of the Catholic Irish. From the beginning, the laity were given an intellectual authority new to Ireland: of Newman's twenty-three appointments, all were confirmed by the hierarchy; though only five of them were priests, and four of these taught only theology.[27]

But when Newman's resignation was at last accepted, at the end of 1858, the bishops ignored his plea to appoint Dr Moriarty in his stead, and chose Dr Woodlock, an opponent of any compromise with the Queen's Colleges. Not till 1879 was the remnant of Newman's idea reconciled with the state. Protestant intransigence, Catholic dogmatism, had an ally in Newman's own Englishness.

The voice of initiative, he was also the embodiment of incompatibility.

In 1854 Oxford was opened to Catholic undergraduates by the abolition of religious tests for BA degrees aside from theology. Newman's mind began to move beyond his 'idea of a University' towards a more specific and long-term strategy.

Like Mill, Arnold and other Victorian thinkers, he responded to the spirit of Carlyle's central challenge to writers, to evolve some way of combining greater fairness with greater efficiency. Fairness would never be achieved for Catholics in the British State, Newman decided, until they took their proper place in the heart of the British Establishment. His own days of usefulness in Ireland were at an end: 'I would rather do good to English Catholics in Oxford than in Dublin', he declared in 1856. At the same time, he began to look beyond the university altogether. Responsive to the arguments of radicals and nationalists in Ireland, he came to see that merely broadening the British Establishment slightly in order to grant access to higher education to a few well-heeled Catholics would not make society fairer or more efficient: 'A gentleman is an evil,' he conceded, '. . . The University is for gentlemen. It is then but a provision for perpetuating a recognised evil and nuisance.'[28]

Newman spent the rest of his life promoting this double strategy. He wanted Catholics to infiltrate the British Establishment: not principally for sectarian reasons, but because he sincerely believed that a 'stiffening' of Catholic moral commitment could help to make society more responsible. At the same time, he wanted to promote the growth of liberal and modern thinking throughout the Catholic Church. If possible – and it was a sizeable ambition – he wanted to help to turn the Church round from being a force for repression to being a great instrument for the divine mission of peaceful change.

Higher education and society

Newman had some qualities in common with Ruskin. In part, both men preferred the quiet life, but their high intelligence and sincerity, combined with a sense of duty derived from early Evangelical convictions which they never really abandoned, drew them inevitably into controversy. A gift for lecturing and for personal influence drew Ruskin away from water-colour drawing and the observation of natural form into highly publicised efforts to reconcile the elitist traditions of Oxford with the demand for justice being made by working-class trade union movements. Similarly, Newman was drawn from his life of prayer and teaching at Edgbaston into equally controversial efforts to reconcile Oxford traditions with new pressures in the Catholic Church – the only major church in the British state with a sizeable working-class following – for a more democratic Church and a greater degree of justice in the State. Because they saw beyond their 'home' subject-matter, Ruskin and Newman were branded as traitors by partisans of those subjects. England's most impassioned aesthete was accused of abandoning art; England's subtlest religious intelligence was condemned for 'minimistic' theology.

In fact, Ruskin and Newman, in their later years, were important precisely because they had outgrown partisanship, and began to formulate a synthesis for the future. Ruskin linked aesthetic and social concerns to generate a gospel of conservation. Newman linked Catholic theology to Protestant respect for conscience to generate a gospel of spiritual reconciliation.

For all his idealism, Newman was engaged in bringing a measure of realism to bear on two opposing fantasies. First, there was the Protestant and agnostic British fantasy which saw the Pope as a blasphemous tyrant whose every move had to be resisted. At Oxford, this had been expressed for centuries in the exclusion of Catholics. Till 1871, religious tests remained for higher degrees and for officials. Moreover, admission to a college remained the practical route to university matriculation: and college fellows (the majority of whom were Anglican clerics till 1882) were not eager to admit Catholics. Newman's University, on the other hand, had admitted Protestants, and even rewarded them with grants and prizes.

The fantasy of diehard Catholics was that any murmur against the Pope's authority or the uses to which it was put was damnable. His temporal power was seen as a sacred principle, his spiritual infallibility as the rider to his every utterance. The declaration of Papal Infallibility as a dogma in 1869 was in fact partly a reaction to the disappearance of the Pope's temporal power, which (outside the Vatican City) became a fact in 1870. The new State of Italy remained unrecognised by the Church, however, till after the First World War.

Newman's view was more realistic. Like all mediators, however, he was subject to misunderstanding. He had always regarded the Pope's temporal power as a secular contrivance, 'destined to fall'.[29] As for Infallibility, it was a reminder of Christ's promise that the spiritual power of Peter would not fail. Like faith itself, it provided security for freedom of thought and discussion among Catholics, in Newman's view. He wanted to see the Pope's spiritual authority made more convincing by becoming more responsive to the whole Church. Religion, for him, was inseparable from education. Repression was poison to both. Both were best engaged in by 'many minds working together freely . . . You cannot make men believe by force and repression.'[30] Among the movements that Newman welcomed was the greater openness among liberal Catholics to scientific ideas and scientific habits of inquiry.

The contemporary Pope – Pius IX – and many powerful ecclesiastical politicians were opposed to any such development. Their idea of education was summarised by agnostic opponents as 'spiritual terrorism',[31] the servitude of young minds to reactionary theologians. Newman's own criticism of these Catholic reactionaries was equally harsh. As late as 1882, and by then a Cardinal, he wrote that in education matters, 'They forbid, but they do not direct or create.'[32] He accused them of 'Nihilism'. They were effectively allies of anarchy and despair, with nothing constructive to offer the modern world.

In small but significant ways, Newman was able to bring a degree of common sense and mutual respect to bear on these opposing groups, the diehard Catholics and their Protestant and agnostic critics. He would live to see only the first signs of real improvement, which came when the reactionary Pius IX was succeeded by a Pope more in touch with the modern world.

However limited the success of Newman's Catholic University, his discourses on its behalf contributed to discussion at Oxford, and anticipated the pattern of reform. Oxford's failings had been exposed by the Royal Commission of 1850. Medicine, physical science, and jurisprudence were virtually wanting; classics had prestige but was taught too narrowly; theology, nominally supreme, was inadequately provided for. Newman's reputation among Anglicans was improved by the publication of his university discourses in 1852. It rose still further with the appearance of his autobiographical *Apologia* in 1864. Occasioned by an attack from the Evangelical Kingsley, it succeeded in creating new understanding between Protestants and Catholics, Christians and agnostics. Newman was seen by many as the obvious choice for a Catholic mission to Oxford. He had the support of many Catholic laypeople and some enlightened clerics. Unfortunately, this failed to persuade the reactionaries.

He was led to believe he might found an oratory, perhaps the nucleus of a college, in Oxford. Twice he negotiated for land there, and twice had to dispose of it because of opposition from his superiors. His mere presence in Oxford would naturally encourage Catholic students to matriculate. The senior Catholic hierarchy did not exactly outlaw such a development, but they wished to inhibit it. As in the case of the Catholic University, Newman was used as a 'fall guy', to raise funds for an institution he would never be allowed to control. He was disappointed, and so were his lay supporters, who withdrew their funds.

University education was for Newman merely the focus of a much broader campaign to 'open men's minds', particularly to new scientific concepts, as he had tried to do with the *Atlantis* magazine. From 1859 he became involved with the *Rambler*, a magazine propagating liberal Catholicism, inspired by new developments on the continent. 'Modern Society,' its editors declared, 'has developed no security for freedom, no instrument of progress, no means of arriving at truth which we look at with indifference or suspicion.'[33] In broad agreement with this view, Newman was briefly persuaded to edit the magazine, his most notable contribution being an article 'On Consulting the Faithful in matters of Doctrine'. Drawing on his research into fourth-century Arianism, he demonstrated that even Popes had stooped to heresy, and that the Church had more than once been rescued from error by enlightened laymen. Dr Brown, Bishop of Newport, delated the article to Rome as heretical. No official action was taken; eventually Dr Cullen was able to plead Newman's cause at Rome: but meanwhile Newman had stirred up prejudices, which may have contributed to the strong dissuasions against Catholic attendance at Protestant universities issued by the English hierarchy in 1864, and repeated by Pius IX in 1867. Newman clung to the fact that there was no absolute prohibition. But from 1865 his Archbishop was Dr Manning, zealot for the temporal power of the Papacy, and for the Pope's far from infallible disparagement of science. Manning's attempts to found a Catholic college in Kensington on Jesuitical lines were a complete failure: a further source of resentment against the 'disloyal' Newman. In 1867, the oratory school at Edgbaston, founded by Newman in 1859, was ordered to prepare no more boys for Oxford.

Pius IX died in 1878. In 1879 his successor Leo XIII made Newman a Cardinal. In 1882 lay supporters showed him Newman's letter[34] asking for action on university access for Catholic students. Leo had a personal interest in science and mathematics. He favoured Newman's request: but routine demanded reference to the wishes of Archbishop Manning. Eventually in 1893, three years after Newman's death, and one year after Manning's, Catholics were allowed to attend Protestant universities.

Notes

1 'Inaugural Address Delivered to the University of St. Andrews' (1867), *Collected Works*, XXI.257. 'reverence and duty': 249. psychology: 242.

2 Ruskin advocated a School of Agriculture, Inaugural Lecture, 1870: *Works*, XX.22. Unable to establish an effective Science Faculty, Newman assigned engineering to Arts: *Catholic University Reports*, p. xiv.

3 Non-Catholic students had access to places, grants and prizes but officers and professors had to be Catholic.

4 Inaugural Address at Edinburgh, 1866: *Critical and Miscellaneous Essays*, III. 562, 575, 579, 581.

5 *Collected Works*, XXI. 250–1.

6 *Works*, XXXIV. 529, n.

7 Robert I. Wilberforce (1802–57), second son of William Wilberforce, the slave emancipator (1759–1833), was received into the Roman Church in 1854. R. Hurrell Froude (1803–36), son of Archdeacon R. Froude, and brother to the scientist William Froude (1810–79), whose discussions with Newman helped to generate the *Grammar of Assent* (1870). John Keble (1792–1866), leading High Churchman, Oxford Professor of Poetry 1831–41. Helped Newman with the *Apologia* (1864).

8 Benjamin Jowett (1817–93), translator of Plato, son of Benjamin Jowett (d. 1859), statistical secretary to the Factory Reform movement, became Master of Balliol in 1870 and was Vice-Chancellor of Oxford 1882–86.

9 *Letters and Diaries*, II. 233.

10 *Life*, II. 380.

11 Edward Bouverie Pusey (1800–82), leading High Churchman, Professor of Hebrew at Oxford 1828–82.

12 Chadwick, *The Victorian Church*, I. 113–21.

13 Isaac Williams, a mild Tractarian, withdrew in favour of the Evangelical Garbett in 1842. Arnold succeeded Garbett in 1857.

14 Newman, *Fifteen Sermons*, p. 63.

15 Matthew 25: 15–28. 'Freewill Calvinism' approximates to the idea.

16 In the *Grammar of Assent* (p. 211) Newman notes that logic, which attempts to 'supersede the need of personal gifts' by 'rule' cannot attain to truth. There is no such thing as 'stereotyped humanity' (p. 224); in 'religious inquiry each of us can speak only for himself'. Catholic doctrine provides rules for the conduct of the Church as a Society. Verbal argumentation is inelastic, and the *words* of dogma are not a stereotype for the contents of an individual mind (pp. 295–300).

17 Note on Liberalism, *Apologia*, pp. 285–8.

18 Mill, *Collected Works*, I. 247.

19 Bruce L. Kinzer, 'John Stuart Mill and the Irish University Question', *Victorian Studies*, 31 (Autumn 1987), pp. 59–77.

20 *The Idea of a University*, pp. 343–61.

21 *Life*, I. 327.

22 *Catholic University Reports*, p. 435. Gross receipts from 9 September 1850 to 4 October 1855 amounted to £58,071, of which £27,616 was subscribed from Ireland, £16,244 from the USA and £4,166 from 'England, Scotland, etc.'. Of all this, £40,000 was invested in Government Stock.

23 *Ibid.*, pp. 3–56, 169–84.

24 Gerard Manley Hopkins (1844–89) was received by Newman into the Roman Church in 1866.

25 *Catholic University Reports*, p. xxxviii.

26 *Catholic University Reports*, p. 308. C. P. Curran, *Newman House and University Church*, Dublin, n.d. Ruskin recommended the basilica style on the same grounds as Newman – visibility and audibility – in *The Stones of Venice*, II (1853): *Works*, X. 446. Pollen, a Catholic convert, heard Newman preach at Oxford and worked with Benjamin Woodward, Ruskin's choice as architect of the University Museum.

27 McGrath, *Newman's University*, pp. 502–7.

28 *Life*, I. 628.

29 *Life*, I. 521.

30 *Life*, II. 49.

31 Kinzer, 'John Stuart Mill', p. 67.

32 *Life*, II. 486–7.

33 *Life*, I. 475, 505.

34 As above, n. 32.

Books

Paperbacks

Owen Chadwick, *Newman*, Oxford, 1983.

John Henry Newman, *The Idea of a University*, edited by Martin J. Svaglic, Notre Dame, Indiana, 1982.

John Henry Newman, *Essay on the Development of Christian Doctrine*, edited by J. M. Cameron, Harmondsworth, 1974.

Life

Ian Ker, *John Henry Newman, a biography*, Oxford, 1989.
John Henry Newman, *Apologia pro vita sua*, with an introduction by Philip Hughes, New York, 1989.
Henry Tristram, editor, *Autobiographical Writings of J. H. Newman*, New York, 1957 (includes 'Memorandum about my connection with the Catholic University').
Wilfrid Ward, *The Life of John Henry Cardinal Newman*, London, 1912.

Letters

The Letters and Diaries of John Henry Newman, edited by Charles Stephen Dessain, London, 1962–72; Oxford, 1973–.

Works

John Henry Newman, *Essay in Aid of a Grammar of Assent*, edited by Ian Ker, Oxford, 1985.
John Henry Newman, *Fifteen Sermons preached before the University of Oxford*, London, 1970.
John Henry Newman, *Historical Sketches*, 3 vols., London, 1872.
Henry Tristram, *The Idea of a Liberal Education*, London, 1952 (selections from Newman, with an introduction).

Background

Richard Brent, *Liberal Anglican Politics: Whiggery, religion and reform 1830–41*, Oxford, 1987.
Owen Chadwick, *The Victorian Church*, 2 volumes, 1966.
V. H. H. Green, *Religion at Oxford and Cambridge*, London, 1964.
Fergal McGrath, SJ, *Newman's University, Idea and Reality*, London, 1951.
My Campaign in Ireland, Part I (no more parts published): *Catholic University Reports and Other Papers* by Cardinal Newman of the Oratory, edited by W. P. Neville (printed for private circulation only), Aberdeen, 1896.
Gerald Parsons and James R. Moore, editors, *Religion in Victorian Britain*, 4 volumes, Manchester, 1989.

Criticism and commentary

A. Dwight Culler, *The Imperial Intellect: A Study of Newman's Educational Ideal*, New Haven, 1955.
Terence Kenney, *The Political Thought of John Henry Newman* (1957) Westport, Connecticut, 1974.
Nicholas Lash, *Newman on Development: the search for an explanation in history*, London, 1975.

CHAPTER SEVEN

Arnold's poetry:
a new beginning

Introduction

In his prose, Arnold constructed 'bridges' linking his English readers' imaginations with the traditions of the Continent, and Ireland,
with Islam and America, and the classical past; with their own
literary inheritance, and the spiritual vitality of a biblical tradition
which had become obscured under rival theologies. He made rhetorical pleas for an educated democracy which would have more
and more access to all these things; and for a state system of co-
operation and endowment to permit democracy to work.

In his prose, this campaign for openness and renewal seems,
however, to be countermanded by an apparent reaction against
many of the 'reforms' beloved of the liberal middle classes. The
whole tenor of his prose is directed to urging his contemporaries
to 'think again'. This is a useful task to perform in prose. But when
Arnold performs, roughly speaking, a similar task in verse, the
difference is enormous.

In Newman's 'idea' of a university, the circle of knowledge is
made up of many segments. Each segment has its own function,
and should not intrude on its neighbours. Presiding over all these
areas is the 'philosophic' or 'liberal' knowledge which deals with
the principles of and relationships between the departments of
knowledge. Arnold's prose works are like 'segments' of such a circle
of knowledge, though he provides far less than a complete circle.
He has some theology, some politics, some educational history and
theory. His major 'segment', which is literary criticism, is in danger
of overstepping its limits (something Newman warned against).
Arnold's habit of trying to make literary criticism do the work of
theology, ethics, even anthropological and political theory, would

141

have been regarded by Newman as symptomatic of the isolation and excess which the shared intellectual life of a University was intended to correct.

By contrast, when we turn to Arnold's poetry we find ourselves in the presence of something much more like that 'philosophic' overview of principles, the central human activity which generates 'liberal' knowledge, in Newman's scheme. The poetry is written by the light of Arnold's other knowledges, but it is also drawn from deep within himself. It is not, however, 'confessional' so much as something he chooses to publish as a conscious act. It nevertheless communicates with a directness and universality that make it altogether more catalytic than his argumentative prose. It provides, as Newman hoped liberal enquiry would provide, not a separate body of knowledge or a set of rules, but a means of cultivating personal gifts and exercising innate capacities.

If prose were all Arnold wrote, he would merely provide a revisionist coda to the Victorian literature of thought initiated by Carlyle. As a literary critic he could, and does, supply some insights into the literary quality of other Victorian thinkers. To a large extent, however, he is too close to his contemporaries to provide impressive criticism of them. T. S. Eliot called him a 'propagandist for criticism . . . a populariser rather than a creator'.[1] The same may be said of his propaganda for a highly civilised democracy. It is excellent propaganda.

Arnold's prose is valuable; but it is his poetry which really performs the task of inner renewal which his prose merely draws attention to. The poetry makes a new and fuller beginning. It gets to grips with the problem posed by the seminal work of the Victorian literature of thought: Carlyle's *Signs of the Times* of 1829. Tinkering with institutions, Carlyle warned, was no way to set free the 'dynamical nature of man'.[2] Changes in individuals would be needed.

In many detailed ways the antithesis of Carlyle, Arnold nevertheless shared with him this important motive of transforming the individual. This was in sharp contrast to Ruskin, Mr and Mrs Mill, and Newman. These four middle-class Londoners assailed the false values of mid-Victorian England in the thoroughly mid-Victorian spirit of the maverick entrepreneur: reminiscent of Palmerston's gun-boat diplomacy, not to say the Charge of the Light Brigade. Ruskin tilted single-handedly against classical political economy;

Mill seems to have thought the he could persuade the House of Commons to accept the 'Hare-brained scheme' of proportional representation. Newman – whom his friends likened to Julius Caesar – calmly accepted the resignations of the entire male staff of his Oratory School rather than withdraw his support from a matron of whom they disapproved. Harriet Taylor Mill refused to allow any man, even Mill, to tell her how, as a woman, she ought to think and feel.

All four of them shared a typically mid-Victorian belief that individual human character was something absolute that could never really be changed. Institutions did not exist for their own sake, but for the sake of all the individuals who belonged to them. In cases of difficulty it was more than likely the institution that needed reforming, not individual human beings who needed to be distorted to fit the institution. 'You cannot alter natures', said Ruskin. The right to pursue eccentricity is the core demand of the Mills' masterpiece *On Liberty*. 'I cannot avoid being sufficient for myself,' wrote Newman, 'for I cannot make myself anything else.'[3] Because of this shared conviction, they all tangled with institutions in order, as Ruskin put it, to promote 'great changes in society'.

For Carlyle, and for Arnold, though, the source of reform must lie in promoting transformations in the individual. Carlyle ends his *Signs of the Times* with this statement: 'To reform a world, to reform a nation, no wise man will undertake; and all but foolish men know, that the only solid, though a far slower reformation, is what each begins and perfects on *himself*.' As he became more Torified, Carlyle turned his doctrine of individual reformation into a case for submission: '*Be* thyself a man able to be governed', he wrote in *Latter-Day Pamphlets* (p.105). To get the spiritual attitude of humanity right is for Arnold, as well as for Carlyle, the key to peaceful change: 'Docile echoes of the eternal voice, pliant organs of the infinite will, such workers are going along with the essential movement of the world; and this is their strength and their happy and divine fortune.'[4]

Compared with the other four, Carlyle and Arnold are both strikingly conservative, in the sense that they regard the transformation of individual spiritual disposition as the priority for social reform. However, Carlyle tends to think that there will only ever be a very few 'best men', sent by God into the world to mould that world according to God's ordinance (uniquely revealed to themselves). A small elite or a single 'best man' have the right to compel the mindless multitudes. Arnold also believes in an elite, but in a special democratic sense. He wishes to encourage, as far as possible, every citizen to develop a 'best self', or inner awareness of the whole organism of society, and of ways in which he, as an individual, may contribute to this. Arnold thinks that a few people already exist at every level of society who can function in this way. He wants to see more, and the paradox 'elitism for all' perhaps best describes the direction of his thought. A chief source of disquiet for Carlyle was the suspicion that no worthy heroic individual would ever arrive to compel changes in society. Arnold's source of anxiety was the fear that there would never be enough 'best selves' to continue to sustain peaceful change as an inner dynamic, not merely of the individual, but of the social organism. Just as one must evoke an entity called 'the poem' to describe how all the qualities of words may come together to form a whole greater than the sum of the parts, so Arnold evoked an entity called 'the State' to suggest a similarly dynamic organisation of society.[5]

Carlyle, anticipating Arnold's poetic motivations, as far as they were conscious, wrote: 'unless poetic faculty means a higher-power of common understanding, I know not what it means. One must first make a *true* intellectual representation of a thing before any poetic interpretation that is true will supervene.'[6] It is his pursuit of such intellectual objectivity and (despite his dandyism) his true inner desire to express and promote a 'common understanding' that make Arnold's poetry a vehicle for peaceful change working at a deep level through individual minds. Just as he wanted each of his poems to present a 'total impression'[7] that was of the highest quality, and avoided the purple passage or glittering phrase that would detract from the effect of the whole, so also he wanted society to promote a life of the highest quality, in which each individual life would be sustained by, and help to sustain, the quality of that whole life to which it belonged. His poetry, which is a synthesis of both quality and awareness, prepares the individual consciousness of readers for participation in democracy, which for Arnold cannot survive without a citizenship qualified to belong to it.

All the great Victorian prose writers touch the individual consciousness, too. Mill is among these because of Harriet's effect upon him. Arnold, however, because he is a poet, and a good one, can touch and transform more deeply than any Victorian writer of prose.

With Arnold, the wheel comes full circle; and we are back again at the beginning, with Carlyle's challenge to the individual. The work of the mid-Victorian thinkers who come between Carlyle and Arnold, however, is among the reasons why Arnold's strategy for transforming the individual is more civilised and more demo-cratic than Carlyle's. The actual quality of that strategy, however, and its effectiveness, depend on Arnold's unique poetic talent.

It is in his poetry that Arnold engaged with the 'dynamical nature of man'. He evolved a new verse technique of spareness and reticence which permits the fullest engagement of the reader. He structured his poems so as to speak to the 'common understand-ing' of readers troubled by the collapse of Christian values and the incursions of a 'scientific' and (literally) 'valueless' view of history. He provides a harder alternative to the Catholicism which enabled Newman's convert Hopkins to fill his verse with predetermined meanings. Arnold's own verse is truly more innovative than that of Hopkins, for its spareness and metrical daring influenced Yeats and Eliot, and its effort to relate philosophical problems to contem-porary emotion anticipated Hardy. More than this, it provides an induction into habits of civilised democracy, rooted in compassion and alert to intellectual challenges.

By delaying the publication of *Dover Beach* till 1867, when it appeared together with *Thyrsis*, his elegy for his dead friend the poet Clough, Arnold transformed what may have begun as a private and fragmented lyric into one of the most powerful and universal poems of the Victorian era, whose metrical technique, strategy of allusion and dispassionate manipulation of persona anticipate *The Waste Land*.

Background

Arnold's background can be described partly in terms of its privi-lege, and partly in terms of certain literary and religious elements which helped to shape it. To these rather abstract factors there must be added the particular qualities, outlooks and characteristics of the people who helped to shape him. Together with his own emerging personality, these more specific details modify the broad pattern considerably. Central to the whole pattern, yet quite unpredictable from the rest of it, there is also the fact of his poetic talent.

Matthew Arnold had a father who was educated at Winchester, went on to Oxford and a fellowship there, became a public school headmaster and eventually Professor of Modern History at Oxford. His mother came from a long line of gentry and clergy. It could have been predicted that with moderate intelligence and application Matthew would get to Oxford and achieve some sort of middle-class career. In the true Victorian fashion he did what was expected of him. He achieved a fellowship at his father's college and later, through family influence, secured a post as secretary to Lord Lansdowne, President of the Privy Council, which was at that time in charge of education. In due course, Matthew moved on to a Schools Inspectorship, and became at last (in 1884) Chief Inspector of Schools.

Stated in outline, this career shows Arnold to have been privileged, and possessed of sufficient competence and energy to justify such privilege, at least to most members of his own class.

The picture becomes more interesting on closer acquaintance with some of its cultural aspects. Arnold's parents were both devout. Both wrote amateur verse. They ensured that literature and religion were implanted in Matthew simultaneously and from an early age. His father made him learn passages of the Bible by heart – not least the magnificent chapters of Isaiah which made up the Evening Lessons of the Church for Advent, the season of Matthew's birth. His mother made him recite *The Christian Year*, an Anglican cycle of poems by John Keble. Privilege and culture come together in the fact that Keble – later Professor of Poetry at Oxford – was actually Matthew's godfather. Equally advantageous was the fact that the Arnolds' 'off-duty' home in the Lake District became a centre for literary visitors, notably Wordsworth, the Poet Laureate. Such a background might be expected to produce professors of poetry: such as Matthew became at Oxford, and his brother Thomas (a Catholic convert) at Newman's university in Ireland.

The intertwining of culture and privilege, and of both with the Established Church, would provide many of the tensions running through Arnold's thought and writing in later life. His background comes still more into focus on asking 'what sort' of culture it was that nurtured him: religious and literary, but of what sort? It is here that there is a contradiction; for the undercurrent of all this privileged culture was a desire for reform.

Dr Arnold combined a view of the Church of England's function that went back to Reformation times with a doctrine of progress which was essentially that of the French Revolution. He wanted the endowed ('public') schools and the ancient universities to remain institutions of the Established Church, whose function it was to educate the people to supply the needs of the State. But at the same time he was convinced that profound changes were inevitable: 'there is nothing so unnatural or convulsive to society as the strain to keep things fixed, when all the world is by the very law of its creation in eternal progress'.[8] This was a widely shared type of dilemma between continuity and renewal. Dr Arnold subscribed to the not uncommon formula of his generation for peaceful change: institutions must be improved from within. The great question that remained, however, was: how far could the Church of England be improved? Dr Arnold's desire for change was restricted by his loyalty to a state church which had been formed and maintained in the interests of the landed classes. How could such a church, and the culture that belonged to it, be 'improved' so as to accommodate the new middle classes and the expanding working-class populations of the industrial towns? Along with Richard Whately and other Oriel 'intellectuals', Dr Arnold tried to argue for a 'broad church', more rational, more generous, less concerned with dogma and tradition. They came to represent a movement in the Church which won the limited approval of agnostic intellectuals like J. S. Mill. Newman however became convinced that a church shorn of essential doctrines while remaining tied to the State would merely become a propaganda weapon in the hands of a materialist and commercial tyranny 'liberal' only in name.

Unlike his brother Thomas, who followed Newman to Rome, Matthew would never reject the principle of a State Church. For him, as for his father, this principle would remain at the centre of the social, political and ecclesiastical problems that clustered round the theme of public education. While these concerns of his father's recur throughout Arnold's prose, his mother and his godfather Keble had a more formative influence on his poetry. They provided him with a pair of sometimes complementary, sometimes opposing responses to the traditions of the State Church.

His mother was nurtured in the Protestant Evangelical tradition which put enormous emphasis on the individual searching of conscience. In part a response of the established church to the success of Methodism among the 'lower' classes, it was perhaps inevitable that Evangelicalism, while being a force for gentlemanly reform in such areas as slave emancipation and factory regulation, should also have its slightly snobbish and narcissistic side: a certain complacency might be involved in an individual Evangelical's contemplation of his or her own special sensibility. Letters survive which provide evidence that Matthew's mother encouraged him in such a tendency, and in the writing of poetry which reflected it.

Keble, however, represented a Catholic movement in the Church of England which sought to meet the limitations of Evangelicalism. In clear, spare and elegant verse which Arnold never ceased to admire, his godfather celebrated the corporate life of the church, the duties of an elect priesthood, the traditional ceremonies and beliefs connected with the seasons of the year. Since Matthew's birthday was on Christmas Eve, it seems likely that Keble's poem for that stage of the Christian calendar would be familiar to him. This advocated setting aside the 'curious . . . maze' of individual introspection in order to listen to the 'inward music' of an ultimate Harmony with 'Love divine'.[9] Not anxious self-regard or ratiocination in pursuit of correct opinions but patience, modesty and reconciliation with others in a context wider than anything definable by human intellect – all those qualities which Matthew would summarise as 'sweetness and light' – were the principles of Keble's Anglo-Catholic position. To his mother's Evangelical individualism must be added this Anglo-Catholic insistence on the corporate. Later followers of Keble would be notable for work in inner-city parishes and for their commitment to forms of socialism. Matthew's social compassion, and desire to see the State take greater responsibility for its citizens are in line with this aspect of his upbringing.

Even more significantly, the tension between the Evangelical search for a faith credible to the individual intellect and the Anglo-Catholic celebration of a shared experience beyond verbal reasoning would be a major presence in Arnold's poetry.

The fourth contributor to Matthew Arnold's background of privileged, ambiguously reformist culture was Wordsworth, family

friend and major Romantic poet. At one time, he had been notable
for radical sympathies in politics and religion. Now he was a figure
of the Establishment. He wrote poems in favour of the Church of
England and capital punishment, to name only two themes
obnoxious to radicals. His Preface to *Lyrical Ballads* (1802) had
proclaimed that poetry was rooted in the life and language of the
peasantry. Yet here he was, like the Arnolds themselves, residing
in what was really a suburban villa set incongruously in the Lake
District.[10] What really was the poet's organic relation with his
society and environment? What was the difference between the
Arnolds and Wordsworths, in their Lakeland retreats, and the
horrid Manchester cotton manufacturers in theirs? Was 'culture'
justified, or even attainable? Must good poetry always be an alienated protest and poetry of celebration always be liable to seques-
tration by the vulgar? Affection, admiration, reverence for Wordsworth, and in a lesser degree the other Romantics, would always
be felt by Arnold. But a certain irony and detachment would be
appropriate too.

In 1843 Arnold, like Ruskin before him, achieved his first
public literary success by winning the Newdigate Prize for Poetry
at Oxford. The theme was chosen by the aggressively Protestant
Garbett, Keble's successor as Professor of Poetry. It was Carlyle's
own favourite: *Cromwell*. Arnold treated it in a radical new way,
almost freakish for its date in its spareness of rhythm and image
and (despite Garbett) introspective and desolating rather than celebratory of Cromwell's achievements. This success was typical of
Arnold's personal style in relation to his privileged upbringing. He
could conform outwardly when it suited him, and outclass the
opposition when he did so. At the same time, he subverted expectations by producing poetry that was not only technically innovative
but also curiously disturbing in its treatment even of familiar or (it
might have been expected) celebratory themes.

That same year, Wordsworth became Poet Laureate. The
older man went on to the nadir of his poetic career and the apex
of his social recognition with an 'Ode on the Installation of Prince
Albert as Chancellor of the University of Cambridge'. Whatever
Arnold wrote, it must never be such things as that. He was determined to draw on the deep sources of his own authentic inner
life, just as Wordsworth, when he was a great poet, had drawn on
his.

Making space for the reader

Arnold's *Cromwell* achieves some moments of uncanny power by meticulously deploying one persistent principle of versification. Just because it was an academic exercise written in cold blood for a prize, it provided a useful opportunity for Arnold to experiment with techniques which would enable him to reinvigorate English verse, and in so doing express important truths about himself and his age. Even in *Cromwell*, the techniques become very complex when examined in detail. Their shaping principle, however, could not be simpler. It is the same as the motto over Apollo's oracle at Delphi: 'Nothing in Excess'. In *Cromwell*, Arnold pursues this classical principle in an almost mannered way. In the volumes of poems he issued between 1849 and 1867, the principle would remain paramount, culminating in *Dover Beach*, not published till 1867, though written earlier. In that poem, Arnold anticipates the technique of *The Waste Land* by making space and silence work as hard as the words to construct the mood and meaning of the poem.

In *Cromwell* and other poems (including *Dover Beach*) Arnold uses the metre of Shakespeare's plays, of *Paradise Lost* and *The Prelude*. The reason for its frequent use is simply that it is the nearest to the sound-patterns and phrasing of everyday speech. It is a disciplined version of ordinary speech. As the reader or hearer gets used to expecting a regular rhythm of five stresses, each on the even syllables, the poem can begin to work its magic by subtly disappointing this expectation of regularity to provide all the nuances of shape and emphasis that build up the distinctive music and meaning of a particular poem. Arnold is so eager to avoid excess that he has a habit of producing 'pentameters' with fewer than five stresses when it suits his purpose, and he in any case avoids anything like melodramatic stress. By the same token, he avoids excess of adjective or vocabulary in general. The words he uses and the patterns in which he deploys them are always chosen to get the maximum effect from the minimum of *apparent* effort. Enormous actual effort has to be expended to achieve this effect, but in accordance with another classical principle – that art should 'hide' its own artfulness – Arnold never throws this effort into the reader's face. Comparison with other users of the iambic pentameter makes these qualities of Arnold's own blank verse particularly clear. The same qualities are equally apparent in his lyric verse: though here direct comparison is not so readily available. Rather than being lulled, or perhaps repelled, by the over-richness of more conventional Victorian poetry and art, the reader of Arnold is in suspense, wondering how to stretch what he is given into the conventional form he expects.

The overall effect of any given poem by Arnold might be described as providing a defined space or enclosure which the reader enters, as one entering a new element. The spare, reticent style, so near to ordinary speech, yet so absolutely distinct from ordinariness, can be disturbing, or consoling; but in any case it inducts the reader into a new kind of clarity.

Arnold was always interested in underwater images. As a child, he 'played' at being a corpse at the bottom of Windermere. His first great critical success came with *The Forsaken Merman*. In his notebooks he wrote: 'We are plunged at birth into a boundless sea: crystal clear, where all may be seen . . . You must plunge yourself down to the depths of the sea of intuition, all other men are trying as far as in them lies to keep you to the barren surface.'[11] Arnold's poetry provides for adults something familiar to the effect on children of reading Lewis Carroll's *Through the Looking Glass*. In both, the reader enters a strange new world which is nevertheless full of disturbing information about the ordinary world which it resembles, yet subverts. Avoiding the eye-catching phrase or the 'purple passage', Arnold's economic style aims at producing a 'total impression' in which to immerse the reader.

Arnold's style is one of metrical spareness and reticence, with a deliberate employment of space and silence, so that not only does every word work hard, but every pause and 'absence' of word or emphasis works equally hard. This technique of refinement and extreme economy may appear at odds with the kind of cluttered exuberance associated with a Victorian drawing room; and is certainly different from the lush atmospherics of Tennyson or the wordy virtuosity of Browning. While their genius created masterpieces by working *with* the sensibility of their age, Arnold's whole style is more obviously a challenge to the Victorian age. In this respect it is not at all like more typically ornate examples of Victorian high art like Holman Hunt's overloaded canvases or the endless elaboration of Manchester Town Hall; but it is very like

Ruskin's watercolours and Ruskin's expressed aesthetic preferences:

> 'Refinement in colour' is indeed a tautological expression, for colour,
> in the true sense of the word, does not exist until it *is* refined . . .
> In every touch laid on canvas, if one grain of the colour is inoperative
> and does not take its full part in producing the hue, the hue will
> be imperfect. The grain of colour which does not work is dead . . .
> The art of painting . . . consists in laying on the least possible colour
> that will produce the required result. . . . THE FINER THE EYE
> FOR COLOUR, THE LESS IT WILL REQUIRE TO GRATIFY
> IT INTENSELY. But that little must be supremely good and pure,
> as the finest notes of a great singer, which are so near to silence.
> And a great colourist will make even the absence of colour lovely,
> as the fading of the perfect voice makes silence sacred. (*Works*, XVI.
> 419, 24)

This aesthetic of reticence, refinement and absence character-
ises Ruskin's private drawings as much as it does Arnold's poems.
Aesthetically concerned to 'tone down' the lushness of Keats (and
thus following an opposite course from Hopkins), Ruskin and
Arnold, in their metaphysical and social thinking, nevertheless
show a desire to relate the insights of Keats to the problematic
Victorian world. Very conscious of the difficulty of maintaining the
position described by Keats as 'Negative Capability', they both
explore the possibility 'of being in uncertainties, Mysteries, doubts,
without any irritable reaching after fact and reason'. Ruskin attained
this condition occasionally without remaining in it. Much of
Arnold's poetry is dedicated to developing a capacity for remaining
in it long enough to deepen the reader's sensibility. As with Ruskin,
there is a correlation between Arnold's aesthetic and metaphysical
capacity for 'Mysteries' and his political orientation, the spirit of
which he shares with Keats: 'Man should not dispute or assert but
whisper results to his neighbour, and thus by every germ of Spirit
sucking the Sap from mould ethereal. . . . Humanity instead of
being a wide heath of Furse and Briars with here or there a remote
Oak or Pine, would become a great democracy of Forest Trees.'[12]

In a transitional age, when so many things were becoming
more and more uncertain, people looked to art for reassurance.
They liked a sense of secure horizons closed by moral meanings
and happy endings. Arnold's spare and open style, which often
left to the reader the task of constructing his own conclusions or

affirmations, in the spaces left open by Arnold, could be disturbing to some, though a blessed relief to others.

Whereas Arnold shared Ruskin's aesthetic and moral excitement about the democratic possibilities for new and positive development that might grow out of the breaking down of old and rigid rules and expectations, he was also haunted by Carlyle's historically-based scepticism. Democracy – apart from a brief period in Athens, when the term applied only to free males, not women or slaves – had never actually worked in human history. The new democracy of the Northern States of the USA – the Southern ones were slave states – seemed to be governed only by money and money-values. In Europe, old faiths and dynasties had collapsed, with little sign of renewal. In such a context, it is understandable that Arnold should share Carlyle's scepticism about democracy, and his sense of the awesome consequences of the collapse of man's ability to generate meaning out of history. Silence, absence of certainty, and a general state of 'not knowing' were seen by Carlyle as a terrible punishment and obligation rather than as a source of opportunity.

This dark sense of speechlessness before history would be of major importance in Arnold's poems. As the son of a Christian historian, Arnold was raised to see God's finger in history; but in his own poetry disturbing mysteries or bleakness and alienation are more noticeable than any benign Providence. Of 'all Bibles the frightfulest to disbelieve in', wrote Carlyle, 'is this "Bible of Universal History" . . . such infidelity you would punish . . . by the most peremptory order, to hold its peace till it got something wiser to say. Why should the blessed Silence be broken into noises, to communicate only the like of this?'[13] While the spaces and silences of Arnold's poems are in part a positive inducement, giving the reader room to expand and deepen his own awareness, they are also in part a reflection of this Victorian bewilderment before a history which no longer offers meaning.

Silence may provide an intensely gratifying opportunity for the audience to make their own creative participations along the lines of Ruskin's aesthetic of painting.

It may be a bleakly chastening device, repulsing optimistic clichés, along the lines of Carlyle's metaphysic of history. What it certainly is, is an opportunity for the audience to think, and reach their own conclusions. This didactic possibility of a technique of silence Arnold may have learned from attending Newman's sermons in Oxford. An observer described Newman's style of delivery: 'Each . . . short paragraph was spoken rapidly, but with great clearness . . . and then at its close there was a pause, lasting for nearly half a minute.'[14] Clearly, the silent reflections of the congregation were as much a part of the sermon as Newman's own words. The authority which Newman thus desired to address and enlist was the authority of the individual and corporate conscience – which was for him the prime source of revelation and meaning. No philosophy of history, or observation of the natural world, could provide meaning or sufficient grounds for faith. It was after he had become a devout Catholic that Newman wrote:

> If I looked into a mirror, and did not see my face, I should have the sort of feeling which actually comes upon me, when I look into this living busy world, and see no reflexion of its creator . . . Were it not for this voice, speaking so clearly in my conscience and my heart, I should be an atheist, or a pantheist or a polytheist when I looked into the world.[15]

Such bleakness was well known to Arnold. In his *Dream of Gerontius*, which shares Arnold's spareness of expression, Newman gives the theological definition of this condition of silence. Gerontius, in death, is momentarily cut off from all meaning. He enters the ambiguous, ultimately horrific, state of limbo:

> Ah! whence is this? What is this severance?
> This silence pours a solitariness
> Into the very essence of my soul;
> And the deep rest, so soothing and so sweet,
> Hath something too of sternness and of pain,
> For it drives back my thoughts upon their spring
> By a strange introversion, and perforce
> I now begin to feed upon myself,
> Because I have nought else to feed upon.
>
> *Dream of Gerontius*, ll. 185–93

For Hopkins, as for Newman, there was no escape from this 'strange introversion' except into the fullness of Catholic doctrine and tradition. Gerontius, like the persona of *The Waste Land*, has reached a point where disintegration or faith must follow. In his personal life, Arnold, like Eliot, found more and more solace in Anglo-Catholicism. But unlike Eliot, he did not explore this solace in his poetry, but largely ceased to write it. His last 'new' volume of 1867 contained pieces written or even published long before.

His verse therefore provides an enlightening contrast to that of Hopkins. There is a necessary connection between Arnold's spareness and his (poetic) refusal to embrace an elaborated system of faith; just as there is between Hopkins's fullness and the rich evidence he finds for his own systematic faith. In finding such external evidence, Hopkins is of course absolutely different not only from Arnold but from Newman himself.

Some short quotations might exemplify how Arnold's space and spareness may evoke not only physical phenomena like vision and sound, and landscape, but also the sort of desolate 'strange introversion' of a mind that will not pretend to see external evidence for inner meaning where no such evidence is visible.

Keats's *Endymion* is full of swirling processions elaborately 'realised' in words. Arnold conveys more in fewer words:

> Faster, faster,
> O Circe, Goddess,
> Let the wild, thronging train,
> The bright procession
> Of eddying forms,
> Sweep through my soul!

The Strayed Reveller, ll. 1–6

If the rhythm of the lines is given space to 'breathe' in our consciousness, the effect is rich and vivid. The reader has to work.

An example of the evocation of sound:

> Come away, away children.
> Come children, come down.
> The hoarse wind blows colder;
> Lights shine in the town.
> She will start from her slumber
> When gusts shake the door;
> She will hear the winds howling,
> Will hear the waves roar.

The Forsaken Merman, ll. 108–15

Again, the reader will hear everything that is necessary if he allows himself to do so.

Here is a piece of landscape which also evokes the idea of the pilgrimage of life:

> PAUSANIAS
> The noon is hot; when we have cross'd the stream
> We shall have left the woody tract, and come
> Upon the open shoulder of the hill.

> See how the giant spires of yellow bloom
> Of the sun-loving gentian, in the heat,
> Are shining on those naked slopes like flame!
> Let us rest here; and now, Empedocles,
> Pantheia's history.

Empedocles on Etna, I, ii, ll. 1–8

'Pantheia' is the goddess whose myth gives meaning to natural phenomena: the classical source of Wordsworthian Pantheism. Empedocles the philosopher refuses to give his friend the comfort of myth:

> Spells? Mistrust them.
> Mind is the spell which governs earth and heaven.
> Man has a mind with which to plan his safety;
> Know that, and help thyself.

ll. 26–9

The spareness, and the refusal of mythic guides to the pilgrimage of life, are both in sharp contrast to Hopkins's sonnet which raises similar questions. Both pieces are in the same metre:

> The world is charged with the grandeur of God.
> It will flame out, like shining from shook foil;
> It gathers to a greatness, like the ooze of oil
> Crushed. Why do men then now not reck his rod?
> Generations have trod, have trod, have trod;
> And all is seared with trade; bleared, smeared with toil;
> And wears man's smudge and shares man's smell: the soil
> Is bare now, nor can foot feel, being shod.

God's Grandeur, ll 1–8

Hopkins turns to his own mythic guide:

> Oh, morning, at the brown brink eastward, springs –
> Because the Holy Ghost over the bent
> World broods with warm breast and with ah! bright wings.

ll. 12–14

Whatever his personal beliefs, such a 'solution' would embarrass Arnold in his poetic stance. Equally embarrassing would be Hopkins's evocation of the stars, so filled with faith that even 'elves' are welcome to join the celebration:

> Look at the stars! look, look up at the skies!
> O look at all the fire-folk sitting in the air!
> The bright boroughs, the circle-citadels there!
> Down in dim woods the diamond delves! the elves'-eyes!

The Starlight Night, ll. 1–4

Arnold's picture requires more co-operation from the reader:

The thoughts that rain their steady glow
Like stars on life's cold sea,
Which others know, or say they know –
They never shone for me.

Thoughts light, like gleams, my spirit's sky,
But they will not remain.
They light me once, they hurry by,
And never come again.

Despondency

Addressing the readership:
Arnold's democratic strategy

Twenty years younger than Arnold, and virtually unknown as a poet, Hopkins was doubly fenced around by the privacy of his poetic output (virtually unpublished in his lifetime) and by the return to traditionalist attitudes which characterised the harsher political and international climate during the period of his output.[16] Hopkins belonged to a time when it was regarded as intellectually permissible to argue *from* first principles: to make moral and metaphysical assumptions, and argue from those. Arnold, on the other hand, was writing poetry just as Mill's *Logic* – with its 'liberal' insistence on empirical induction – was coming into fashion. Intellectually nothing could be assumed; everything had to be based on empirical observation. Just like Newman, Arnold was aware that no convincing system of belief could be founded solely on empirical observation. Just like Mill and Newman (who learnt his logic from Whately, who shared Mill's basic approach), Arnold rooted his thinking in his own consciousness. But he found different things in that consciousness than Mill or Newman did. For Mill, moral conscience had to be constructed by reason dealing with observed experience. For Newman, conscience was primary. It could become the nurturer of right reason: but by the same token, a religious 'conscience' which tried to *dictate* to reason was no true conscience at all. For Hopkins, the act of faith was like going through a door into a safe haven within which emotions and fancies could be consecrated to God: reason almost ceased to count. An agnostic like Mill might have said that Hopkins allowed his religious 'conscience' to dictate to his reason (something Newman would never do).

Arnold's position was the most vulnerable of all. He was exposed from without and from within. The son of a famous father, a public servant, Professor, and published poet, he was inwardly exposed to two awesome challenges: the Evangelical conscience *and* the intellectual demand for an empirical process of reasoning rooted in observation: Mill's scientific logic, which could never supply the *grounds* of conscience. In exploring his *personal* outlook, Arnold often relied on intuition – something Mill regarded as degrading – in order to resolve this dilemma. In his poetry, which he regarded as in some measure a public act, he rarely allowed himself this luxury. Poems like *Obermann Once More* or the *Grande Chartreuse* may be said to be founded on the intuition that solutions will one day be found by others: but Arnold is scrupulous not to parade his own personal intuitions or private convictions in his poetry. His is not a 'confessional' type of poetry in this sense. Even when he began to 'solve' his personal religious crisis by practising Anglo-Catholicism, he did not consider that this absolved him from the duty of reinterpreting scripture and doctrine for his own age. This task (a Protestant version of Newman's campaign for liberal thought within the Catholic Church) Arnold pursued in his later prose.

His poetic stance – which is different from what he may 'really' have felt or thought – is in part that of an empiricist and (lapsed) Evangelical who is seeking the sort of harmonious reconciliations and certainties, beyond words, which have been characteristic of the Catholic tradition and may be characteristic of some future tradition which has not yet arrived.

An even more primal function of his poetry, however, is to provide an enclosure of verse within which the consciousnesses of poet and reader may be open to all the disturbing considerations which assail them at unguarded moments. In a number of poems – notably *Dover Beach* – the reader is invited to look over the ramparts of this enclosure towards some oceanic commitment to the elemental reconciliations characteristic of love poetry or religious verse. Arnold's own poems are not exactly in either category, and offer nothing that absolutely compels either emotional or spiritual commitment. They clear the way, and even invite, towards such commitment, but the final choice is left with the reader. What Arnold is not doing is displaying his own personal emotions or private thoughts; and what he never allows is easy solutions. The reader has to be both attentive to Arnold and open to his own thoughts and feelings. He needs to make some positive effort to generate from the poem a meaning that will satisfy the intelligence. Much easier to discover, unless we allow intellectuality to shut it out, is the civilised (rather than merely personal) emotion of compassion present in Arnold's poetry. To the critical mind, the technical power of Arnold is always apparent. Different minds – or aspects of mind – are most fruitfully engaged, however, when they are drawn together into a balanced and unhurried meditation of the poem. Many minds, working together, are unlikely to exhaust the complexity below Arnold's surface. Yet Arnold's apparent simplicity and sincerity are also real: the primal emotions he works with are not negated by his fine technique, or the intellectual context he brings to our attention.

This process can be linked to Arnold's view of democracy. Often, poems deal with situations which call for compassion. A humane but uncomplicated mind can respond to this emotion without necessarily troubling to make technical explorations. A more 'sophisticated' mind may be wary of emotion, and prefer to exercise itself by analysing Arnold's fine technique. As different types of mind – or the same mind in different moods – explore the poem, the 'simple and emotional' will discover that closer reading enriches and broadens the emotive appeal very considerably. The 'sophisticated', on the other hand, will find that Arnold's technical brilliance leaves no escape from the poem's emotive demands. Reading an Arnold poem, therefore, can reconcile persons to each other and themselves, and provide an education in right feeling and thinking. Technical 'appreciation' and emotive 'response' centre on the quest for a new intelligence that goes deeper than either, and which is capable of generating the kinds of affirmation Arnold seeks. In this way, the reading of the poem is an induction into Arnold's criteria for a civilised democracy. His hopes for the American democracy, reunited after civil war, are relevant here:

> When American intellect has not only broken, as it is breaking, the leading strings of England, but has also learnt to assimilate independently the intellect of France and Germany and the ancient

world as well as of England, then, and not till then, may the spiritual construction of an American be a 'many-gated temple'.[17]

Arnold's poems relate to each other, but he did not create 'books' of interanimated poems – each inadequate without the others – as Yeats did, or one multi-styled epic like Whitman. Each Arnold poem is its own fortress of concentrated sensibility. Comparisons between poems are useful, but each poem is distinct. If the volumes of Yeats speak as a series of elite concourses, and Whitman's volume spreads and achieves itself like a democratic banner, each of Arnold's poems is a 'bridgehead' into new territory, an area within whose cool domain many of the concerns of other Victorian writers are lucently apparent; a refuge from which to observe Arnold's period and some of our own still unacknowledged inner life. 'No single literature is adequately comprehended except in its relation to other events', said Professor Arnold.[18] Not with the 'superficial affectations' of Arnold's prose, but with masterly appearance of helplessness, within the citadel of verse, Matthew Arnold releases those 'movements of the imagination' at variance, for him as for Wordsworth, with 'the proceedings of the middle and upper classes among us'.[19]

Each poem of the mature Arnold is a bridgehead for the recovery of the English soul from the kind of (Clough's word) 'factitious' effectiveness of English education at all levels.[20] Arnold's poetic style makes a space for the reader. He does not tell the reader how to occupy that space. Nevertheless, there is at work in his poetry a subtle strategy that promotes the kind of intellectual and emotional awareness he saw as necessary to democracy. Each reader is likely to become aware of much that is new to him. Occupying for himself the space that exists within this strange new environment, the Victorian reader, particularly, must have felt that an old structure was being eroded, and a more primal atmosphere was becoming apparent in the spaces beyond it. Beneath the eroding label of the tribe, 'know your place', a more disquieting and energising manifesto was emerging: 'know yourself'.

Arnold's poems are carefully constructed. Readers are not able to lose themselves in them. Yet neither are rhetorical demands made requiring a particular response or the adoption of a particular set of values. Their verse economy is like a new element within which the pressures of a world outside the poem can be experi-

enced at a distance that makes them informative rather than inhi-
biting. Images of water frequently enhance this sense of difference,
yet connection. Remembering Arnold's pet-name of 'Crab', one
might resort to an out-of-the-water image to suggest the strategic
relation of the verse to other forms of thought and activity, including Arnold's own prose. If the technical nuances of the verse
provide rock pools of transformative reflection and danger, each
poem in aggregate is also a bridgehead of rescue or capture to
bring us beyond the borderland we enter if we engage with it. We
have to choose to enter the poems and to co-operate with what we
find there; but there is always an implied route our imaginations
are free to pass on to as we leave them. *The Strayed Reveller* or
the *Grande Chartreuse*, for instance, both disclose oases of reflection; forbid wallowing; but refuse to preach directives. Not even
an imperative emotional poem like *Longing* ('Come to me in my
dreams . . .') is an exercise in persuasion. It is rather the statement
of a general need; implying, not that someone should dab Arnold's
forehead with eau-de-Cologne, or assimilate his prose ideas, but
that all might be more sensitive to the needs of others. If we enter
the 'bridgehead' of such a poem, we can also investigate beyond
it, along an implied line of thought and feeling: deeper into Arnold,
ourselves and others. Hints for the conduct of the journey may be
derived from his prose only if we wish.

An example: reading *Dover Beach*

Dover Beach

The sea is calm to-night,
The tide is full, the moon lies fair
Upon the Straits; – on the French coast, the light
Gleams, and is gone; the cliffs of England stand,
Glimmering and vast, out in the tranquil bay.   5
Come to the window, sweet is the night air!
Only, from the long line of spray
Where the ebb meets the moon-blanch'd sand,
Listen! you hear the grating roar
Of pebbles which the waves suck back, and fling,   10
At their return, up the high strand,
Begin, and cease, and then again begin,
With tremulous cadence slow, and bring
The eternal note of sadness in.

Sophocles long ago   15
Heard it on the Aegean, and it brought
Into his mind the turbid ebb and flow
Of human misery; we
Find also in the sound a thought,
Hearing it by this distant northern sea.

The sea of faith
Was once, too, at the full, and round earth's shore
Lay like the folds of a bright girdle furl'd;
But now I only hear
Its melancholy, long, withdrawing roar,   25
Retreating to the breath
Of the night-wind down the vast edges drear
And naked shingles of the world.

Ah, love, let us be true
To one another! for the world, which seems   30
To lie before us like a land of dreams,
So various, so beautiful, so new,
Hath really neither joy, nor love, nor light,
Nor certitude, nor peace, nor help for pain;
And we are here as on a darkling plain   35
Swept with confused alarms of struggle and flight,
Where ignorant armies clash by night.

In his essay on 'The Study of Poetry', Arnold claims that 'the best poetry will be found to have a power of forming, sustaining and delighting us, as nothing else can'. In poetry, he writes, 'which is thought and art in one, it is the glory, the eternal honour, that charlatanism shall find no entrance'. Thus, poetry's power to renew the individual consciousness has also a potential for guarding society from the manipulations of that consciousness by various forms of vested interest. The study of poetry, often regarded as an elitist activity, is therefore in fact one of the surest safeguards of democracy. He warns, however, that mere emotive response to poetry, based on the 'personal estimate', will not get us very far, and will eventually betray us. On the other hand, the 'historical estimate', which seeks to learn about a 'poet's life and historical relationships' will degenerate into 'literary dilettantism' unless it retains a sense of its ultimate purpose: which is to support, but never distract from, the ability to 'feel and enjoy . . . as deeply as ever we can', work that belongs 'to the class of the very best'.[21]

In making a case for his own poetry, he is anxious to argue for the 'total impression' rather than 'single lines and passages'. He insists always on the need for familiarity with the classics, especially Greek tragedy; and he is anxious to 'transmit' to future generations 'the practice of Poetry, with its boundaries and wholesome regulative laws under which excellent work may again, perhaps, at some future time, be produced'.[22]

With these warnings in mind, let us see what happens when we read *Dover Beach*.

Dover Beach was begun during the summer of the Great Exhibition, in 1851, when Arnold and his wife visited Dover on their honeymoon, but it was not published till 1867, when it appeared with *Thyrsis*, Arnold's elegy for Clough, and other poems.

Clearly, Arnold drew on his own experience to write the poem, and readers are free to draw on Arnold's biography to help them to read it. Nevertheless, the poem speaks for itself. It is not autobiography. Thus, if we identify a certain emotional timidity in the poem, we do not have to distort our response by imagining that this timidity is something Arnold is insisting on as a personal characteristic of his own for which he demands our respect. Speculation *in vacuo* about Arnold's 'real' character will not illuminate our reading. On the other hand, objective accounts by observers *can*, if used with discrimination, help to get into focus how the *poem* works. Once we know that an American observer saw Arnold as an 'educated brick-layer – spokesman of a strikers' delegation',[23] we shall be released from the trap of confusing Arnold's evocation of mood in *Dover Beach* with an attempt at objective self-portraiture. If we have read Clough's masterpiece *Amours de Voyage*, first published in 1858 in the *Atlantic Monthly*, we shall have encountered the concept of a poet's using a hypersensitive persona as a means of exploring aspects of human feeling. If we further recognise that the persona of *Dover Beach* has things in common with Eliot's Prufrock, this is another helpful way of avoiding confusion. Eliot is not Prufrock: nor 'is' Arnold the persona of *Dover Beach*. In both poems, however, the persona embodies feelings common to Arnold, Eliot, and the rest of humanity.

The fact that *Dover Beach* was published as part of a volume permits us to draw on that volume to illuminate *Dover Beach*. But the poem's own integrity must not be infringed by unwarranted importation of moods and ideas from other poems.

In dealing with the allusions in the poem, a similar discrimination and balance are required. The only human being mentioned by name is Sophocles. Given Arnold's deep interest in Sophocles, it is likely to be true that the more we know about Sophocles, the more we shall unlock the mysteries of the poem. Wispy fantasies about Sophocles are unlikely to be helpful, however: and so are pedantic attempts to turn the whole poem into a footnote to Sophocles.

When approaching less clearly signalled allusions, we are entitled to develop and check our response by drawing on objective information. But the poem is not an encyclopaedia: nor, on the other hand, will *any* fantasy we care to import necessarily be of interest to anyone but ourselves. Thus, if we 'spot' the 'ignorant armies' that 'clash by night' at the end of the poem as implying (among other things) a reference to the defeat of the Athenian democracy in the western land of Sicily – a defeat which destroyed democracy until its reappearance in modern times – this may be useful to us. If we happen to know that the account of this epochal night battle is given in the histories of Thucydides, of which Arnold's father supplied a standard edition, so much the better. We might even know, from reading Clough's poem *The Bothie*,[24] that Arnold's friend shared his interest in this historical catastrophe. None of this information should distort our reading of the poem, however. Arnold is not parading his classical knowledge in order to alienate the reader, only hinting at it in case the reader cares to make use of the hint to enrich his reading.

Not even a cultural propagandist of Arnold's determination could have dared to hope that Sophocles would be reborn – in this century – as a dramatist filling theatres all over the world; or that Thucydides would become widely available in paperback translations. If we have read Arnold's sonnet *To a Friend*, we know that he was particularly drawn to Sophocles's last play, *Oedipus at Colonus*. The Penguin introduction will tell us that this last play, with its memorable chorus likening human life to a high strand besieged by the sea, was first staged after the dramatist's death and the defeat of Athens. It is our choice whether we regard Arnold's classical 'references' as fossils of a defunct elitism or seeds for the flowering of a more accessible cultural life.

Single adjectives may work in the same way: but caution is required here. Arnold's persona stands on a 'darkling' plain. This strange adjectival form is chosen for its own sake. Arnold does not demand that we remember Keats's *Ode to a Nightingale*, where it is memorably used:

> Darkling I listen; and, for many a time
> I have been half in love with easeful Death

vi. 1–2

What the reader does with his memory of the Keats poem is his own business. On the one hand, the memory provides a poignant insight into the way the egotistical Romantic sensibility is being swept away by harsher new realities. On the other hand, the same memory may reconcile us to the stoicism of Arnold's own stance, and help to throw into relief, and to motivate, the almost inaudible, yet impassioned, cry to another human being made in Arnold's poem:

> Ah, love, let us be true
> To one another!

We may be able to respond to this quite directly, and thus to enter the heart of the poem without needing to puzzle over it. But the chances are that we may be just sufficiently skilled at reading to detect the feebleness and uncertainty of these lines, without being able to account for such a 'failure', or being at all sure whether the failure is ours, or Arnold's, or is atrributable to some deeper source. If we estimate that the poem is not a confessional outpouring designed to make us cry, what is it? A cynical parody to be read with a smirk and tossed aside?

Looking again at *Dover Beach*, with eyes and ears beginning to become familiar with its rhythms and hints at meaning, we may find ourselves excited, yet disturbed, by this supreme example of Arnold's poetic habit of deploying space – many of the lines fall far short of the five stresses we have learned to expect – and we may begin to try to use the hints of meaning which he gives us in an attempt to generate some way of resolving the poem. Having become more deeply drawn into Arnold's 'bridgehead', we may begin to feel a certain bleakness and oppressiveness, like someone trapped in a labyrinth. Is there no comfort in it at all? Is there any way out? Can we resolve the structure of the poem sufficiently to find some comfort in it, and at least some gate of exit? We do not need to establish that the poem is a complete model of culture as defined by Arnold in America – 'a many-gated temple' – but it is only human to seek some spiritual consolation, and some sense of access and withdrawal, or the poem will become a trap: formless and meaningless.

Distracted by the Romantic 'clue' of Keat's 'darkling', we may have entered a dead end. Perhaps the 'historical estimate' can come to the aid of the 'personal estimate'. Bewildered as we may be by our own latent romanticism and unexamined post-modernist cynicism, we might seek consolation from the Victorians.

Our world is in many ways even more mechanical, more agnostic and bewildered than the world Arnold was addressing. If we have time to consider this, we may find that we want to echo Charles Darwin's lament for the loss of his ability to respond to poetry: 'My mind has become a kind of machine . . . but why this should have caused the atrophy of that part of the brain alone, on which the higher tastes depend, I cannot conceive . . . The loss of these tastes is a loss of happiness . . . enfeebling the emotional part of our nature.'[25] This kind of testimony may take us a little beyond mere emotion, or merely pedantic 'historical explanations', for it is a personal testimony. Looking at other poems in the Arnold volume of 1867, we may find that Darwin's condition has been confronted by Arnold in *Growing Old*, which tells of a Victorian condition of feeling 'but half, and feebly, what we feel . . . But no emotion – none' (27, 30).

Victorian intellectuals can enhance our appreciation of the cultural context of *Dover Beach*, and of the aesthetic means by which Arnold depicts and confronts Victorian difficulties of thought and feeling. Carlyle can remind us of the 'silence' enforced on thinkers in the face of a meaningless history populated by 'ignorant armies'. Newman can identify the 'silence' to which even Christians were reduced by the ebbing of the 'sea of faith'. Ruskin can tell us how an aesthetic of reticence, absence and refinement, such as is exemplified in *Dover Beach*, can at least permit the structuring of some kind of response to the Victorian condition. Victorian imaginative writers are even more helpful. If we have read *Middlemarch* or *Villette* or Clough's *Amours de Voyage*, we know that many writers shared Arnold's sense that personal commitment was almost impossibly difficult, and the achievement of any human contact and sympathy was correspondingly valued more highly, perhaps, than ever before.

Victorian literature can thus help us to sympathise with the situation described in *Dover Beach*, and so enable us to find positive qualities and values within the poem. We need no longer be trapped within our own unconsidered modern assumptions. But while feeling more kindly disposed to Arnold's poem, we may still feel trapped within it. We may feel only futility, and not vital expectancy in a line like:

> Begin, and cease, and then again begin

In his Preface to his *Poems* of 1853, Arnold identifies two kinds of dilettanti, those who care only for 'spirituality and feeling' and those who care only for 'the indispensable mechanical part'. He reiterates his commitment to the spirit of Greek tragedy, and his determination to continue the technical 'practice of Poetry' for the sake of the future.[26]

Perhaps if we set aside the dilettantism of 'spirituality and feeling' for a moment, and confront this apparently repellent central paradox of Arnold's thought, we may find that what seems an insuperable barrier is really a gate that offers a way out of our dilemma. We may need help for this, which is always embarrassing, but we are not alone in the world, and have only to ask.

A Dryasdust classical scholar could tell us, for example, that the precedent for Arnold's truncated lines is to be found in the *Oedipus at Colonus*, where Sophocles avails himself of one of the advantages of having strict rules, which is to break them for unique effect. The truncated iambic line in the following passage is an extremely rare thing in Greek tragedy:

> Since even God accommodates Himself,
> Showing restraint in all He does, so father,
> Make room for compromise: my sins must be
> More than enough for your forgiveness, surely?
> > Why silence?[27]
> Say something, father! Don't abandon me!

> (1167–72)

Immediately before this scene comes a passage for the chorus, and the 'thought' Arnold found in the play:

> this wretched person here, not I alone, just as some high strand all open to the cold, wave-battered, wintry, is tumultuously tumbled, so this person, too, the direful strokes of misery harass, and persistently haunt, breaking like waves over him, forever: some from the setting of the sun; some from the quarter of the dawn; some from the noon time; some from the northern Night. (1239–48)

That was the sea of Greek tragedy 'at the full'. No more high tragedy would be possible till Renaissance times:

> The sea of faith
> Was once, too, at the full . . .

Neither tragedy nor faith is possible in Arnold's world. Arnold's evocation of the sound-patterns of Sophocles reduces them to an infinite distance. But Arnold has planned his poem in such a way that even a pedantic literary dilettante, pursuing 'references' and metrical precedents, cannot escape the primal emotions of the volume of 1867. Arnold's difficulties with his father, and his guilt[28] and desolation over his early death, perhaps the major trauma of his life, are set out in acceptable Victorian form in *Rugby Chapel*. We have to pursue the 'indispensable mechanical part' of metrical precedent to get at his deepest feelings, as expressed 2,000 years before by Sophocles. In pursuing this 'academic reference' we also confront what Arnold intends us to find: 'this wretched person here, not I alone'.

The 'historical estimate' can help the 'personal estimate' a little more, and find a way out of the poem. When Athens had destroyed herself in the battle by night in Sicily, it was not the conservative Sophocles, but his disturbing, psychologically compli-cated and technically innovative rival the 'atheist' Euripides who provided some means of redemption for the remnant of the Athenian army:

> there is a tradition that many of the Athenian soldiers who returned home safely visited Euripides to thank him for their deliverance which they owed to his poetry. Some of them told him that they had been given their freedom in return for teaching their masters all they could remember of his works, while others, when they took to flight after the final battle, had been given food and water for reciting some of his lyrics.[29]

Arnold has not made the discovery of this point of exit from the poem easy. It is difficult, perhaps slightly far-fetched: just as all grounds for transcendental or historical affirmation are difficult and slightly far-fetched. Arnold has, however, provided clues elsewhere in the volume. In the light of the above Athenian 'tradition', the Sicilian myths of resurrection to which Arnold grants Clough access in *Thyrsis* appear less like pastoral fantasy and more like a modern allegory for cultural renewal. Arnold strove to be a classical poet in the spirit of Sophocles. His 1867 volume has a 'fragment' of a classical tragedy based on Sophocles's play about Hercules and Deianeira. Clough, by contrast, was more like Euripides: psychologically upsetting, subversive in politics and religion, far too distressingly 'modern' to win the approval of conservatives in his home country.

Clough was partly educated, and first appreciated and published in America. At Rugby, his nickname was 'Yankee'. Like Euripides, the rebel Clough found his truest admirers among the new cultural leaders of the West.

England, and Europe with her, may collapse into ruin, but the pattern of life and history is not merely one of deterioration, but also of renewal, of:

> Begin, and cease, and then again begin

By reading the poem in the context of the whole volume, it is possible to understand what makes the affirmation of personal commitment so difficult for the persona of *Dover Beach*, and also to sympathise with the courage required for making this commitment. Over and above these things, however, the clue of the 'battle by night' *may* lead (if we wish it to do so) towards an affirmation of renewal. Just as the retreating sea *will* once again return, so also, despite its defeats, that 'democratic fervour' which Clough associated with the rising tide in his own poetry *may* once again return.[30] This affirmation is made more credible for the reader by Arnold's careful laying of 'clues' elsewhere in the 1867 volume. These clues are not like a crossword puzzle with only one answer, but suggestions which hint to the reader that there are indeed grounds for confidence in the human destiny. The persona of *Dover Beach*, however – like all of us when we are making choices within our own lives, rather than surveying human history through the medium of poetry – has to make his (or her)[31] commitment without any such confidence. The persona, for instance, cannot 'hear' the fact that the poem is in rhyme. The device of rhyme was a Christian innovation in European poetry, to help the memory, and to act as an image of return and renewal. The persona, trapped in the dramatic present, cannot be aware of these things, as the reader can.

If we seek an actual geographic source for the sustaining and renewal of the civilised democracy Arnold believes in, the 1867 volume seems to point westward, hints at America, and again reminds us of Clough:

> Ah! now 'tis changed. In conquering sunshine bright
> The man of the bold West now comes array'd;
> He of the mystic East is touch'd with night.
>
> *East and West* ll. 12–14

As a propagandist for culture, Arnold would actually go on lecture tours of America, bringing some of the spiritual ideas of the 'East' to the 'bold West', and renewing his confidence in democracy from the evidence of vigorous cultural life at every level which he found there.

If we can find our own way of 'resolving' *Dover Beach* – and there are as many ways as there are readers – we can read the accompanying poem, *Calais Sands*, as something other than a piece of Victorian sentimentality, with its celebration of the 'lovely presence' of the beloved. We can know what Arnold's allegory of the *Austerity of Poetry* means; and not find facile his sonnet called *Anti-Desperation*. We may even be inclined to read without wincing his *Last Word*. Much lighter and more straightforward than *Dover Beach*, it tells the same story with a different emphasis. If the old culture of Europe has degenerated into 'folly' and lapsed into silence, Arnold will nevertheless still fight for it, because only by fighting for it can he affirm the values it once had and provide an example for the future of commitment to value:

> Charge once more, then, and be dumb!
> Let the victors, when they come,
> When the forts of folly fall,
> Find thy body by the wall.

The American victor, when he came, turned out to be on Arnold's side. Arnold's 'practice of Poetry': his disinterestedness, and care for values, his complex strategy of allusion, deployment of persona, and even his metrical device, borrowed from Sophocles, of iambic lines with great spaces and silences in them; would all be born again in *The Waste Land*.

Notes

1 *The Sacred Wood*, 3rd edition, 1932, p. 1.
2 *Thomas Carlyle: Selected Writings*, p. 73.
3 *Essay in aid of a Grammar of Assent* (1870), p. 272.

4 *Culture and Anarchy*, p. 212.

5 *Culture and Anarchy*, pp. 94–5.

6 Carlyle to Robert Browning, 21 June 1841, Charles Richard Sanders, *The Carlyle-Browning Correspondence and Relationship*, John Rylands Library, Manchester, 1975, pp. 13–14: 'Not that I deny your poetic faculty . . . But unless . . .', etc.

7 Preface to *Poems* (1853). *Matthew Arnold: Selected Prose*, p. 47.

8 Trilling, *Matthew Arnold*, p. 54.

9 John Keble, 'Fourth Sunday in Advent', *The Christian Year* (1827), 1885, p. 26.

10 Honan, *Arnold*, illustrations between pp. 194–5.

11 Honan, *Arnold*, pp. 3, 81.

12 John Keats to George and Tom Keats, December 1817; to John Hamilton Reynolds, 19 February 1818, reprinted e.g. Harold Bloom and Lionel Trilling, *The Oxford Anthology of English Literature, Romantic Prose and Poetry*, 1981, pp. 768, 772.

13 *Past and Present*, Book IV, Chapter 1, 'Aristocracies', para. 3.

14 John Campbell Shairp, *Studies in Poetry and Philosophy*, Edinburgh, 1868, p. 11.

15 *Apologia*, Chapter 5, para. 5. Newman composed hymns while shaving.

16 Mark Pattison, *Memoirs* (1885), quoted Klingopulos, 'Notes on the Victorian Scene', *Pelican Guide to English Literature* (1968), volume 6, p. 42: 'the clerical party . . . since the Franco-German War [1870] have been advancing upon us . . . accompanied by a renewed attempt to accredit an *a priori* logic'.

17 Honan, *Arnold*, p. 402.

18 Oxford Inaugural (1857). *Matthew Arnold: Selected Prose*, p. 59.

19 Honan, *Arnold*, pp. 220, 197.

20 Arthur Hugh Clough (1819–61), Head Boy of Rugby; Fellow of Oriel 1842–48, *Amours de Voyage*, II. 273, *The Poems*, edited by A. L. P. Norrington, 1968, p. 195, 'I tremble for something factitious,/ Some malpractice of heart and illegitimate process;/We are so prone to these things with our terrible notions of duty.'

21 *Matthew Arnold: Selected Prose*, pp. 341–4.

22 *Selected Prose*, p. 54.

23 Honan, *Arnold*, p. 398.

24 *The Bothie*, IX. 51: 'If there is battle, 'tis battle by night: I stand in the darkness.'

25 Francis Darwin, *Life of Charles Darwin* (1887), quoted Klingopulos, p. 55.

26 *Selected Prose*, p. 54.

27 Greek classical tragedy, rather like the French, almost invariably uses *regular* iambic hexameters (i.e. almost always of twelve syllables) for its dialogue lines. Choruses are in lyric verse. This truncated line (of three syllables, literally, 'Why [are you] silent?') is therefore much more striking in the original than in this English pentameter version. Polyneices is speaking to his father Oedipus. The play is set in Sophocles's home village of Colonus, where his blinded hero comes to achieve

forgiveness in death, leaving the next generation to destroy themselves in vendettas. There are only two more examples of truncated hexameters in this play of 1,779 lines, both suggestive. Polyneices's sister Antigone has two syllables only at line 315: 'What [shall I] say?'; and three syllables at line 317: 'Unhappy'. In the chorus passage (1239–48) a sea-threshed pebbly headland is implied. The root here translated 'harass' (like disturbed bees) and 'tumbled' (like fish) may connote with 'trembling' in later Greek (*Greek-English Lexicon*, compiled by H. G. Liddell and R. Scott (1st edition 1843), 9th edition 1940, reprinted 1958, p. 962, under κλον-). Not a translation or a falsification, Arnold's evocation of Sophocles holds the (ironic?) memory of his own 'tremulous' over-refined youthful interpretation. Commoner minds have made 1.1225 of this chorus the commonest and most depressing of Sophocles' quotations (*The Oxford Dictionary of Quotations*, 1966, p. 506).

28 Dr Arnold arrived in Oxford as Professor of History in December 1841. His son Matthew parodied the event by writing a burlesque tragi-comedy featuring the 'Spirit of Propriety' led on stage sick, in a witty pastiche of Oedipus's arrival at Colonus, led on stage by Antigone. Propriety declaims: 'A little further lead me, good my friends,/ That I may gaze on High Street ere I die.' The following June, Dr Arnold died of heart failure. Matthew's burlesque quoted in Honan, *Arnold*, p. 56.

29 Plutarch, 'Nicias', 'The Rise and Fall of Athens', translated by Ian Scott-Kilvert, Harmondsworth, 1960, pp. 242–3. Clough valued Plutarch as 'one who had lived into good times out of evil' (*Plutarch's Lives . . .* Revised by Arthur Hugh Clough, 5 vols, Boston, Massachusetts, 1882, I.xvii).

30 *The Bothie*, IX. 73, 81: 'As at return of tide the total weight of ocean . . . Comes back, swelling and spreading, the old democratic fervour.'

31 Arnold occasionally employs a female persona, as in *A Modern Sappho* (1849).

32 *The Poems of Matthew Arnold*, World's Classics Series, Oxford, 1906, etc., p. 377. Used throughout this chapter for its handy format, durability and historical interest. Readers may enjoy comparing it with more recent editions listed below, while reflecting that Arnold, like Sophocles, is constantly being revised by his readers.

Books

Paperbacks

Matthew Arnold, *Culture and Anarchy*, edited by J. Dover Wilson, Cambridge, 1932, etc.

Matthew Arnold (Oxford Authors series), edited by Miriam Allott and Robert H. Super, Oxford, 1986.

Matthew Arnold: Selected Prose, edited by P. J. Keating, Harmondsworth, 1982.

The Portable Matthew Arnold, edited by Lionel Trilling, Harmondsworth, 1980.

Lionel Trilling, *Matthew Arnold* (1939), London, 1963, etc.

Life

Park Honan, *Matthew Arnold: A Life*, London, 1981.

Letters

The Letters of Matthew Arnold to Arthur Hugh Clough, edited by H.
F. Lowry, Oxford, 1932, reprinted 1968.

Works

The Complete Prose Works of Matthew Arnold, edited by R. H. Super,
Ann Arbor, Michigan, 1960–.

Matthew Arnold, *Essays in Criticism: First Series*, edited by Sister
Thomas Marion Hoctor, SSJ, Chicago and London, 1968.

Matthew Arnold, *The Poems*, edited by K. Allott, second edition by M.
Allott, London, 1979.

Criticism and commentary

Matthew Arnold: the Critical Heritage, edited by Carl Dawson, London,
1973.

Joseph Bristow, editor, *The Victorian Poet: poetics and persona*,
London, 1987.

Vincent Buckley, *Poetry and Morality*: studies in the criticism of Matthew Arnold, T. S. Eliot and F. R. Leavis, with an introduction by
Basil Willey, London, 1959.

Robert Giddings, editor, *Matthew Arnold: Between Two Worlds*,
London, 1986.

James C. Livingston, *Matthew Arnold and Christianity*, Columbia,
South Carolina, 1986.

Mary W. Schneider, *Poetry in the Age of Democracy: the Literary
Criticism of Matthew Arnold*, Lawrence, Kansas, 1989.

Gillian Sutherland, editor, *Matthew Arnold on Education*, Harmondsworth, 1973.

Kathleen Tillotson, 'Matthew Arnold and Carlyle' (Warton Lecture),
from *Proceedings of the British Academy*, vol. 42, Dover, New
Hampshire, 1956.

Lionel Trilling, *Matthew Arnold* (1939), with an additional essay, 'Matthew Arnold, poet', Oxford, 1982.

Fred George Walcott, *The origins of 'Culture and Anarchy': Matthew
Arnold and popular education in England*, Toronto, 1970.

CHAPTER EIGHT

Conclusion

Three of our writers were graduates of Oxford; four of them were middle-class Londoners; all of them were deeply influenced by classical literature and the Bible. Their creative heyday – from about 1830 to about 1870 – seems equally narrow. Yet their significance – and people all over the world are still reading them and arguing about them – becomes less surprising when it is remembered that they were representatives, and extraordinarily articulate ones, of those 'respectable' classes who were the mainstay of the largest empire the world has known; that their productive years were spent while the commercial strength and international prestige of that empire were at their height; and that the language in which they wrote has, since their day, become more and more the international language for the kinds of cultural and political 'liberalism' (in its broadest sense) to which they contributed their enabling, defining, and warning criticism. Four of them had 'Evangelical' childhoods in the narrow sense; and all six were imbued with the Evangelical interpretation of the parable of the talents. They considered it their duty to spend their talents to benefit the world: a childlike idealism from which they never wavered, and of which we are the beneficiaries. In the non-political sense 'conservative', all of them really believed the spiritual principles instilled into them as children: and caused a creative disturbance in the 'real' world by fulfilling, with truly Victorian pertinacity, the implications of what they found in their own brains and hearts. In this area, for instance, Mill's Evangelical mother – despite the would-be-adult disregard for her which he has transmitted to his rationalist admirers – was probably as important as his famous father.

Ruskin was the only one of the six to express admiration for Whitman; and the admiration was apparently not mutual. It is useful, however, to try to re-imagine the nineteenth-century sense of enterprise and commitment whose most outspoken utterance is found in the American poet, in order to understand these Victorian pioneers:

> See, my children, resolute children,
> By those swarms upon our rear, we must never yield or falter,
> Ages back in ghostly millions, frowning there behind us urging,
>   Pioneers! O pioneers! . . .
>
> These are of us, they are with us,
> All for primal needed work, while the followers there in embryo
>   wait behind,
> We to-day's procession heading, we the route for travel clearing,
>   Pioneers! O pioneers!
>
> *Pioneers! O Pioneers!*, ll. 45–8, 77–80

Despite differences of taste and environment, Arnold – the man Whitman dubbed the 'dude of literature' – and all five of our other thinkers shared this same perspective on history, and much of Whitman's sense of mission. Our six 'resolute children' of the Victorian age were convinced that they owed a debt of effort to all the 'ghostly millions' of the past, and a debt of responsibility to the future millions 'in embryo'; and that the opportunity of their day for creative innovation would be short-lived. They were pioneers of a transitional age, whose contribution would affect the future of humanity, and they never forgot it.

Writing after the Second World War, when Britain had completed her role as a first-class world power, the economic historian W. W. Rostow looked back at the 'British Economy of the Nineteenth Century' in his book of that title (1948):

> In the period 1790–1914, the eighteenth century notion of responsible aristocratic government gave way to concepts of representative democracy; notions of *laissez-faire* and self-help triumphed over older concepts of paternalism and then quite promptly began to lose ground to a revived conception of state responsibility for the general welfare. (p. 137)

Our six writers made their contribution to this revival of 'state responsibiity'; and were part of the prompting which kept alive an awareness of the inadequacy of '*laissez-faire*' and the potentialities and dangers of 'representative democracy'. They were in different degrees beneficiaries of the newer middle-class hegemony; yet all of them retained some of those 'older concepts of paternalism'. As responsible members of a literary middle class, they fulfilled the duty of goading their contemporaries away from the suicidal opportunism of gang-politics towards the more permanently useful statesmanship of responsibility for the 'general welfare'.

The mid-nineteenth-century period to which their work mainly belongs was one of confidence for Britain, and also of more than usual tolerance, at least as far as new ideas were concerned. It was not, however, a time of obvious practical reform. It was a period of consolidation between the limited reforms of the late 1820s and early 1830s and the more drastic ones of the late 1860s and early 1870s. The former period saw political emancipation for Protestant dissenters and Roman Catholics, the abolition of slavery through the empire, a modest Parliamentary Reform Act. All these things tended to promote middle-class commercial interests. The new Poor Law of 1834, designed to make any work by which the 'independent' poor could survive – or even hope to survive – preferable to the savage 'dependency culture' of the Workhouse, was even more clearly in the interests of the middle-class employer.

The later group of reforms were more far-reaching: a new Reform Act brought the vote to 'respectable' working-class males; an Education Act established the principle of elementary education for all; a Married Woman's Property Act initiated the long process of female emancipation. These reforms of the late 1860s and early 1870s tended to undermine the middle-class hegemony. They raised the hopeful possibility of a broad, educated democracy. Without continuing prosperity, however, together with commitment by the state to paying for real democracy, there was a danger that these reforms – the foundation-stones, as it were, of modern Britain – would do more harm than good. It is these possibilities and dangers – which are indeed still very much with us – that our six writers were already addressing in the 1840s, 1850s and early 1860s.

This intervening period between two bursts of reform was marked by a slightly spurious confidence on the part of the well-to-do middle classes. The earlier reforms had suited them; any increase in the quantum of social justice might undermine their position. On the whole they liked things the way they were. Whatever might happen abroad or out of sight at home, Ruskin told them in 1859, 'You think it is all right.' Gladstone noted in 1860 that these were 'anti-reforming times'. The reforming Liberal Richard Cobden even detected a 'reaction against . . . "humanitarianism" '. The aggressive stance occasionally adopted by all our six thinkers, and the general sharpness of their humour, are to be understood in this context. Generally speaking, their audience were willing to be persuaded that things were not necessarily 'all right': but the 'message' had to be clear; and the promoter of the 'message' had to have some authoritative base from which to deliver it.

The Victorian bourgeois public appreciated talent (as opposed to 'genius'), respectability, and an appetite for hard work. Anyone who combined all three had a chance of being heard over a wide range of subjects: a specific feature of Victorian 'liberalism' which no longer obtains. This latter point helps to explain certain strategies of behaviour which might otherwise strike the modern reader as odd.

Modern readers may find it incomprehensible, for instance, that Ruskin's Appendices in the *Stones of Venice* on 'Austrian Government in Italy' or 'Modern Education' should be 'mixed up' with page after page of meticulous outlines of the profiles of Byzantine and Gothic Archivolts, and other merely 'technical' drawings. In the Victorian context, however, these particular drawings – evidence only of talent, application and 'seriousness', with none of the suspect brilliance of Ruskin's principal illustrations elsewhere in the volume – help to 'validate' the radical ideas with which they are – however incongruously – associated. A similar strategy helps to explain Arnold's decision to publish his academically unexceptional classical tragedy *Merope* as part of his campaign to revolutionise the functions of the Oxford Professorship of Poetry. His 'outrageous' Inaugural of November 1857 on the 'Modern Element in Literature' (given in English, too – Latin was still the official language on these occasions) was offset by his Preface to *Merope*, of the following month, to which the most pedantic classicist could hardly take exception. A similar pattern explains Newman's annual re-reading of Jane Austen, as a means of maintaining a lucid and flawless public style of writing. His letters are much more pungent, and say much riskier things than he allowed himself in the disciplined conservatism of his public prose.

In the same way, Mill could always refer those who suspected his championship of women's emancipation and other 'risky' topics during the 1860s to his *Logic* of 1843: a monument to the kind of meticulous empirical hard thinking that Victorians respected. Indeed, Mill's salvo against *The Subjection of Women*, not published until 1869, relies on the strict empiricism of the *Logic* just as that empiricism was going out of fashion with 'advanced' intellectuals. Harriet Taylor's anxiety to avoid any breath of scandal over her friendship with Mill was essentially part of the same necessary strategy for acceptance. Carlyle's doctrine of 'work' was validated, if by nothing else, by his encyclopaedic knowledge of German literature and by the sheer bulk and density of his allusive prose. The massive *Frederick the Great*, designed to crown Carlyle's achievement, had an argument for its own respectability in its very massiveness.

Since the passing away of the sort of consensus which our writers addressed, there has been a series of reactions to that consensus, and to the writers who achieved their best work in terms of it.

John Holloway's *The Victorian Sage* of 1953, for instance, deals with Carlyle, Newman and Matthew Arnold as discursive prose writers, together with Disraeli, George Eliot and Hardy as novelists. Holloway is anxious to offset the kind of debunking of all things Victorian which became fashionable in the wake of Lytton Strachey's *Eminent Victorians* of 1918. For Strachey's generation, Victorian 'progress' and all its products seemed to have led only to the obscene farce of the First World War. Strachey strengthened his indictment by steering clear of truly eminent Victorians like Newman or Matthew Arnold, and keeping to softer targets like Arnold's father and Newman's fanatical and self-righteous rival Cardinal Manning. Holloway's reassessment of Victorian personalities of the highest eminence shows a return to 'earnestness' and respect for moral considerations which seemed natural and proper to many in the England of the early 1950s: shorn of empire, exhausted by war, but greatly relieved to feel that democracy had survived the monstrous threat of Nazism. Holloway's text implies that the prose of the Victorians promoted the values which, at as deep level, the war fought by Holloway's generation had been *about*: on the Allied side, a belief, however vague, in what Carlyle had advocated in *On Heroes* (1841) as the political need to establish a system that would combine fairness with efficiency: on the Axis side, the resurgence of what Carlyle had denounced as the 'charlatan element' of Napoleon's dictatorship, based on the fallacy that military force alone can *create* value. Never at his most authoritarian did Carlyle believe that: though he was clear that force might have to be resorted to in the defence of value. In his own historical context, Holloway's 'liberal' concern for moral values is understandably also combined with a greater sympathy than some critics have since shown to Carlyle's grim awareness that such values need strong defences.

Moving on to the early 1960s, we find that W. L. Burn looks back with some sympathy to the effort by mid-Victorian writers to achieve a dialogue with a broader audience. But he no longer has Holloway's moral confidence. The title of his book, *The Age of Equipoise: a Study of the Mid-Victorian Generation* (1964), describes not only his subject-matter but his own sense of being poised between two points of view. It was during the early 1960s that the physical aspect of urban England underwent traumatic changes: shops, streets, factories, public buildings and road-systems still preponderately Victorian were swept away and replaced by the high-rise, the concrete box and the motorway. Medieval and renaissance pastiche yielded to parodies of Gropius and Le Corbusier. At the same time, England was being informed by her allies that she had lost an empire and not yet found a role. Burn's book belongs to this period of introverted reassessment for England, and it is interesting to see him draw on a pair of opposing contributions from the 1950s to make his double case about the mid-Victorians. On the one hand, he cites J. H. Buckley's *The Victorian Temper: a Study in Literary Culture* of 1952. Like Holloway, Buckley is still sympathetic to the kind of public-spirited attempt at communication and compromise, the strengths of the western liberal tradition as embodied by the mid-Victorians. On the other hand, John Wain's article, 'The Strategy of Victorian Poetry' of 1953, which Burn also quotes, already embodies the essence of the 'angry young man' movement of the later 1950s which Wain helped to promote. John Osborne, Wain, and other 'angry young men' had no time for the slack compromises of older men. They were ashamed of England's paltering deference to two incompatible but equally repellent systems: Yankee capitalist imperialism and Stalinist Soviet imperialism. When they turned their sights on mid-Victorian literature they tended to see it as too bourgeois: lacking aesthetic and ideological rigour on the one hand, and lacking real sympathy with the masses of the poor on the other. They recognised that England had had her opportunity in mid-Victorian times, but thought she had thrown it away. Wain naturally disapproved of the middlebrow tendencies of poets like Tennyson and Browning, and other Victorian writers who achieved wide recognition in their lifetime. Their style suggested to him 'a fatal lowering of vital energy'. Their 'liberalism' was a betrayal.

On balance, Burn seems more attracted to Buckley's approach, which he exemplifies by quoting a judgement about Ruskin which may be felt to apply to all our six thinkers and also to other Victorians who have survived Wain's reproof: ' "Throughout Ruskin's criticism runs his desire for synthesis, his will to discover the universal harmony to which his age aspired.' " Nevertheless, although Burn's sympathy may lie with this kind of commitment to achieving synthesis and consensus, he is also clear as a historian that while on the whole factors existed in the mid-Victorian age that made such reconciliatory effort possible, 'there were signs that they might not exist much longer'. Quoting Buckley again, he adds: ' "for better or worse, a private impressionism began to eclipse the social concern of the high Victorians" '.

Moving back to consider the period that opens with the defeat of France in 1870 by the new united Germany and closes with Hitler's suicide in 1945 and the partition of Germany, we may get the impression that the kind of confidence which gave mid-Victorian writers their sense of mission and desire for harmony became less and less tenable, but more and more desirable. By the 1870s the writing careers of our six intellectuals were over, or drawing to an end: but more than that, the world to which they had belonged was changing. On the one hand, their ideas became absorbed by the British Establishment, though only in such doses as suited prevailing policies and fashions. In the face of new economic expectations and requirements, Arnold's rhetoric on behalf of state support for education, for instance, began to look like a plea for the inevitable: the principle of free education, where needed, was established in 1891. Philistine politicians since have had to reason the need. Again, Mill and Taylor's critical suggestions, Ruskin's scathing attacks, on the subject of *laissez-faire* economics began to look less eccentric as professional economists came to share a similar view of the limitations of rampant capitalism. Vested interests since have had to block the view. On the other hand, partial acceptance of viewpoints articulated by our six writers has implied the partition of their influence among rival political groupings. Various forms of socialism, conservatism, nationalism, internationalism, rationalism, mysticism, atheism and even Church-of-Englandism are all capable of being 'derived' from our five male writers, severally and together. Taylor's contribution to Mill's work has come only more recently to general knowledge. She, too, has been pillaged like the others. For some she provides an argument for an aggressive feminism, for others proof positive of women's unfitness for intellectual activities. Rarely indeed has her collaboration with Mill been recognised as a pioneering contribution to human liberation.

While all our writers were critics of 'liberalism' in its narrow political sense, they all relied on the confidence and openness to persuasion which characterised mid-Victorian England at its best. This situation did not last for very long. The breakdown of consensus which is still the experience of many was already beginning in the late 1860s. A decisive factor was the shift in the world economy which brought to an end the high-Victorian creed of *laissez-faire*. From about the mid-1870s, Britain was losing against industrial competition from a unified Germany, and agricultural competition from the post-bellum American Mid-West. Entrepreneurs began the pattern of planned unemployment in the interests of 'productivity'. The raising of the odds in the class war at home was part of a heightening of the international commercial and imperial 'cold war'. 'Protection' was sought for the British Empire against outside economic aggression; new mechanical efficiency made its own contribution to an eventual rise in exports, and to an imperial triumphalism moving towards the 'show-down' with Germany for which the Boer War was a kind of curtain-raiser, the First World War being its terrible first phase. Dynastic government in Russia and the Austro-Hungarian Empire did not survive the war. The western democracies survived, at a price. The peculiar German system was damaged, but not successfully replaced by anything better.

From Bismarck to Hitler, with a brief interlude under the Weimar Republic, Germany had a state 'socialism' without democracy. The Reichstag, though elected on universal suffrage, was hardly a shadow of the British Parliament. An executive appointed by and responsible solely to the head of state presided over welfare systems designed to make Germany economically and militarily invincible. The head of state (the Kaiser at the Chancellor's prompting, or Hitler as Chancellor-Führer) declared war and entered into treaties on Germany's behalf. She had no resource, it transpired, but a vicious recrudescence of socialism without democracy after her economic crippling by the 'victorious' Allies in 1919.

Carlyle had been an admirer of Bismarck because he brought order to Germany; and Ruskin and Arnold had promoted the idea of state responsibility: but all of them, at their most extreme, retained an element of Mill's insistence on the right to argue for different ideas; and held sacred, as Newman did, the individual moral conscience.

If Germany could have benefited from Mill's message of intellectual freedom and Newman's crusade for the individual conscience, England had to learn the validity of Carlyle's idea of public discipline for the sake of peace, and the force of Ruskin's demand for decent material provision, and of Arnold's demand for better educational facilities.

If only in order to prepare herself for war, Britain found herself, from the turn of the century on, wobbling spasmodically towards some equivalent for German state efficiency in welfare and education: from the National Insurance Act of 1911 to the Education Act of 1944. Looking back in 1948, when a Labour government was consolidating this process, Rostow could see the pattern over the previous century as a groping towards the stability of 'peace, democracy, and universal prosperity' (p. 144).

Rostow's book of 1948 represents the sense of relief and hopefulness shared by many in the western democracies at their own survival. His own intellectual training was undertaken partly in America and partly in England. He provides a context of economic thinking which helps to explain Holloway's reaffirmation of the best aspects of the mid-Victorian openness to ideas, in *The Victorian Sage*. Burn's book of 1964 brings us forward to a crossroads. He combines a sense of the transitory nature of those moments in history – like the mid-Victorian period – when there is time for reassessment and renovation, with a sense of nostalgia for their passing. He introduces the voice of the 'angry young men' who were demanding during the 1950s harder criteria in literary criticism and truer commitment to radical change. They were unpersuaded by the kinds of appeal to a home-made 'common sense' which lies at the root of many of the arguments of the mid-Victorian writers. Such an appeal may be regarded as typically British, and is certainly at odds with the great nineteenth-century theorists of continental extraction like Comte and Marx. Common sense and compromise became less and less convincing criteria (though more and more desperately needed) as the 'cold war' of the 1950s and early 1960s moved nearer and nearer to nuclear confrontation. Hard theory and revolution became the watchwords of many young intellectuals, especially those with Marxist sympathies.

But as the 1960s advanced, a sense of disillusionment and unreality became more widespread. The end of the war had seen the beginning of a polarisation of world affairs between the camps represented by the Soviet empire and American economic imperialism. This pair of unattractive and incompetent 'realities', in their dinosaur struggle, were exhausting the world's resources in an arms race which made the Third World poorer, and failed to justify the hypocrisy of the rival claims to 'socialism' and 'freedom'. There was a bizarre repetition of certain features of the mid-nineteenth-century world. America proposed to shore up a corrupt regime in South Vietnam in order to prevent Russia from extending her 'sphere of influence'. Young men were sacrificed to the political and military incompetence of their elders: just as they had been in the Crimean War, when France and England had 'gone to the aid' of a corrupt Turkey in order to repel the same Russian 'threat'. In both cases, the well-to-do young reacted by developing a hatred of authority, and by retreating into dream-worlds. Pre-Raphaelite fashion was back on the streets in the late 1960s. Disillusioned young people refused intellectual allegiance to a 'free' America in which armed police were drawn up against student protestors, or a 'socialist' Russia where the elite shopped for caviar while the poor queued for bread. In 1968, Russian troops, under orders from the old men in the Kremlin, invaded Czechoslovakia to destroy the first signs of the recovery of democracy. The struggles for freedom in mid-nineteenth-century Italy and Austro-Hungary had been thwarted by similar means. Despite official protests, the action – or inaction – of western politicians, in 1968 as in Victorian times, seemed to declare that they thought it was 'all right'.

Ben Knights's book, *The Idea of the Clerisy in the Nineteenth Century*, was born out of this context. Begun as a Cambridge PhD thesis, and published in 1978, it is as much a product of its own time as the work of Burn or Holloway. At one level, it traces Coleridge's idea of a clerisy – or superior minority educated through religion and literature – as it seems to manifest itself in the texts of Carlyle, Arnold, Mill and Newman. At another level – which is exposed with perfect frankness – the book is a document of the disaffections of the late 1960s and early 1970s. Knights makes clear his dislike of the 'clerisy', which he sees as an idea formulated and accepted out of psychic need. Authoritarian and repressive, and perhaps greedy for their privileges (for Knights sees them as a class or at least a pressure group as well as an idea), the clerisy should be abolished, he feels, and replaced by new habits of awareness. Knights wants a Blake-inspired reverence for children, and for spontaneous expression, to replace the malign Coleridgean fantasy of an elite intellectual class. Drawing on the work of the anarchist theoretician Max Stirner, Knights looks forward to a time when, in an atmosphere of supervised permissiveness, schoolteachers, for instance, would be able to let literature enter the children's talk, and not 'drown' it with its own structures and assumptions. The claim that there are 'traditional values' to be transmitted is seen as spurious: from the earliest age, the citizens of a democracy need to be in charge of their own responses. What Knights regards as the preference of Mill and Newman for 'liberal' over 'useful' education is seen as threatening. The traditional 'liberal' education – especially anything to do with Latin and Greek – is seen as advantaging those with the money and leisure to acquire an elitist 'culture' whose main purpose is to exclude the underprivileged from its codes, leaving them exposed to its manipulations.

Knights's book reflects a distaste for English academics of the opinionated, self-admiring type, rewarded with comfortable jobs during the university-building boom of the 1960s. He voices the radical aspirations of those employed in the new comprehensive schools of the same period, with their non-selective admission policy and stated commitment to breaking the class snobberies of English culture and education. Knights was himself engaged in extra-mural teaching: the 'Cinderella' branch of university work, committed to enlarging the intellectual experience of disadvantaged mature students. These pioneers promoted a new idea of 'cultural studies' which rejected 'tradition' in favour of an empirical response to the individual condition, interests and needs of students. These developments were truly a possibility only in the context of a highly developed, confident and affluent democracy. Since the mid-Victorian thinkers Knights finds fault with were among the pioneers of a fairer and more accessible political and educational system, it seems a little hard to condemn them.

It is when they are seen in their own historical context that it becomes possible to sympathise with them. Knights's core objection to the mid-Victorians is their demand that specially gifted people should be funded by the State to pursue their special interests. Carlyle, however, only made this claim in his *On Heroes* lectures, after he had achieved financial independence by a lifetime of hard work. Arnold made similar claims in prose written in moments snatched from the grind of the Schools Inspectorship. Like Mill – also a busy civil servant – Arnold wanted to see more and more people educated to the point where they would be emancipated from the manipulations of politicians and other vested interests. Newman, in particular, wanted more Irishmen to get the kind of mental training that would equip them to get a fair deal from the British State. Ruskin – whom Knights does not deal with in denouncing Ruskin's 'master' Carlyle – is at his most characteristic when he is making Knights's case for him: urging artists, for instance, in the closing letters of *Fors Clavigera*, to love and learn from the intuitive vividness of the drawings of young children, unspoiled by academic training. Harriet Taylor, as a crusader, not merely for female, but for human liberation, is someone who belongs even more clearly among those of whom Knights might surely approve. Yet Mill's best work would have been impossible without her, and Knights, in rebuking Mill, does not discuss her. Ruskin and Taylor, it might be noted, had something in common which helps to explain their comparative acceptability within the context of anarchist theory: neither of them ever had to work for their keep.

During the decade that has passed since Knights's book was published, there has been a series of unforeseeable developments in Britain, and in the wider world.

Mill's nightmare of a reactionary populist government, elected on a minority of the votes cast under the antiquated English electoral system, has been realised. A secure majority in the House of Commons has permitted a return to the 'Victorian values' which our six Victorian thinkers spent their lives attacking. The undue dominance of commercial and materialist vested interests, the 'rolling back of the frontiers of the state', the crippling of working-class movements like the unions, the shoring up of private means of enrichment by drafts on the public funds, have been accompanied by policies like making 'willingness to pay' a prime criterion for university entry, and financial 'reforms' like the institution of a 'Poll Tax', levied on all alike, regardless of ability to pay (something Mill regarded as too unsympathetic a measure for any government to attempt). All these and many similar developments are evidence of an attempt to make Britain great again by reverting to the inequalities that blemished her period of greatness in the mid-Victorian era. This is surely nostalgia, rather than renewal.

Mill, the calmest of our thinkers, is also the most telling critic of the Thatcher regime. Without proportional representation, he wrote, in a Pamphlet on Parliamentary Reform of 1859, 'The party who was numerically strongest would rule without opposition until by its abuse of power it had provoked a change of public sentiment.' This applied, he thought, regardless of the slogans favoured by the governing party, though he added: 'Could we be disposed to give "unchecked ascendancy" in Parliament to any type of any description, the small tradesman is scarcely the one we would select'. The small tradesman would always be likely, Mill thought, to miss the point that 'laws of property have to depend upon considerations of a public nature . . . not upon motives of a more personal character operating on the minds of those who have control of the Government' (*Collected Works*, V. 706).

The world has changed, too, since 1979. The Victorian summer, to which our writers belonged, was a breathing-space for reassessment between periods of more brutal compulsion. If they helped to nag and goad the British into retaining and developing the awareness that the humane values are the workable ones, they are benefactors of the whole world. This is particularly apparent wherever English is available as a language of ideas. Ruskin, Arnold, Mill and Carlyle fed, and continue to feed, the minds of India's awakening democracy. A small but hopeful outcome of the pollution of 'prosperous' Tokyo has been the recent opening of a Ruskin Library there. Despite China's brutal attempt to hold back her own revolution, the humane discourse richly seeded by the Victorians is alive now in the English Corner of the People's Park of Beijing.

As a year of revolution, 1989 was as remarkable as 1848. The peoples of Eastern Europe, making new demands for democracy, now face the same challenge that was outlined in Carlyle's *On Heroes* of 1841, and pursued in detail by a great range of Victorian thinkers: how to find some workable synthesis that combines efficiency with fairness. The members of the Polish Solidarity Trade Union who shout 'Long Live England!' are cheering an *idea* of England which is the idea of fairness and democracy, despite England's incapacity to realise her own ideal.

Our six thinkers need no longer be seen as merely concerned with English affairs. We may smile, for instance, at Newman's vision, but we need not belittle it. He saw a great future for the faith and wit of Catholic Ireland, nurtured by the heritage of British constitutionalism, and enlarged by the free spirit of America and Australasia. Ruskin had equally large ideas. Food, clothing, and shelter he considered to be the rights of all. A world economy which did not meet those needs could not be efficient. His own observations led him further to believe that an untramelled industrialism, without safeguards against pollution, was poisoning the planet. Few would now call either of these insights 'crazy', as many did a century ago. Taylor's vision of human liberation, which for her included economic and sexual liberation, has become, like Ruskin's 'crazy' demands, so evident a need that political leaders pay lip-service to it. Its realisation must attend on the arrival of Mill's vision of a democracy that works 'in detail'. Awareness of other cultures, and of the classical basis of all western culture, together with a general improvement in educational standards, regardless of 'willingness to pay', will become economic and political necessities, as Arnold can still remind us. Whatever it calls itself, any scheme of international co-operation will need Carlyle's 'authoritarian' insight that laws must be seen to be worth obeying if they are to command the spirit of the people.

As the hole-in-corner manoeuvres of British class-warriors of various shades are brought more and more into the light of the European Community – all of whose members have some form of proportional representation for minorities – there is some chance that common sense and workability rather than gamesmanship may become respectable. German thoroughness – which has now again become something fearful, as Germany achieves reunification – requires correction, not ostracism, by English traditions of liberty and French habits of civilisation and taste.

The beginnings of the restoration of democracy and religious and intellectual toleration in the Soviet Union are not without their dangers, and have not been won without the martyrdom of its 'clerisy' – if one may employ that doubtful word to describe a real thing. Thwarted during the 1950s and 1960s, the 'intellectual' resistance in Eastern Europe has been joined, albeit briefly, by the people: a triumph for something more profound than an urge to be exposed to 'market forces'. Now that the Pope and the successor of Lenin have met, it becomes less credible to insist that religion must be reactionary or socialism unspiritual.

At the same time there has been a recrudescence, all over the world, of the kind of 'political religion' all six of our writers regarded as being essentially in retreat; and a reclaiming of nationalist values and frontiers which enlightened Victorians too confidently expected to crumble before the benefits of commerce, common sense and rational morality. Bossing and ignoring people, in the Russian manner; exploiting and dumping them, in the American manner, have not, in themselves, provided any major improvement over English assumptions of Empire. Like them, they have left unused the best talents of those trapped into compliance; and have provoked reactions almost worse than themselves.

The disaster of Chernobyl, which scattered the radiation from one inefficient Soviet nuclear power station over Europe, takes us back in spirit to Carlyle's *Past and Present*. A poor Irish widow, he wrote, sought help from her respectable Edinburgh neighbours. No help arrived. What had they to do with her? Disease and dirt reduced her to exhaustion and typhus-fever. Dying, she infected 'seventeen other persons'. 'Would it not have been *economy*', wrote Carlyle, 'to help this poor Widow?' The central 'idea' of our Victorian writers: that the world is a single economy, and falls or stands together: is still a hope, but more than ever a warning.

In his Conclusion to *Culture and Society* (1958), Raymond Williams wrote of the idea of solidarity as 'potentially the real basis of a society'; but added that 'in our time . . . it has been . . . a defensive attitude, the natural mentality of the long siege' and that 'the negative elements this produced will have to be converted into positives in a fully democratic society' (p. 319). All this remains true, is becoming more urgently true, and not only in Poland or South Africa.

If we look back at our six writers, we might decide that the two whose work centres most cogently on resistance are also the two who provide the most positive prospect. It is rather a childish game to imagine our Victorian writers in different contexts: but there is some value in it. Thus, it has been the fashion to imagine Carlyle as a mouthpiece of fascism: he was occasionally so abused, in Italy and Germany. G. B. Shaw called Ruskin a 'bolshevist', explaining that by this he meant a 'Tory-communist', who wished to impose good on the masses. Neither of these characterisations is fair; nor is it fair to conclude that Newman's writings are compatible with the Vatican concordat with Hitler, or Arnold's with the smooth running of an elitist bureaucratic nominal democracy. There is plenty in the writings and character of all of them to make these fantasies invalid. But the usefulness of such speculation is that it highlights the essential contribution of Taylor and Mill.

Taylor, alone, might appear 'neurotic'; Mill, alone, might appear a formalist. It is when we appreciate their collaboration that we begin to see the value of their refusal of tyranny, their persistence in finding ways to win minds and influence laws, through all the illnesses and sillinesses and failures of their lives. There is plenty of evidence that might be drawn from the lives of all six writers – and from our own lives – which would corroborate the need for the human emancipation which Taylor envisioned.

Now that Britain is part of Europe, and the world's great powers are beginning to see that what Mill called 'democratic institutions in detail' – the dream of the nineteenth century – are going to have to be implemented in the twenty-first century if we want to see the twenty-second, it becomes possible to imagine that Taylor's kind of defiance and Mill's kind of persistence may be given their chance.

Books

Discussed in this chapter (listed in chronological order)

Lytton Strachey, *Eminent Victorians*, London, 1918.

W. W. Rostow, *The British Economy of the Nineteenth Century*, Oxford, 1948.

J. H. Buckley, *The Victorian Temper: a Study in Literary Culture*, Cambridge, 1952.

John Holloway, *The Victorian Sage*, London, 1953.

John Wain, 'The Strategy of Victorian Poetry', *Twentieth Century*, May 1953.

Raymond Williams, *Culture and Society*, London, 1958; Harmondsworth, 1961. Reprinted with a postscript, 1963.

W. L. Burn, *The Age of Equipoise: a Study of the mid-Victorian Generation*, London, 1964.

Ben Knights, *The Idea of the Clerisy in the Nineteenth Century*, Cambridge, 1978.

Background (see also under individual chapters)

Richard D. Altick, *The English Common Reader: A Social History of the Mass Reading Public, 1800–1900*, Chicago, 1957.

Geoffrey Best, *Mid-Victorian Britain 1851–1875*, London, 1971.

Asa Briggs, *Victorian Cities*, London, 1963.

G. Kitson Clark, *The Making of Victorian England*, London, 1962.

J. M. Golby, editor, *Culture and Society in Britain, 1850–1890: A Source Book of Contemporary Writings*, Oxford, 1986.

Elie Halévy, *A History of the English People in the Nineteenth Century*, 6 volumes, Ernest Benn: London, 1962.

Walter E. Houghton, *The Victorian Frame of Mind 1830–1870*, New Haven, 1957.

Harold Perkin, *The Origin of Modern English Society 1780–1880*, London, 1985.

Keith Robbins, *Nineteenth-Century Britain: England, Scotland and Wales*, Oxford, 1989.

Ninian Smart, John Clayton, Steven Katz and Patrick Sherry, editors, *Nineteenth Century Religious Thought in the West*, 3 volumes, Cambridge (paperback reissue), 1988.

F. M. L. Thompson, *The Rise of Respectable Society: a social history of Victorian Britain 1830–1900*, London, 1988.

Comparative criticism

Edward Alexander, *Matthew Arnold, John Ruskin and the Modern Temper*, Columbus, Ohio, 1973.

Gillian Beer, *Darwin's Plots: Evolutionary Narrative in Darwin, George Eliot and Nineteenth-century Fiction*, new edition (paperback), London, 1985.

Peter Allan Dale, *The Victorian Critic and the idea of history: Carlyle, Arnold, Pater*, Cambridge, Massachusetts, 1977.

George Levine, *The Boundaries of Fiction: Carlyle, Macaulay, Newman*, Princeton, 1968.

Herbert L. Sussman, *Fact into Figure: typology in Carlyle, Ruskin and the Pre-Raphaelite Brotherhood*, Columbus, Ohio, 1979.

Kathleen and Geoffrey Tillotson, *Mid-Victorian Studies*, London, 1965.

Some further reading

A. J. Ayer, *Russell*, London, 1972.

William Berkson and John Wettersten, *Learning from Error: Karl Popper's Psychology of Learning*, Chicago, Illinois, 1984.

Asa Briggs, editor, *William Morris: Selected Writings and Designs*, Harmondsworth, 1962.

Antony Easthope, *British Post-Structuralism since 1968*, London and New York, 1988.

Christina Howells, *Sartre: the Necessity of Freedom*, Cambridge, 1988.

Paisley Livingston, *Literary Knowledge: Humanistic Inquiry and the Philosophy of Science*, Ithaca, New York, 1988.

David Marquand, *The Unprincipled Society: New Demands and Old Politics*, London, 1988.

Rosalind Miles, *The Women's History of the World*, Topsfield, Massachusetts, 1989.

Martin Sprinker, *Imaginary Relations: aesthetics and ideology in the theory of historical materialism*, London, 1988.

Michael Walzer, *The Company of Critics: social criticism and political commitment in the twentieth century*, London, 1989.

Raymond Williams, editor, *George Orwell: a Collection of Critical Writings*, London, 1974.

Virginia Woolf, *A Room of One's Own*, London, 1929.

INDEX